Fourth Workshop on Structured Prediction for NLP 2020

Online
20 November 2020

ISBN: 978-1-7138-1990-5

EMNLP 2020

Structured Prediction for NLP

Proceedings of the Fourth Workshop

November 20, 2020

Introduction

Welcome to the Fourth Workshop on Structured Prediction for NLP!

Structured prediction has a strong tradition within the natural language processing (NLP) community, owing to the discrete, compositional nature of words and sentences, which leads to natural combinatorial representations such as trees, sequences, segments, or alignments, among others. It is no surprise that structured output models have been successful and popular in NLP applications since their inception. Many other NLP tasks, including, but not limited to: semantic parsing, slot filling, machine translation, or information extraction, are commonly modeled as structured problems, and accounting for said structure has often lead to performance gain.

Of late, continuous representation learning via neural networks has been a significant complementary direction, leading to improvements in unsupervised and semi-supervised pre-training, transfer learning, domain adaptation, etc. Using word embeddings as features for structured models such as part-of-speech taggers count among the very first uses of continuous embeddings in NLP, and the symbiosis between the two approaches is an exciting research direction today.

This year we received 26 submissions and, after double-blind peer review, 16 were accepted (4 of which are non-archival papers) for presentation in this edition of the workshop, all exploring this interplay between structure and neural data representations, from different, important points of view. The program includes work on structure-informed representation learning, energy-based learning, and structured fine-tuning of language models. Our program also includes six invited presentations from influential researchers.

Our warmest thanks go to the program committee – for their time and effort providing valuable feedback, to all submitting authors – for their thought-provoking work, and to the invited speakers – for doing us the honor of joining our program. We are looking forward to seeing you online!

Priyanka Agrawal
Zornitsa Kozareva
Julia Kreutzer
Gerasimos Lampouras
André Martins
Sujith Ravi
Andreas Vlachos

Organizers:

Priyanka Agrawal, Booking.com, Netherlands
Zornitsa Kozareva, Google, USA
Julia Kreutzer, Google, Canada
Gerasimos Lampouras, Huawei, UK
André F. T. Martins, Unbabel and Instituto de Telecomunicações, Portugal
Sujith Ravi, Amazon, USA
Andreas Vlachos, University of Cambridge, UK

Program Committee:

Sweta Agrawal, University of Maryland, USA
Naveen Arivazhagan, Google Research, USA
Yoav Artzi, Cornell University, USA
Wilker Aziz, University of Amsterdam, Netherlands
Colin Cherry, Google Research, Canada
Gonçalo Correia, Instituto de Telecomunicacoes, Portugal
George Foster, Google Research, Canada
Kevin Gimpel, TTI Chicago, USA
Parag Jain, University of Edinburgh, UK
Arzoo Katiyar, Cornell University, USA
Yoon Kim, MIT-IBM Watson AI Lab, USA
Parisa Kordjamshidi, Tulane University, USA
Chunchuan Lyu, University of Edinburgh, UK
Pranava Madhyastha, Imperial College London, UK
Zita Marinho, Sacoor Brothers, Portugal
Musie Meressa, Sapienza University of Rome, Italy
Sabrina J Mielke, Johns Hopkins University, USA
Toan Q Nguyen, University of Notre Dame, USA
Vlad Niculae, University of Amsterdam, Netherlands
Marek Rei, University of Cambridge, UK
Hiko Schamoni, Heidelberg University, Germany
Tianze Shi, Cornell University, USA
Vivek Srikumar, University of Utah, USA
Sean J Welleck, New York University, USA

Invited Speakers:

Isabelle Augenstein, University of Copenhagen
Jonathan Berant, Tel-Aviv University
Mark Johnson, Macquarie University
Alexander Rush, Cornell Tech
Sunita Sarawagi, IIT Bombay
Ivan Titov, University of Edinburgh

Table of Contents

Syntax-driven Iterative Expansion Language Models
for Controllable Text Generation

Noe Casas[†*],   **Jose A. R. Fonollosa**[*],   **Marta R. Costa-jussà**[*]

[†] Lucy Software, United Language Group

[*] TALP Research Center, Universitat Politècnica de Catalunya

{noe.casas,jose.fonollosa,marta.ruiz}@upc.edu

Abstract

The dominant language modeling paradigm handles text as a sequence of discrete tokens. While that approach can capture the latent structure of the text, it is inherently constrained to sequential dynamics for text generation. We propose a new paradigm for introducing a syntactic inductive bias into neural text generation, where the dependency parse tree is used to drive the Transformer model to generate sentences iteratively.

Our experiments show that this paradigm is effective at text generation, with quality between LSTMs and Transformers, and comparable diversity, requiring less than half their decoding steps, and its generation process allows direct control over the syntactic constructions of the generated text, enabling the induction of stylistic variations.

1 Introduction

The currently dominant text generation paradigm is based on generating a sequence of discrete tokens in a left-to-right autoregressive way. Most neural language models (LMs) fall into this autoregressive generation category. Some neural architectures are sequential in nature, such as those based on recurrent neural networks (RNNs), lending themselves naturally to the autoregressive approach when used together with teacher forcing (Williams and Zipser, 1989). Other architectures, such as Transformer (Vaswani et al., 2017), while not intrinsically sequential, have also been targeted for sequential generation. On the other hand, some recent lines of research have focused on nonsequential generation. In this work, we propose a new paradigm for text generation and language modeling called Iterative Expansion Language Model, which generates the final sequence following a token ordering defined by the sentence dependency parse by iteratively expanding each level of the tree.

2 Related Work

In this section, we provide an overview of works related to ours, including dependency tree-driven LMs (§2.1), syntax-driven generation (§2.2), insertion-based approaches (§2.3) and iterative refinement approaches (§2.4).

2.1 Dependency LMs

The use of dependency parse trees to drive a language model was first proposed by Chelba et al. (1997), with a similar structure to an n-gram LM, but where the context of a word is its preceding bigram plus a list of preceding words whose parent does not precede it. Shen et al. (2008) make use of the dependency tree in a probabilistic LM, computing the probability of each word conditioned on its parent and the sibling words between both.

Mirowski and Vlachos (2015) propose a dependency LM based on RNNs, where the dependency tree is decomposed into a collection of unrolls, that is, paths from the root to one of the leaves, and where the probability of a word can be predicted from these unrolls. Buys and Blunsom (2018) propose a shift-reduce transition-based LSTM (Hochreiter and Schmidhuber, 1997) dependency LM that can be used for language modeling and generation by means of dynamic programming.

2.2 Syntax-driven Generation

Recurrent neural network grammars (Dyer et al., 2016) are recursive models that operate with a stack of symbols that can be populated with terminals or nonterminals, or "reduced" to generate a syntactic constituent, obtaining as a result a sentence and its associated constituency parse tree.

Shen et al. (2018) use skip-connections to integrate constituent relations with RNNs, learning the underlying dependency structures by leveraging a syntactic distance together with structured

1

Proceedings of 4th Workshop on Structured Prediction for NLP, pages 1–10

November 20, 2020. ©2020 Association for Computational Linguistics

attention.

Akoury et al. (2019) use a simplified constituency tree as latent variables, modeling it autoregressively to later use it as input for a non-autoregressive transformer that generates the output sentence.

Ordered neurons (Shen et al., 2019) are modified LSTMs where the latent sentence tree structure is used to control the dependencies between recurrent units with a special "master" input and forget gates.

2.3 Insertion-based Generation

Stern et al. (2019) propose a conditional generative model that iteratively generates tokens plus the position at which they should be inserted within the sequence. Emelianenko et al. (2019) further propose to optimize the generation order by sampling from the ordering permutations. Instead, Chan et al. (2019) optimize a lower bound of the marginalized probability over every possible ordering.

Gu et al. (2019a) handle the generation order as a latent variable that is captured as the relative position through self-attention, optimizing the ELBO to train the model.

Levenshtein Transformer (Gu et al., 2019b) is a non-autoregressive approach trained with reinforcement learning (RL) to generate token insertion and deletion actions. While it benefits from the same generation speed-ups over autoregressive models as our model, it has the added difficulty of learning an insertion/deletion policy using RL without any linguistically or empirically motivated priors, which can be slow or difficult to obtain convergence in practice. By comparison, our approachmakes uses a linguistically motivated prior for word insertion in a fully supervised way, avoiding the optimization difficulties of RL.

Welleck et al. (2019) use cost minimization imitation learning to learn a policy to generate a binary tree that is used to drive the token generation.

2.4 Iterative Refinement

Lee et al. (2018) propose a latent variable non-autoregressive machine translation model where first the target length is predicted by the model, and then, the decoder is iteratively applied to its own output to refine it.

Mask-predict (Ghazvininejad et al., 2019) also predicts the target sentence length and then non-autoregressively predicts the sentence itself, iteratively refining it a fixed number of times, masking out and regenerating the tokens it is least confident

about. Lawrence et al. (2019) follow a similar approach and start with a sequence of placeholder tokens (all the same) of a specified length, and they iteratively replace them with normal tokens via masked LM-style inference. As the masking strategy for the training data, the authors propose different stochastic processes to randomly select which placeholders are to be uncovered.

3 Iterative Expansion LMs

Our proposal is to train a new kind of language model where the token generation order is driven by the dependency parse tree of the sentence and where the generation process is iterative.

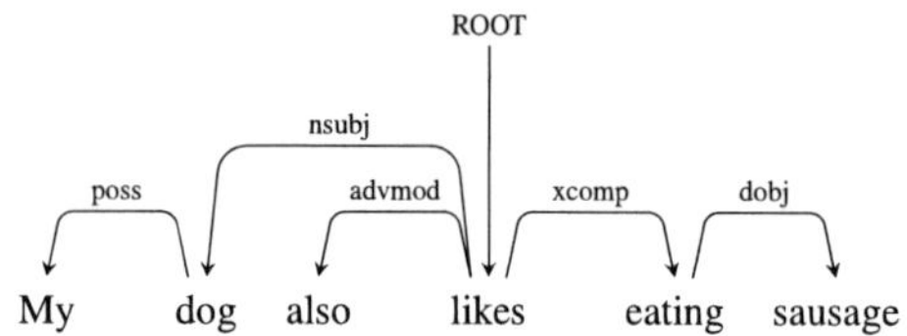

Figure 1: Example of dependency parse tree.

The input vocabulary contains terminal tokens as well as non-terminal special tokens called dependency placeholders, each of which is associated with one of the possible dependency relations to the heads. For the dependency tree in Figure 1, the dependency placeholders are `[poss]`, `[nsubj]`, `[advmod]`, `[xcomp]`, `[dobj]` and `[ROOT]`.

The input of the first iteration is the sequence with the `[ROOT]` element. At each iteration, the model receives as input a sequence I_{tok} with tokens from the input vocabulary and non-autoregressively generates two new sequences, each with the same length as the input.

The first output sequence, O_{tok}, contains tokens from a vocabulary with all possible textual tokens (terminal tokens). The second output, O_{exp}, is a sequence of tokens called expansion placeholders, which are taken from a separate vocabulary. Each expansion placeholder is associated with a pattern describing the left and right dependencies of the token at that position in the O_{tok} sequence. An example of dependency expansion could be `[nsubj-advmod-HEAD-xcomp]` for the word "likes" in the dependency parse tree from Figure 1.

After each iteration, the output of the model is expanded.[1] This consists of creating a new sequence

---

[1] The expansion of the output to be fed as input in the next iteration occurs in the CPU outside of the neural model itself.

by combining the tokens from I_tok, O_tok and O_exp. This process is illustrated in Figure 2, making use of the dependency tree from Figure 1.

When there is a padding token `[pad]` in the output (either O_tok or O_exp), this means that the output at that position is ignored when computing the loss function. This occurs when the terminal token has already been computed in previous iterations and has therefore been received as part of I_tok, and the model does not need to compute it again.

Note also that an empty dependencies token `[HEAD]` marks the end of a branch and that there is no need for an end of sequence token `<eos>`. As shown in the example from Figure 1, the generation of different branches occurs in parallel, needing only 3 iterations to generate a 6-token sentence.

Iteration 1

I_tok:	`[ROOT]`		
O_tok:	likes		
O_exp:	`[nsubj-advmod-HEAD-xcomp]`		

Iteration 2

I_tok:	`[nsubj]`	`[advmod]`	likes	`[xcomp]`
O_tok:	dog	also	`[pad]`	eating
O_exp:	`[poss-HEAD]`	`[HEAD]`	`[pad]`	`[HEAD-dobj]`

Iteration 3

I_tok:	`[poss]`	dog	also	likes	eating	`[dobj]`
O_tok:	my	`[pad]`	`[pad]`	`[pad]`	`[pad]`	sausage
O_exp:	`[HEAD]`	`[pad]`	`[pad]`	`[pad]`	`[pad]`	`[HEAD]`

Figure 2: Example of iterative text generation.

The strategy for composing tree expansion tokens (e.g., `[nsubj-advmod-HEAD-xcomp]`) may not scale well when single words have many direct dependencies. To alleviate this, we introduce a preprocessing step to modify the dependency tree so that every word has at most one dependency to the left and one to the right. For each word with more than one dependency on any of its sides, we rearrange the tree to force left-to-right dependencies. Although this **tree binarization** reduces the degree of parallelism, it reduces data sparsity and allows handling constructions with a number of dependencies may otherwise be too large for the model to properly capture, such as enumerations (e.g., "I bought a pair of shoes, an umbrella, a beautiful jacket and a bracelet").

Iterative expansion LMs can be naturally extended to subword vocabularies, like byte-pair encoding (BPE; Sennrich et al., 2016): for each word, we decompose its node in the tree into as many nodes as subwords in the word, rearranging the tree so that the head of the old word is now the head of the first subword, and each subsequent subword depends on the previous one, while every dependency of the old word node now depends on the last subword.

3.1 Neural Architecture

The neural architecture proposed is based on a Transformer decoder (Vaswani et al., 2017). To generate the dual output (terminal tokens and expansion placeholders) we condition the generation of terminals on the expansions: the probability distribution over the expansion token space is generated first by projecting from one of the intermediate layers' hidden states. We sample from it and use the resulting expansion IDs as an index to a trainable expansion embedding layer; the embedded vectors are added to the hidden state used to generate them for use as input to subsequent layers.

As described in Section 3, the input and output token vocabularies are different: the latter only contains terminal tokens (plus some special tokens such as `[PAD]`); the former also contains dependency placeholders. However, for practical purposes, at the model level, we define both vocabularies to be the same, both with terminal tokens and dependency placeholders, and we mask the entries of dependency placeholders in the final softmax.

To inject the syntactic dependency information as input into the model, we add a layer of learned positional embeddings containing the position of the head of each token, and we refer to this embedding layer as head position embedding.

The self-attention mask used in Transformer to force causality is not used in our proposal. The input is therefore not masked at all, and the token predictions have access to the full input sequence.

3.2 Training

For training iterative expansion LMs, the main input of the model is the tokens at one of the levels of the dependency parse tree (I_tok), while the output is the following level tokens (O_tok) and expansion placeholders (O_exp). A secondary input to the model are the dependency indexes, which are used in the head position embedding.

The model is trained with the categorical cross-entropy for both tokens and expansion placeholders, then adding both sublosses into the final loss (with equal weights). Tokens generated in previous iterations appear as [PAD] tokens in the expected output and are ignored when computing the loss.

Training takes place in batches; as the trainable unit is a level transition, a training batch is composed of level transitions from different sentences.

3.3 Inference and Text Generation

In iterative expansion LMs, inference takes place iteratively. The initial state is a batch of [ROOT] tokens, together with the head positions initialized to the special value representing the root node and, in constrained attention variants, a mask with the self-dependency of the single node in each sentence in the batch. At each iteration, the model generates the probability distributions for terminal tokens and expansion tokens. We use nucleus sampling (Holtzman et al., 2020) to sample from them. The terminal token sequences are expanded according to the expansion tokens (see §3), and these are the inputs for the following iteration if there are still unfinished branches. Before sampling from the token and expansion probability distributions, we mask the <unk> token and the dependency placeholders to avoid generating them.

Although iterative expansion LMs could be subject to beam search across iterations, we have not covered such a possibility as part of this work.

4 Experimental Setup

4.1 Unconditional Text Generation

We conducted experiments on unconditional text generation following the methodology used by Caccia et al. (2020). The goal is to assess both the quality and diversity of the text generated by the model and the baselines. For the quality evaluation, we use the BLEU score (Papineni et al., 2002) over the test set, where each generated sentence is evaluated against the whole test set as a reference. For diversity, we used the self-BLEU score (Zhu et al., 2018), computed using as references the rest of the generated sentences. For each model, the temperature of the final softmax τ is tuned to generate text in the closest quality/diversity regime to the training data.

Iterative expansion LMs are compared against a standard LM baselines, namely, AWD-LSTM[2] (Merity et al., 2018) and a Transformer LM (Vaswani et al., 2017), both with word (w) and BPE subword (sw) vocabularies. The models

---

[2]Abbreviation of ASGD weight-dropped LSTM, where ASGD stands for averaged stochastic gradient descent.

were trained on the EMNLP2017 News dataset, which contains news in English, enriched with dependency annotations by corenlp, an automatic annotation tool that provides pre-trained models. Syntax-driven generation baseline models were not included because the only model with an available implementation that is able to do unsupervised text generation are RNNGs, but they proved not to scale even to medium-sized datasets like EMNLP2017 News. When sampling from models, we use nucleus sampling (Holtzman et al., 2020), a form of ancestral sampling that constrains the candidate pool by discarding the distribution tail. Samples from the training and validation data are included for reference. Full hyperparameters and data processing details are described in Appendices D and B.

4.2 Style Variation

Iterative expansion LMs drive the generation of text with the dependency parse tree. It is possible to influence the generated trees by altering artificially the probability of the different expansion tokens. To demonstrate this, we modified the decoding process of iterative expansion LMs to force the probability of generating adjectival constructions to be higher than normal, aiming at generating a more descriptive style: during decoding, we multiply the probabilities of the expansion placeholders that express adjectival dependencies (i.e. those containing adjectival modifier "amod" relations), and renormalize the probabilities by dividing by the sum.

We conducted this experiment with the word-level models trained on EMNLP2017 News data. We compute the ratio of adjectives per sentence to verify the increased presence of adjectives, while controlling quality and diversity measures over the generated text for potential degradation.

5 Results and Analysis

We assess the ability of iterative expansion LMs to unconditionally generate text in terms quality (BLEU-5) vs. diversity (self BLEU-5), comparing against sequential baselines, each with a softmax temperature τ tuned separately.

In order to tune the output softmax termperature τ, we generated text with each model at different temperatures and chose the value of τ that was the most similar to a sample from the training data in terms of BLEU-5 against a sample from the validation set (proxy for quality) and self BLEU-5

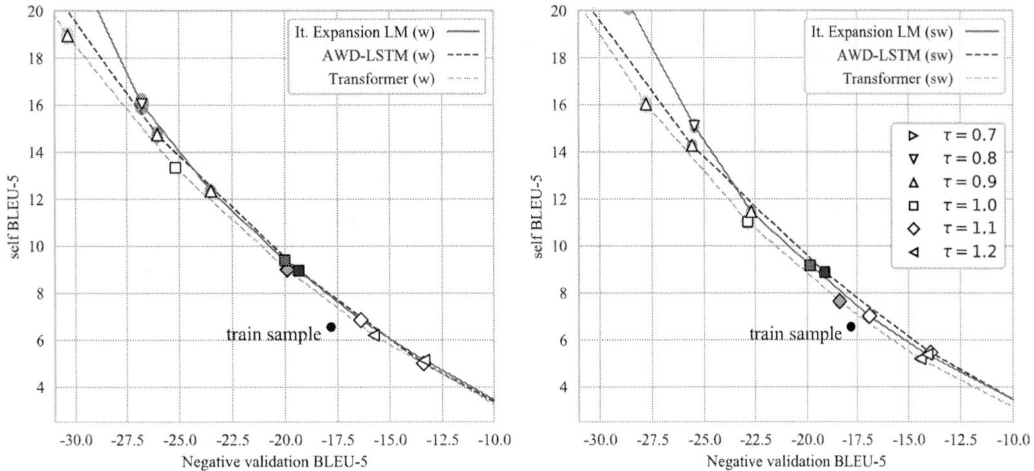

Figure 3: Quality vs. diversity on EMNLP2017 News (BLEU-5). Models with **word-level vocabulary on the left** and **subword-level on the right**. The point marker is color-filled for the chosen value of τ. Each point represents the average over 20 generated text samples, and is surrounded by a small colored ellipse representing the standard deviation.

τ	ITEXP (w)		AWD-LSTM (w)		Transformer (w)	
	valid ↑	self ↓	valid ↑	self ↓	valid ↑	self ↓
0.70	30.1 ± 0.8	22.3 ± 1.0	39.2 ± 0.9	33.4 ± 1.1	40.5 ± 0.6	35.0 ± 1.1
0.80	26.8 ± 0.8	16.0 ± 1.0	33.0 ± 0.7	23.2 ± 1.0	35.8 ± 0.7	26.3 ± 0.8
0.90	23.5 ± 0.7	12.4 ± 0.7	26.0 ± 0.6	14.7 ± 0.8	30.4 ± 0.7	19.0 ± 0.8
1.00	$\mathbf{20.0 \pm 0.6}$	$\mathbf{9.4 \pm 0.5}$	$\mathbf{19.4 \pm 0.6}$	$\mathbf{9.0 \pm 0.6}$	25.2 ± 0.5	13.3 ± 0.5
1.10	16.4 ± 0.5	6.8 ± 0.5	13.4 ± 0.4	5.0 ± 0.4	$\mathbf{19.9 \pm 0.6}$	$\mathbf{9.0 \pm 0.6}$
1.20	13.4 ± 0.6	5.1 ± 0.4	9.0 ± 0.5	2.9 ± 0.3	15.8 ± 0.5	6.2 ± 0.5

τ	ITEXP (sw)		AWD-LSTM (sw)		Transformer (sw)	
	valid ↑	self ↓	valid ↑	self ↓	valid ↑	self ↓
0.70	28.6 ± 0.9	20.3 ± 1.1	39.0 ± 0.8	33.5 ± 1.1	36.9 ± 0.7	30.6 ± 1.2
0.80	25.5 ± 0.5	15.1 ± 0.7	32.3 ± 0.7	22.4 ± 0.7	32.5 ± 0.7	22.4 ± 1.0
0.90	22.7 ± 0.6	11.5 ± 0.7	25.6 ± 0.6	14.3 ± 0.6	27.8 ± 0.7	16.0 ± 0.8
1.00	$\mathbf{19.9 \pm 0.6}$	$\mathbf{9.2 \pm 0.5}$	$\mathbf{19.2 \pm 0.5}$	$\mathbf{8.9 \pm 0.5}$	22.9 ± 0.8	11.0 ± 0.7
1.10	16.9 ± 0.8	7.0 ± 0.6	13.9 ± 0.5	5.5 ± 0.4	$\mathbf{18.4 \pm 0.7}$	$\mathbf{7.6 \pm 0.6}$
1.20	14.1 ± 0.6	5.4 ± 0.5	9.7 ± 0.4	3.3 ± 0.3	14.5 ± 0.5	5.2 ± 0.5

Table 1: Validation and self BLEU-5 scores of the text generated by the **word-level (top)** and **subword-level (bottom)** models under study at different temperatures τ, showing the average and standard deviation over 20 different generated text samples. The selected generation regime is highlighted for each model, being the closest to the training sample, which has a validation BLEU-5 of 17.8 and a self BLEU-5 of 6.6.

(proxy for diversity). Each model was used to generate 20 samples of 400 sentences, and self-BLEU5 and validation-BLEU5 were computed over each of them, taking the average and the standard deviation. Figure 3 and Table 1 show these BLEU values, highlighting the chosen τ for each model. Given the low values for the standard deviation, we decided not to include it in subsequent tables to avoid unnecessary clutter. Note that in all BLEU vs. self-BLEU figures, each model is shown as a different line (each with its own color and/or dashed pattern) and that the data points computed for each temperature value are plotted with a specific marker shape (square, diamond, triangle, or flipped triangle).

Apart from BLEU scores, we also include extra quality measures, namely the perplexity obtained

	τ	Test BLEU-5 (quality ↑)	Self BLEU-5 (diversity ↓)	AWD-LSTM perplex. ↓	Transformer perplex. ↓	GPT-2 perplex. ↓
AWD-LSTM (w)	1.0	22.9	8.9	37.0	47.9	99.5
Transformer (w)	1.1	23.8	9.0	33.6	18.6	66.5
ITEXP (w)	1.0	23.7	9.4	40.8	40.7	85.2
AWD-LSTM (sw)	1.0	22.7	8.9	43.5	56.9	113.5
Transformer (sw)	1.1	22.1	7.6	37.5	31.6	77.1
ITEXP (sw)	1.0	23.6	9.2	45.2	49.2	97.1
Train sample	-	21.5	6.6	49.5	29.1	37.7
Valid sample	-	21.2	7.2	53.3	44.7	36.7

Table 2: Quality and diversity on EMNLP2017, with τ generating the closest text to the validation data.

by other language models: an AWD-LSTM word-level LM and a Transformer word-level LM, both trained on EMNLP2017 News, plus OpenAI GPT-2 (1.5 B parameters) (Radford et al., 2019). The results are shown in Table 2.

These results show how the generated text improves over AWD-LSTM in terms of quality by all measures, with a comparable level of diversity. In comparison to the Transformer, while the quality measured with BLEU-5 is better for ITEXP, the rest of the quality measures indicate that the text generated by the Transformer is of better quality.

Adjective probability	Adjs. per sentence	Test BLEU-5	Self BLEU-5
×1	1.2	23.7	9.4
×10	3.4	21.3	8.4
×20	4.2	20.6	8.8
×50	5.2	19.8	8.9

Table 3: ITEXP (w, $\tau = 1.0$) with increased adjectives.

The results of the styled text generation experiments, shown in Table 3, confirm that the style of the resulting text can be successfully modulated to the desired degree and that the quality and diversity are only slightly degraded at moderate increases of the probability of adjectival clause generation.

5.1 Human Evaluation

In order to better assess the quality of the generated text, we also include a human evaluation. For this, we took a sample of 60 sentences of each model under study, including also a sample of the same size from the validation data, to serve as reference. The sentences were evaluated by a pool of annotators, who were requested to rate the sentence in an integer scale from 1 to 5, taking into account its fluency and correctness.

The pack of sentences rated by each annotator contained 10 sentences from each of the models under evaluation. Each sentence under evaluation was part of the packs of 3 evaluators; this redundancy was used to measure the discrepancies in the rating of each sentence among annotators, which was quantified by means of the average per-sentence standard deviation.

Model	Average rating	Per sentence avg. stddev
AWD-LSTM (w)	3.08	0.74
Transformer (w)	3.43	0.78
ITEXP (w)	3.28	0.73
AWD-LSTM (sw)	2.66	0.68
Transformer (sw)	3.33	0.83
ITEXP (sw)	3.09	0.70
Valid sample	4.49	0.61

Table 4: Human evaluation for the different models.

Table 4 shows the statistics of the obtained ratings, were we can see the average rating of the sentences generated by each model, together with the average per-sentence standard deviation, to understand how different the ratings for each sentence were among the different evaluator ratings. We can see that the highest human ratings were obtained by the Transformer, both with word and subword-level vocabularies, followed by ITEXP and then AWD-LSTM.

Table 5 shows the human evaluation for the models from the style variation experiments presented in Table 3. As we can see, there is a small degradation in quality as we force high levels of adjectival presence.

Adjective probability	Average rating	Per sentence avg. stddev
×1	3.28	0.73
×10	3.16	0.79
×20	2.98	0.84
×50	3.19	0.70

Table 5: Human evaluation for ITEXP (w) models with increased adjectival construction probability.

6 Further Comparison with Real Text

Given that the generation process in iterative expansion LMs is not sequential, we studied the distribution of the sentence lengths it generates. This is shown in Figure 4 for the text generated by a word-level iterative expansion LM trained on EMNLP2017 News, along with the lengths of a sample from the training data.

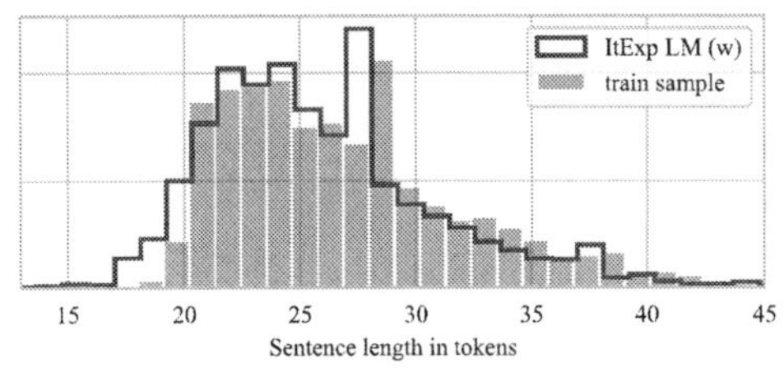

Figure 4: Distribution of generated text length.

Iterative expansion LMs generate the dependency parse tree as they generate text. We studied the depths of the dependency trees of generated text in relation to those parsed from the training data, as shown in Figure 5.

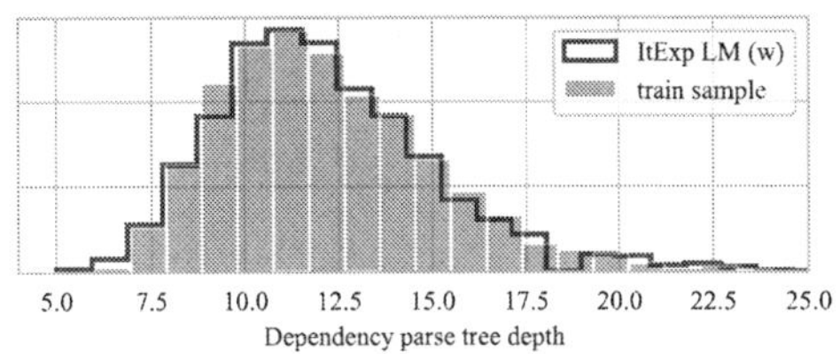

Figure 5: Histogram of generated text tree depth.

We also measured the degree to which the generated trees adhere to the trees obtained by parsing their lexicalized representation. Specifically, we computed the labeled and unlabeled attachment scores between both for the text generated at different softmax temperatures τ. Attachment scores are the standard performance measure in dependency parsing and are computed as the percentage of words that have been assigned the same head as the reference tree, over a test set. The attachment score is "labeled" if the dependency label is taken into account or "unlabeled" otherwise. As shown in Table 6, the obtained labeled attachment scores (LAS) and unlabeled attachment scores (UAS) are very high across the different values of the generation temperature τ.

τ	0.7	0.8	0.9	1.0	1.2
LAS	96.4	95.3	94.2	92.3	86.2
UAS	98.0	97.3	96.5	95.2	90.7

Table 6: Attachment scores of the generated trees.

6.1 Quantification of the Generation Speedup

Text generation with autoregressive models like LSTM or Transformer models offers a linear computational complexity with respect to the length of the generated sequence. In comparison, the dependency tree-driven decoding used by iterative expansion LMs generates text in parallel for each branch in the tree. If the tree was a perfectly balanced binary tree, then the computational complexity would be logarithmic. However, dependency trees in general are not balanced and, given the tree binarization postprocessing that we introduce, the parallelization is slightly reduced.

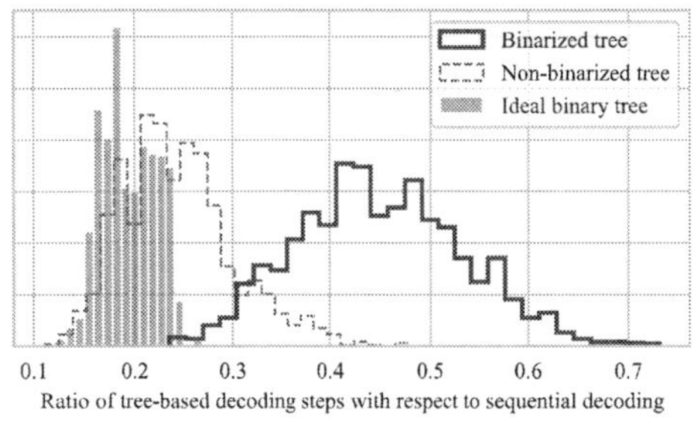

Figure 6: Histogram of the ratio of the decoding steps needed to generate a sentence with tree-based decoding with respect to sequential generation.

Figure 6 shows the speedup of the needed decoding steps of tree-based decoding with respect of auto-regressive decoding, taking a sample of the training data and computing the needed steps to decode them should the sentences have an idealized binary dependency parse tree, a normal parse tree, and a binarized parse tree. On average, the binarized parse tree, which is the decoding used by iterative expansion LMS, needs only 45% of the decoding steps needed by autoregressive decoding.

American students were 62 percent more likely to die in a heart attack during the first week of 2004, according to the study.

For 150 days, Hillary Clinton will do more to improve access to affordable quality care, support and education funding for millions of Americans, she says.

For those on this list, it's likely that I would rather be able to train them up, she said.

He made it clear the SNP repeated on Friday as a response, saying they discussed a contract getting the extra cost here.

He'll pay $25, 000 for rent and more buses and bring his collection to The Academy on Channel 31.

Six years later, at least eight people died as a result of the shooting.

The health prime minister told CNN Thursday that he was willing to back up against the US and remove all of the relevant items at the end of the transition.

Then, another man told police that was a friend's friend, and as a child, he made the decision to call his mother.

They are 40 - 60 among the top 50, 000 women in the last year in that group since 2014 - 15.

They've worked hard on Twitter and they think they've tried to focus on our sport, she said.

We like to think that if you try to get this game done, we can get a lower success rate out of 15.

Table 7: Samples of text generated by iterative expansion LMs with word vocabulary.

I feel that they're going to Syria because we had this explanation, that they have an indication of their advance.

The girl's mother told the group of three she needed treatment and the family said her daughter would still be alive with another child.

But she added: "The data is important to the EU that the UK can attract more businesses.

Though he also spoke to Mr Wilson on Saturday morning at the Netherlands Police trial, Johnson referred it to the No. 1 commission.

It's a collective belief and it's a statement to us, he said.

It's just the first thing we're feeling now and I don't like it.

So if you want to be sitting in a garden, you have to wait for something to make sure that this does not end.

So, for example, we need to argue about what the president did, but I'm just interested in having any talk.

The British defence ministry confirmed action had been taken at the hospital but could not confirm the details until now.

We'll ask for a fair share of Russia to stop border security, particularly for people of color, he added.

Table 8: Samples of text generated by iterative expansion LMs with subword vocabulary.

6.2 Generation Examples

Table 7 shows a selection of text samples generated by iterative expansion LMs with a word-level vocabulary, while Table 8 shows samples generated with a subword-level vocabulary. We can see that, despite being generated non-sequentially and each branch of the dependency parse tree being generated in parallel, the resulting sentences maintain coherence and syntactic agreement, confirming that conditioning on the token dependencies in the parse tree provides enough information to generate it while speeding up the decoding process.

7 Conclusion

In this work, we presented iterative expansion LMs, which are iterative non-autoregressive text generation models that rely on syntactic dependency trees to generate sentence tokens in parallel. As opposed to other syntax-driven generation mechanisms, the training of iterative expansion LMs can be naturally computed in batches and they are amenable to subword-level vocabularies.

We showed that our proposed method generates text with quality between LSTMs and Transformers, with comparable diversity, both regarding automatic measurements and human judgement, while generating text in half of the decoding steps needed by sequential LMs, and also allowing direct control over the generation process at the syntactic level, enabling the induction of stylistic variations in the generated text.

Our code is available as open source at `https://github.com/noe/iterative_expansion_lms` .

Acknowledgments

This work is partially supported by Lucy Software / United Language Group (ULG) and the Catalan Agency for Management of University and Research Grants (AGAUR) through an Industrial Ph.D. Grant. This work also is supported in part by the Spanish Ministerio de Economía y Competitividad, the European Regional Development Fund through the postdoctoral senior grant Ramón y Cajal and by the Agencia Estatal de Investigación through the projects EUR2019-103819, PCIN-2017-079 and PID2019-107579RB-I00 / AEI / 10.13039/501100011033

References

Nader Akoury, Kalpesh Krishna, and Mohit Iyyer. 2019. Syntactically supervised transformers for faster neural machine translation. In *Proceedings of the 57th Annual Meeting of the Association for Computational Linguistics*, pages 1269–1281, Florence, Italy. Association for Computational Linguistics.

Jan Buys and Phil Blunsom. 2018. Neural syntactic generative models with exact marginalization. In *Proceedings of the 2018 Conference of the North American Chapter of the Association for Computational Linguistics: Human Language Technologies, Volume 1 (Long Papers)*, pages 942–952, New Orleans, Louisiana. Association for Computational Linguistics.

Massimo Caccia, Lucas Caccia, William Fedus, Hugo Larochelle, Joelle Pineau, and Laurent Charlin. 2020. Language gans falling short. In *International Conference on Learning Representations*.

William Chan, Nikita Kitaev, Kelvin Guu, Mitchell Stern, and Jakob Uszkoreit. 2019. KERMIT: Generative insertion-based modeling for sequences. *arXiv preprint arXiv:1906.01604*.

Ciprian Chelba, David Engle, Frederick Jelinek, Victor Jimenez, Sanjeev Khudanpur, Lidia Mangu, Harry Printz, Eric Ristad, Ronald Rosenfeld, Andreas Stolcke, and Dekai Wu. 1997. Structure and performance of a dependency language model. In *In Proceedings of Eurospeech*, pages 2775–2778.

Chris Dyer, Adhiguna Kuncoro, Miguel Ballesteros, and Noah A. Smith. 2016. Recurrent neural network grammars. In *Proceedings of the 2016 Conference of the North American Chapter of the Association for Computational Linguistics: Human Language Technologies*, pages 199–209, San Diego, California. Association for Computational Linguistics.

Dmitrii Emelianenko, Elena Voita, and Pavel Serdyukov. 2019. Sequence modeling with unconstrained generation order. In *Advances in Neural Information Processing Systems 32*, pages 7698–7709. Curran Associates, Inc.

Marjan Ghazvininejad, Omer Levy, Yinhan Liu, and Luke Zettlemoyer. 2019. Mask-predict: Parallel decoding of conditional masked language models. In *Proceedings of the 2019 Conference on Empirical Methods in Natural Language Processing and the 9th International Joint Conference on Natural Language Processing (EMNLP-IJCNLP)*, pages 6114–6123, Hong Kong, China. Association for Computational Linguistics.

Jiatao Gu, Qi Liu, and Kyunghyun Cho. 2019a. Insertion-based decoding with automatically inferred generation order. *Transactions of the Association for Computational Linguistics*, 7:661–676.

Jiatao Gu, Changhan Wang, and Junbo Zhao. 2019b. Levenshtein transformer. In *Advances in Neural Information Processing Systems 32*, pages 11179–11189. Curran Associates, Inc.

Sepp Hochreiter and Jürgen Schmidhuber. 1997. Long short-term memory. *Neural computation*, 9(8):1735–1780.

Ari Holtzman, Jan Buys, Li Du, Maxwell Forbes, and Yejin Choi. 2020. The curious case of neural text degeneration. In *International Conference on Learning Representations*.

Carolin Lawrence, Bhushan Kotnis, and Mathias Niepert. 2019. Attending to future tokens for bidirectional sequence generation. In *Proceedings of the 2019 Conference on Empirical Methods in Natural Language Processing and the 9th International Joint Conference on Natural Language Processing (EMNLP-IJCNLP)*, pages 1–10, Hong Kong, China. Association for Computational Linguistics.

Jason Lee, Elman Mansimov, and Kyunghyun Cho. 2018. Deterministic non-autoregressive neural sequence modeling by iterative refinement. In *Proceedings of the 2018 Conference on Empirical Methods in Natural Language Processing*, pages 1173–1182, Brussels, Belgium. Association for Computational Linguistics.

Edward Loper and Steven Bird. 2002. Nltk: The natural language toolkit. In *In Proceedings of the ACL Workshop on Effective Tools and Methodologies for Teaching Natural Language Processing and Computational Linguistics. Philadelphia: Association for Computational Linguistics*.

Stephen Merity, Nitish Shirish Keskar, and Richard Socher. 2018. Regularizing and optimizing LSTM language models. In *International Conference on Learning Representations*.

Piotr Mirowski and Andreas Vlachos. 2015. Dependency recurrent neural language models for sentence completion. In *Proceedings of the 53rd Annual Meeting of the Association for Computational Linguistics and the 7th International Joint Conference* on *Natural Language Processing (Volume 2: Short Papers)*, pages 511–517, Beijing, China. Association for Computational Linguistics.

Kishore Papineni, Salim Roukos, Todd Ward, and Wei-Jing Zhu. 2002. Bleu: a method for automatic evaluation of machine translation. In *Proceedings of the 40th Annual Meeting of the Association for Computational Linguistics*, pages 311–318, Philadelphia, Pennsylvania, USA. Association for Computational Linguistics.

Alec Radford, Jeff Wu, Rewon Child, David Luan, Dario Amodei, and Ilya Sutskever. 2019. Language models are unsupervised multitask learners.

Rico Sennrich, Barry Haddow, and Alexandra Birch. 2016. Neural machine translation of rare words with subword units. In *Proceedings of the 54th Annual Meeting of the Association for Computational Linguistics (Volume 1: Long Papers)*, pages 1715–1725, Berlin, Germany. Association for Computational Linguistics.

Libin Shen, Jinxi Xu, and Ralph Weischedel. 2008. A new string-to-dependency machine translation algorithm with a target dependency language model. In *Proceedings of ACL-08: HLT*, pages 577–585.

Yikang Shen, Zhouhan Lin, Chin wei Huang, and Aaron Courville. 2018. Neural language modeling by jointly learning syntax and lexicon. In *International Conference on Learning Representations*.

Yikang Shen, Shawn Tan, Alessandro Sordoni, and Aaron Courville. 2019. Ordered neurons: Integrating tree structures into recurrent neural networks. In *International Conference on Learning Representations*.

Mitchell Stern, William Chan, Jamie Kiros, and Jakob Uszkoreit. 2019. Insertion transformer: Flexible sequence generation via insertion operations. In *Proceedings of the 36th International Conference on Machine Learning, ICML 2019, 9-15 June 2019, Long Beach, California, USA*, pages 5976–5985.

Ashish Vaswani, Noam Shazeer, Niki Parmar, Jakob Uszkoreit, Llion Jones, Aidan N Gomez, Łukasz Kaiser, and Illia Polosukhin. 2017. Attention is all you need. In *Advances in neural information processing systems*, pages 5998–6008.

Sean Welleck, Kianté Brantley, Hal Daumé III, and Kyunghyun Cho. 2019. Non-monotonic sequential text generation. In *Proceedings of the 36th International Conference on Machine Learning*, volume 97 of *Proceedings of Machine Learning Research*, pages 6716–6726, Long Beach, California, USA. PMLR.

Ronald J Williams and David Zipser. 1989. A learning algorithm for continually running fully recurrent neural networks. *Neural computation*, 1(2):270–280.

Yaoming Zhu, Sidi Lu, Lei Zheng, Jiaxian Guo, Weinan Zhang, Jun Wang, and Yong Yu. 2018. Texygen: A benchmarking platform for text generation models. In *The 41st International ACM SIGIR Conference on Research & Development in Information Retrieval*, pages 1097–1100. ACM.

CopyNext: Explicit Span Copying and Alignment in Sequence to Sequence Models

Abhinav Singh[1,2]   Patrick Xia[1]   Guanghui Qin[1]
Mahsa Yarmohammadi[1]   Benjamin Van Durme[1]
[1]Johns Hopkins University   [2]Bloomberg L.P.
`abhinavsingh282@gmail.com, {paxia,vandurme}@cs.jhu.edu,`
`{qin,mahsa}@jhu.edu`

Abstract

Copy mechanisms are employed in sequence to sequence models (seq2seq) to generate reproductions of words from the input to the output. These frameworks, operating at the lexical *type* level, fail to provide an explicit alignment that records where each *token* was copied from. Further, they require contiguous token sequences from the input (spans) to be copied individually. We present a model with an explicit token-level copy operation and extend it to copying entire spans. Our model provides hard alignments between *spans* in the input and output, allowing for nontraditional applications of seq2seq, like information extraction. We demonstrate the approach on Nested Named Entity Recognition, achieving near state-of-the-art accuracy with an order of magnitude increase in decoding speed. [1]

1   Introduction

Sequence transduction converts a sequence of input tokens to a sequence of output tokens. It is a dominant framework for generation tasks, such as machine translation, dialogue, and summarization. Seq2seq can also be used for Information Extraction (IE), where the target structure is *decoded* as a linear output based on an encoded (linear) representation of the input.

As IE is traditionally considered a structured prediction task, it remains today that IE systems are assumed to produce an annotation on the input text. That is, predicting which specific tokens of an input string led to, e.g., the label of PERSON. This is in contrast to text generation which rarely, if ever, needs *hard alignments* between the input and the desired output. Our work explores a novel extension to seq2seq that provides such alignments.

The luxury auto maker last year sold 1,214 cars in the U.S.
(a) *last year* DATE *last* REL *year* DUR *<UNK>* CARD *U.S.* CTRY
(b) *last year* DATE *last* REL *year* DUR *1,214* CARD *U.S.* CTRY
(c) 4 5 DATE 4 REL 5 DUR 7 CARD 11 CTRY
(d) 4 CN DATE 4 REL 5 DUR 7 CARD 11 CTRY

Figure 1: Sequence transduction outputs for nested named entities in an example sentence using: (a) seq2seq, (b) pointer network, (c) Copy-only, and (d) CopyNext model. The numbers are predictions of *indices* corresponding to the tokens in the input sequence. CN refers to the CopyNext symbol, our proposed method of denoting the operation that copies the next token from the input. In (d), the next token from token 4 would be 5.

Specifically, we extend pointer (or copy) networks. Unlike the algorithmic tasks originally targeted by Vinyals et al. (2015), tasks in NLP tend to copy *spans* from the input rather than discontiguous tokens. This is prevalent for copying named entities in dialogue (Gu et al., 2016; Eric and Manning, 2017), entire sentences in summarization (See et al., 2017; Song et al., 2018), or even single words (if subtokenized). The need to efficiently copy spans motivates our introduction of an inductive bias that copies contiguous tokens. Like a pointer network, our model copies the first token of a span. However, for subsequent timesteps, our model generates a "CopyNext" symbol (CN) instead of copying another token from source. CopyNext represents the operation of copying the word following the last predicted word from the input sequence. Figure 1 highlights the difference between output sequences for several transductive models, including our CopyNext model.

We apply our model for the Nested Named Entity Recognition (NNER) task (Ringland et al., 2019). Unlike traditional named entity recognition, named entity mentions in NNER may be subsequences of

Proceedings of 4th Workshop on Structured Prediction for NLP, pages 11–16
November 20, 2020. ©2020 Association for Computational Linguistics

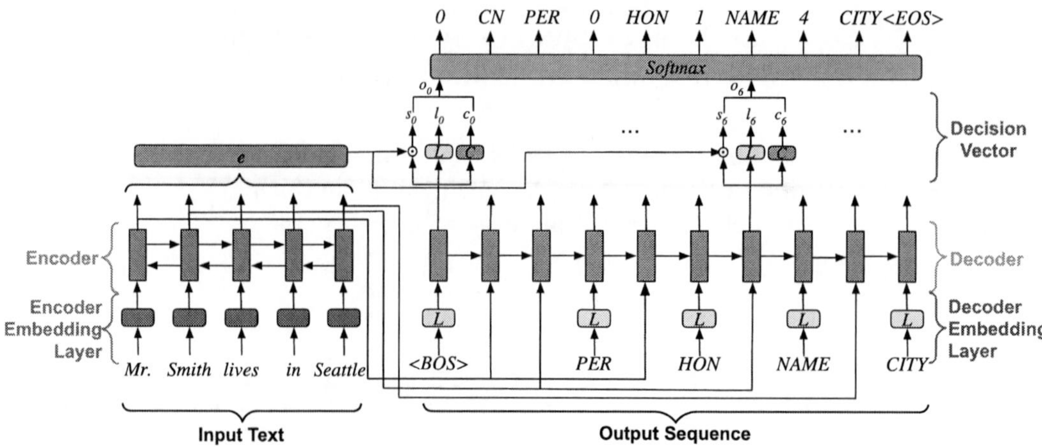

Figure 2: For each decoder timestep a decision vector chooses between labeling, a CopyNext operation, or pointing to an input token. The decoder input comes from either an encoder state or a label embedding.

other named entity mentions (such as *[[last] year]* in Figure 1). We find that both explicit copying and CopyNext lead to a system faster than prior work and better than a simple seq2seq baseline. It is, however, outperformed by a much slower model that performs an exhaustive search over the space of potential labels, a solution that does not scale to large complex label sets.

2 Related Work

Pointer networks (Vinyals et al., 2015; Jia and Liang, 2016; Merity et al., 2016) are seq2seq models that employ a soft attention distribution (Bahdanau et al., 2014) to produce an output sequence consisting of values from the input sequence. Pointer-generator networks (Miao and Blunsom, 2016; Gulcehre et al., 2016, *inter alia*) extend the range of output types by combining the distribution from the pointer with a vocabulary distribution from a generator. Thus, these models operate on the *type* level. In contrast, our model operates at the *token* level. Instead of using soft attention distribution of the encoder states, we use hard attention, resulting in a single encoder state, or a single token, to feed to the decoder. This enables explicit copying of span offsets.

Closest to our work, Zhou et al. (2018) and Panthaplackel et al. (2020) have tackled span copying by extending pointer-generator networks and predicting both start and end indices of entire spans that need to be copied. Using those offsets, they perform a forced decoding of the predicted tokens within the span. These works focus on text generation tasks, like sentence summarization, question

generation, and editing. In contrast, we are concerned with information extraction tasks as transduction, where hard alignments to the input sentence are crucial and output sequences must represent a valid linearized structure. Specifically, we study nested named entity recognition (NNER).

Prior work uses several approaches to model NNER: machine reading comprehension (Li et al., 2019), transition-based methods (Wang et al., 2018), mention hypergraphs (Lu and Roth, 2015; Wang and Lu, 2018; Katiyar and Cardie, 2018), and seq2seq models (Straková et al., 2019).

3 Model Description

We formulate the task as transforming the input sentence X to a linearized sequence Y which represents the gold structure: labeled spans. Specifically, Y contains input word indices, CopyNext symbols, and labels from a label set $\mathcal{L}$.

As described earlier, the model (Figure 2) is reminiscent of pointer networks. We extend its capabilities by introducing the notion of a "Copy Next" operation where the network predicts to copy the word sequentially after the previous prediction.

3.1 Encoder

Embedding Layer This layer embeds a sequence of tokens $X = \langle x_1, x_2, ..., x_{N'} \rangle$ into a sequence of vectors $\mathbf{x} = \langle \mathbf{x}_1, \mathbf{x}_2, ..., \mathbf{x}_N \rangle$ by using (possibly contextualized) word embeddings. The gold labels are adjusted to account for tokenization.

Architecture The input embedding is further encoded by a stacked bidirectional LSTM (Hochreiter and Schmidhuber, 1997) into encoder states $\mathbf{e} = \langle \mathbf{e}_1, \mathbf{e}_2, ..., \mathbf{e}_N \rangle$ where each state is a concatenation of the forward ($\overrightarrow{f}$) and backward ($\overleftarrow{f}$) outputs of the last layer of the LSTM and $\mathbf{e}_i \in \mathbb{R}^D$:

$$\mathbf{e}_i^j = [\overrightarrow{f}^j(\mathbf{e}_i^{j-1}, \mathbf{e}_{i-1}^j); \overleftarrow{f}^j(\mathbf{e}_i^{j-1}, \mathbf{e}_{i+1}^j)], \quad (1)$$

where $\mathbf{e}_i^j$ is the j-th layer encoder hidden state at timestep i and D is the hidden size of the LSTM.

3.2 Decoder

The target for the transducer is the linearized representation of the nested named entity spans and labels. We generate a decision y that either points to (a) a timestep in the encoder sequence, marking the starting index of a span, or (b) the CopyNext symbol, which operates by advancing the right boundary of the span to include the next (sub)word of the input sequence, or (c) a label $l \in \mathcal{L}$, signifying both the end of the span and classifying the span.

Input Embeddings We learn D-dimensional embeddings for each label $l \in \mathcal{L}$. The vectors corresponding to the start index of a span and the Copy-Next operation are the encoder outputs $\mathbf{e}_i$ where i is equal to the start index or index pointed to by CopyNext and are fed directly to the decoder.[2]

Architecture The decoder is a stacked LSTM taking as input either an encoder state $\mathbf{e}_i$ or a label embedding and produces decoder state $\mathbf{d}_t \in \mathbb{R}^D$.

Decision Vector We predict scores for making a labeling decision, a CopyNext operation, or pointing to a token in the input. At each decoding step t, for labels, we train a linear layer $W_L \in \mathbb{R}^{D \times |\mathcal{L}|}$ with input $\mathbf{d}_t$ and output scores $\mathbf{l}_t$. Likewise, we do the same for the CopyNext symbol using a linear layer $W_C \in \mathbb{R}^{D \times 1}$ with input $\mathbf{d}_t$ and output score c_t. The score of pointing to an index i in the input sequence is calculated by dot product: $s_t^i = \mathbf{e}_i \cdot \mathbf{d}_t$. The decision distribution $\mathbf{y}_t$ is then:

$$\mathbf{y}_t = \text{softmax}([\mathbf{s}_t; \mathbf{l}_t; c_t]), \ \mathbf{y}_t \in \mathbb{R}^{N+|\mathcal{L}|+1}. \quad (2)$$

3.3 Training and Prediction

Our training objective is the cross-entropy loss:

$$\ell = \sum_t \sum_k \delta_{y_t^k, y_t^\star} \log(y_t^k) \quad (3)$$

where $y^\star$ is the gold decision, $k \in [0, N + |\mathcal{L}| + 1)$ (representing all three kinds of possible decisions:

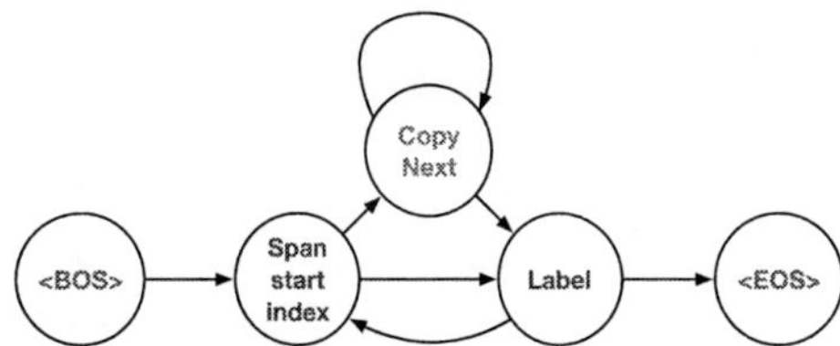

Figure 3: State machine of a well-formed predicted sequence for masking of the decision vector at inference.

Embedding	P	R	F1
RoBERTa	**90.6**	**82.6**	**86.4**
BERT large cased	90.4	78.2	83.9
XLNet large cased	79.1	52.6	63.2
SpanBERT large cased	89.1	80.2	84.4
ELMo	82.1	73.3	77.4
GloVe	76.5	67.8	71.9

Table 1: A comparison of networks used for embedding input tokens before feeding them into the encoder LSTM. These are evaluated on NNER.

index, label or CopyNext) and $\delta_{y_t^k, y_t^\star}$ is 1 if $y_t^k = y_t^\star$ and 0 otherwise. The summation over index t covers the whole dataset.

At prediction time we find the decision $\overline{y}_t$ with the greatest probability ($\overline{y}_t = \arg\max_i(y_t^i)$) at decoder step t.[3] The input to the decoder at $t+1$ timestamp can be one of three things: (1) the output $\mathbf{e}_i$ of the encoder when $\overline{y}_t$ points to the index i of the input sequence, (2) the embedding of the label l predicted at t when $\overline{y}_t$ points to the label $l \in \mathcal{L}$, or (3) the output $\mathbf{e}_{i+1}$ of the encoder where i was the input to the decoder at t when $\overline{y}_t$ points to the CopyNext operation. The decoder halts when the $\langle EOS \rangle$ label is predicted or the maximum output sequence length is reached.

To ensure well-formed target output sequences, we use a state machine (Figure 3) to mask parts of $\overline{\mathbf{y}}_t$ that would lead to an illegal sequence at $t+1$.

4 Experiments and Results

Our experiments analyze the effects of various choices in different components of the system. We use the NNE dataset and splits from Ringland et al. (2019), resulting in 43,457, 1,989, and 3,762 sentences in the training, development, and test splits. Experiments for model development and analysis use the development set.

Text Representation We first establish the best performing text embeddings which we fix for the

---

[2] We will use $\mathbf{e}_i$ to refer to $\mathbf{e}_i^{(-1)}$.

[3] Initial experiments with beam search suggest an expensive tradeoff between time and performance (Appendix A.1).

Model	P	R	F1	Speed
Hypergraph	91.8	91.0	91.4	1.0x
Transition	77.4	70.1	73.6	6.3x
Seq2seq	86.6	63.6	75.4	(*)
Copy	85.8	81.3	83.5	16.7x
CopyNext	88.7	84.7	86.7	16.7x

Table 2: NNER accuracy and speed on the test set for external baselines and our models. *Seq2seq is based on a reference implementation to ensure correctness, but not efficiency: it has the same asymptotics as the Copy and CopyNext models, and can be considered similar in speed.

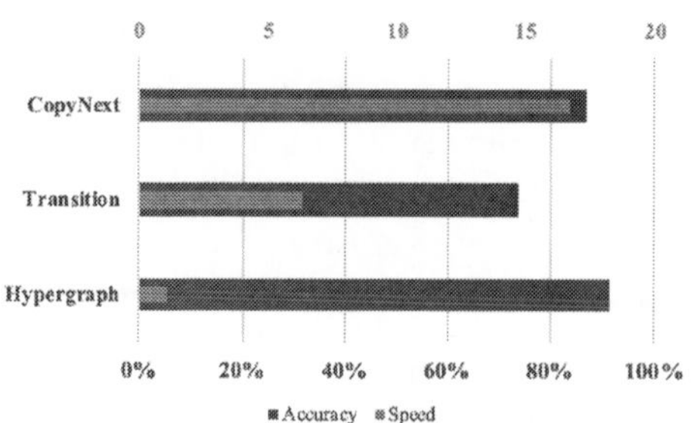

Figure 4: Performance in terms of Accuracy (%F1) and Speed (relative to Hypergraph). The CopyNext model is nearly as accurate as Hypergraph while over 16 times faster.

rest of the experiments. The rationale is that the embedding will provide an orthogonal boost in accuracy to the network with respect to the other changes in the network structure. We find in Table 1 that RoBERTa large (Liu et al., 2019) is best.[4]

Linearization Strategy Previous work (Zhang et al., 2019) has shown that linearization scheme affects model performance. We experiment with several variants of sorting spans in ascending order based on their start index. We also try sorting based on end index and copying the *previous* token instead. We find sorting based on end index performs poorly, while sorting by start all perform similarly. Our final linearization strategy sorts by start index, then span length (longer spans first). Additional ties (in span label) are broken randomly.

RoBERTa Embedding Layer Recent work suggests that NER information may be stored in the lower layers of an encoder (Hewitt and Manning, 2019; Tenney et al., 2019). We found using the 15th layer of RoBERTa rather than the final one (24th), is slightly helpful (see Appendix A.1).

NNER Results In Table 2, we evaluate our best-performing (dev.) model on the test set. We compare our approach against the previous best approaches reported in Ringland et al. (2019): hypergraph-based (Hypergraph, Wang and Lu, 2018) and transition-based (Transition, Wang et al., 2018) models proposed to recognize nested mentions. We also contrast the CopyNext model against a baseline seq2seq model and one with only a hard copy operation (see (a) and (c) in Figure 1). Prior

work (Wang and Lu, 2018) has given an analysis of the run-time of their approach. Based on their concern about asymptotic speed we also provide the following analysis and practical speed efficiency of the systems and their accuracies.[5]

We find that Hypergraph outperforms the Copy-Next model by 4.7 F1 with most of the difference in recall. This is likely due to the exhaustive search used by Hypergraph, as our model is 16.7 times faster. An analysis of their code and algorithm reveals that their lower bound time complexity $\Omega(mn)$ is higher than ours $\Omega(n)$, n is length of input sequence and m is number of mention types. Since the average decoder length is low, the best case scenario often occurs. The Transition system has 6.3 times faster prediction speed compared to Hypergraph, however, it comes with 17.8% absolute drop in F1 accuracy. Our model is substantially faster than both. Furthermore, we show that both an explicit Copy and the CopyNext operation are useful, resulting in gains of 8.1 F1 and 11.3 F1 over a seq2seq baseline.

NNER Error Analysis The errors made by the model on the development set can be clustered broadly into four main types: (1) correct span detection but mislabeled, (2) correct label but incorrect span detection (either subset or superset of correct span), (3) both span and label were incorrectly predicted, and (4) missing spans entirely. Table 7 in Appendix A.1 provides examples.

5 Conclusion and Future Work

We propose adopting pointer and copy networks with hard attention and extending these models

---

[4]We experimented with mean pooling RoBERTa vectors for subwords (Zhang et al., 2019) to maintain the same span lengths as input. Pooling subword units led to poorer performance (see Appendix A.1 Table 3).

[5]Efficiency is measured using wall clock time for the entire test set, performed with Intel Xeon 2.10GHz CPU and a single GeForce GTX 1080 TI GPU.

with a CopyNext operation, enabling sequential copying of spans given just the start index of the span. On a traditionally structured prediction task of NNER, we use a sequence transduction model with the CopyNext operation, leading to a competitive model that provides a 16.7x speedup relative to current state of the art (which performs an exhaustive search), at a cost of 4.7% loss in F1, largely due to lower recall.

Our model is a step forward in structured prediction as sequence transduction. We have found in initial experiments on event extraction similar relative improvements to that discussed here: future work will investigate applications to richer transductive semantic parsing models (Zhang et al., 2019; Cai and Lam, 2019).

Acknowledgments

This work was supported in part by IARPA BETTER (#2019-19051600005), DARPA AIDA (FA8750-18-2-0015) and KAIROS (FA8750-19-2-0034). The views and conclusions contained in this work are those of the authors and should not be interpreted as necessarily representing the official policies, either expressed or implied, or endorsements of DARPA, ODNI, IARPA, or the U.S. Government. The U.S. Government is authorized to reproduce and distribute reprints for governmental purposes notwithstanding any copyright annotation therein.

References

Dzmitry Bahdanau, Kyunghyun Cho, and Yoshua Bengio. 2014. Neural machine translation by jointly learning to align and translate. *arXiv preprint arXiv:1409.0473*.

Deng Cai and Wai Lam. 2019. Core semantic first: A top-down approach for AMR parsing. In *Proceedings of the 2019 Conference on Empirical Methods in Natural Language Processing and the 9th International Joint Conference on Natural Language Processing (EMNLP-IJCNLP)*, pages 3799–3809, Hong Kong, China. Association for Computational Linguistics.

Jacob Devlin, Ming-Wei Chang, Kenton Lee, and Kristina Toutanova. 2019. BERT: Pre-training of deep bidirectional transformers for language understanding. In *Proceedings of the 2019 Conference of the North American Chapter of the Association for Computational Linguistics: Human Language Technologies, Volume 1 (Long and Short Papers)*, pages 4171–4186, Minneapolis, Minnesota. Association for Computational Linguistics.

Mihail Eric and Christopher Manning. 2017. A copy-augmented sequence-to-sequence architecture gives good performance on task-oriented dialogue. In *Proceedings of the 15th Conference of the European Chapter of the Association for Computational Linguistics: Volume 2, Short Papers*, pages 468–473, Valencia, Spain. Association for Computational Linguistics.

Jiatao Gu, Zhengdong Lu, Hang Li, and Victor O.K. Li. 2016. Incorporating copying mechanism in sequence-to-sequence learning. In *Proceedings of the 54th Annual Meeting of the Association for Computational Linguistics (Volume 1: Long Papers)*, pages 1631–1640, Berlin, Germany. Association for Computational Linguistics.

Caglar Gulcehre, Sungjin Ahn, Ramesh Nallapati, Bowen Zhou, and Yoshua Bengio. 2016. Pointing the unknown words. In *Proceedings of the 54th Annual Meeting of the Association for Computational Linguistics (Volume 1: Long Papers)*, pages 140–149, Berlin, Germany. Association for Computational Linguistics.

John Hewitt and Christopher D. Manning. 2019. A structural probe for finding syntax in word representations. In *Proceedings of the 2019 Conference of the North American Chapter of the Association for Computational Linguistics: Human Language Technologies, Volume 1 (Long and Short Papers)*, pages 4129–4138, Minneapolis, Minnesota. Association for Computational Linguistics.

Sepp Hochreiter and Jürgen Schmidhuber. 1997. Long short-term memory. *Neural computation*, 9(8):1735–1780.

Robin Jia and Percy Liang. 2016. Data recombination for neural semantic parsing. *arXiv preprint arXiv:1606.03622*.

Mandar Joshi, Danqi Chen, Yinhan Liu, Daniel Weld, Luke Zettlemoyer, and Omer Levy. 2020. Spanbert: Improving pre-training by representing and predicting spans. *Transactions of the Association for Computational Linguistics*, 8(0):64–77.

Arzoo Katiyar and Claire Cardie. 2018. Nested named entity recognition revisited. In *Proceedings of the 2018 Conference of the North American Chapter of the Association for Computational Linguistics: Human Language Technologies, Volume 1 (Long Papers)*, pages 861–871.

Xiaoya Li, Jingrong Feng, Yuxian Meng, Qinghong Han, Fei Wu, and Jiwei Li. 2019. A unified mrc framework for named entity recognition. *arXiv preprint arXiv:1910.11476*.

Yinhan Liu, Myle Ott, Naman Goyal, Jingfei Du, Mandar Joshi, Danqi Chen, Omer Levy, Mike Lewis, Luke Zettlemoyer, and Veselin Stoyanov. 2019. Roberta: A robustly optimized BERT pretraining approach. *CoRR*, abs/1907.11692.

Wei Lu and Dan Roth. 2015. Joint mention extraction and classification with mention hypergraphs. In *Proceedings of the 2015 Conference on Empirical Methods in Natural Language Processing*, pages 857–867.

Stephen Merity, Caiming Xiong, James Bradbury, and Richard Socher. 2016. Pointer sentinel mixture models. *arXiv preprint arXiv:1609.07843*.

Yishu Miao and Phil Blunsom. 2016. Language as a latent variable: Discrete generative models for sentence compression. In *Proceedings of the 2016 Conference on Empirical Methods in Natural Language Processing*, pages 319–328.

Sheena Panthaplackel, Miltiadis Allamanis, and Marc Brockschmidt. 2020. Copy that! editing sequences by copying spans.

Jeffrey Pennington, Richard Socher, and Christopher D. Manning. 2014. Glove: Global vectors for word representation. In *Empirical Methods in Natural Language Processing (EMNLP)*, pages 1532–1543.

Matthew Peters, Mark Neumann, Mohit Iyyer, Matt Gardner, Christopher Clark, Kenton Lee, and Luke Zettlemoyer. 2018. Deep contextualized word representations. In *Proceedings of the 2018 Conference of the North American Chapter of the Association for Computational Linguistics: Human Language Technologies, Volume 1 (Long Papers)*, pages 2227–2237, New Orleans, Louisiana. Association for Computational Linguistics.

Nicky Ringland, Xiang Dai, Ben Hachey, Sarvnaz Karimi, Cecile Paris, and James R. Curran. 2019. NNE: A dataset for nested named entity recognition in English newswire. In *Proceedings of the 57th Annual Meeting of the Association for Computational Linguistics*, pages 5176–5181, Florence, Italy. Association for Computational Linguistics.

Abigail See, Peter J. Liu, and Christopher D. Manning. 2017. Get to the point: Summarization with pointer-generator networks. In *Proceedings of the 55th Annual Meeting of the Association for Computational Linguistics (Volume 1: Long Papers)*, pages 1073–1083, Vancouver, Canada. Association for Computational Linguistics.

Kaiqiang Song, Lin Zhao, and Fei Liu. 2018. Structure-infused copy mechanisms for abstractive summarization. In *Proceedings of the 27th International Conference on Computational Linguistics*, pages 1717–1729, Santa Fe, New Mexico, USA. Association for Computational Linguistics.

Jana Straková, Milan Straka, and Jan Hajič. 2019. Neural architectures for nested ner through linearization. *arXiv preprint arXiv:1908.06926*.

Ian Tenney, Dipanjan Das, and Ellie Pavlick. 2019. Bert rediscovers the classical nlp pipeline. *arXiv preprint arXiv:1905.05950*.

Oriol Vinyals, Meire Fortunato, and Navdeep Jaitly. 2015. Pointer networks.

Bailin Wang and Wei Lu. 2018. Neural segmental hypergraphs for overlapping mention recognition. In *Proceedings of the 2018 Conference on Empirical Methods in Natural Language Processing*, pages 204–214, Brussels, Belgium. Association for Computational Linguistics.

Bailin Wang, Wei Lu, Yu Wang, and Hongxia Jin. 2018. A neural transition-based model for nested mention recognition. In *Proceedings of the 2018 Conference on Empirical Methods in Natural Language Processing*, pages 1011–1017, Brussels, Belgium. Association for Computational Linguistics.

Zhilin Yang, Zihang Dai, Yiming Yang, Jaime Carbonell, Russ R Salakhutdinov, and Quoc V Le. 2019. Xlnet: Generalized autoregressive pretraining for language understanding. In *Advances in Neural Information Processing Systems 32*, pages 5753–5763. Curran Associates, Inc.

Sheng Zhang, Xutai Ma, Kevin Duh, and Benjamin Van Durme. 2019. AMR parsing as sequence-to-graph transduction. In *Proceedings of the 57th Annual Meeting of the Association for Computational Linguistics*, pages 80–94, Florence, Italy. Association for Computational Linguistics.

Qingyu Zhou, Nan Yang, Furu Wei, and Ming Zhou. 2018. Sequential copying networks. In *Thirty-Second AAAI Conference on Artificial Intelligence*.

Generating Synthetic Data for Task-Oriented Semantic Parsing with Hierarchical Representations

Ke Tran
Amazon Translate
Berlin, Germany
trnke@amazon.com

Ming Tan
Amazon Alexa
Cambridge, MA, USA
mingtan@amazon.com

Abstract

Modern conversational AI systems support natural language understanding for a wide variety of capabilities. While a majority of these tasks can be accomplished using a simple and flat representation of intents and slots, more sophisticated capabilities require complex hierarchical representations supported by semantic parsing. State-of-the-art semantic parsers are trained using supervised learning with data labeled according to a hierarchical schema which might be costly to obtain or not readily available for a new domain. In this work, we explore the possibility of generating synthetic data for neural semantic parsing using a pretrained denoising sequence-to-sequence model (*i.e.*, BART). Specifically, we first extract masked *templates* from the existing labeled utterances, and then fine-tune BART to generate synthetic utterances conditioning on the extracted templates. Finally, we use an auxiliary parser (AP) to filter the generated utterances. The AP guarantees the quality of the generated data. We show the potential of our approach when evaluating on the Facebook TOP dataset[1] for navigation domain.

1 Introduction

In this work, we investigate semantic parsing with hierarchical representations (Gupta et al., 2018) instead of the traditional logical forms (Zettlemoyer and Collins, 2005). Given an utterance x, our goal is to produce a tree-structured representation y of the utterance where additional information about intents and slots is introduced at the non-terminal nodes of the tree. We define a *template* z of a given annotation y as a result of replacing all terminal nodes by a generic [mask] node. Figure 1 shows an example of such an utterance x, its annotation y and the corresponding template z.

---

[1] http://fb.me/semanticparsingdialog

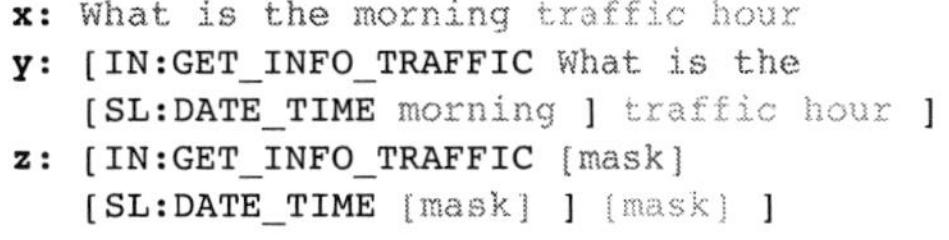

Figure 1: An example of an input utterance x, its desired output y, and the template z inferred from y . By definition, the template z above can be used to generate other utterances such as *"how is the 5:00 traffic looking"* or *"Any construction on my morning route"*.

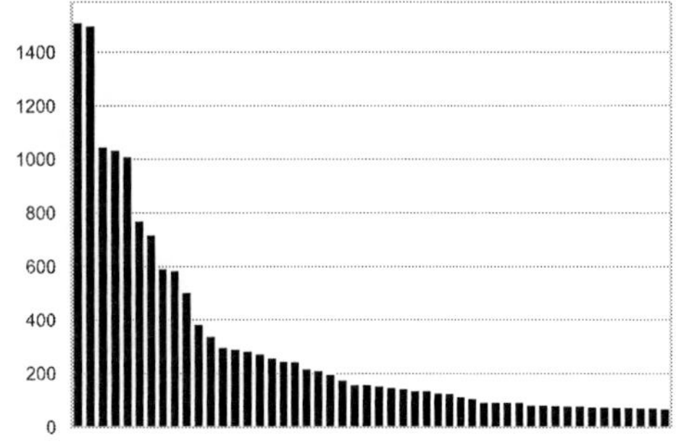

Figure 2: Frequency of most 50 common templates in Facebook TOP dataset. The frequency of z follows a power-law probability distribution.

The hierarchical representation for task-oriented parsing proposed in (Gupta et al., 2018) aims for ease of annotation and expressiveness. The dataset in their work, Facebook TOP, is the largest publicly available dataset in English for hierarchical semantic parsing. It has more than 44K annotated queries. We look at the distribution of the templates in Facebook TOP and found that the dataset is highly unbalanced (Figure 2). The 10 most frequent templates account for 30% of the training data and 14% of the data are singletons, which are utterances with only a single occurrence. This analysis suggests that it is beneficial to generate more synthetic data for templates with low frequencies. In the field of Natural Language Processing, us-

Proceedings of 4th Workshop on Structured Prediction for NLP, pages 17–21
November 20, 2020. ©2020 Association for Computational Linguistics

ing synthetic data via back-translation (Sennrich et al., 2016) has shown a great success for machine translation (Edunov et al., 2018). Unlike machine translation, generating synthetic data for hierarchical semantic parsing is less straightforward. Our work positions itself as one of the first to explore the possibility of generate text from graph (template) for semantic parsing.

In this paper, we propose a generic framework for augmenting a semantic parser with synthetic data. Our framework consists of two steps. First, we train a generator, followed by top-p sampling to generate diverse synthetic utterances conditioning on the above-mentioned templates. Generated utterances share similar hierarchical structures (*i.e.*, templates) with real training utterances while providing a wide spectrum of lexical variety. Second, we use an auxiliary parser for filtering on the generated candidates. The filtering step guarantees the quality of the synthetic data. Our generator is a sequence to sequence (seq2seq) model that is pretrained on massive amount of monolingual data with text infilling objective (§2). We utilize BART (Lewis et al., 2020), a recently proposed denoising autoencoder, as our generator to avoid training it from scratch. The auxiliary parser can be arbitrary. We experiment with BART-based parser as well as state-of-the-art pointer network parser (s2s-pointer; Rongali et al., 2020).

The paper is structured as follows. We introduce our generative model for synthetic data in Section §2. Experimental results on Facebook TOP dataset and sub-sampled datasets to simulate low-resource scenario are presented in Section §3. Section §5 concludes the paper.

2 Denoising Sequence-to-Sequence as Generator

The generative story for generating synthetic data $\mathcal{Y}_{\text{syn}} = \{\widetilde{y}_i\}_{i=1}^{M}$ is given by

1. draw a template $z \sim p_\phi(z)$;[2]

2. draw an annotation $y \sim p_\theta(y \mid z)$ by filling each [mask] token in z by a word or sequence of words from vocabulary $\mathcal{V}$;

Note that the transformation from annotation y to utterance x is deterministic by removing non-terminals from y. While $p_\phi(z)$ can be modeled by

---

[2]During inference for generating synthetic data, we draw z uniformly in order to generate more annotations for templates in the long tail.

an autoregressive neural language model or a Probabilistic Context Free Grammar (Johnson, 1998), in this work we sample template z from seen templates in the data. We leave the possibility of generating new templates to future work.

We need a powerful conditional model $p_\theta(y \mid z)$ to generate annotation y. Thus, we choose BART, a pretrained denoising autoencoder for sequence-to-sequence, as our model. Figure 3a illustrates the idea behind BART. Given an input sequence (a stream of text), one of five types of noise (Figure 3b) is used to corrupt the input sequence. Then BART reconstructs the original sequence by maximizing the likelihood of the original sequence.

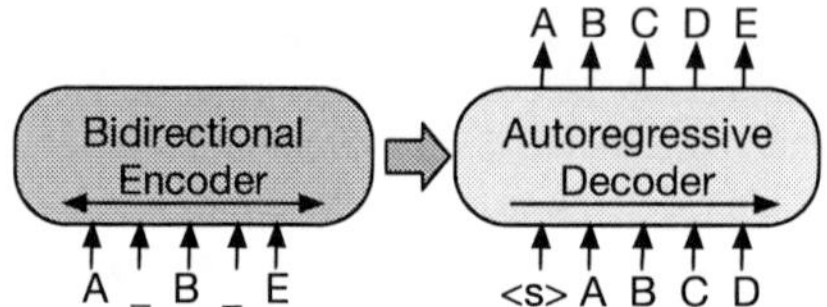

(a) BART is trained to reconstruct the corrupted input.

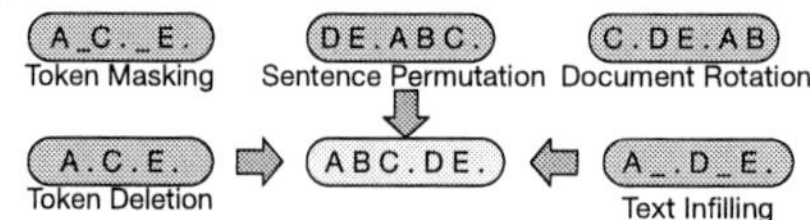

(b) Five different types of noise introduced in BART.

Figure 3: Overview of BART.

Since pretrained BART uses *text infilling* as noise to corrupt the input sequence, naturally we can use BART to infill the templates. Text infilling is the task where a number of spans in the original input sequence are replaced by a token [mask] and BART is trained to predict the replaced spans in the position of [mask] tokens. For our purpose of generating synthetic data, we fine-tune BART on an infilling dataset where the input is a template z with [mask] and the output is a linearized tree representation y where [mask] tokens are replaced by lexical words as shown in Figure 4.

BART source/target construction: We call out a few processing steps to construct this infilling dataset. First, non-terminal words are lowercased. We find this is necessary since the input will be tokenized by BART tokenizer and lowercasing non-terminal words prevents over-segmentation. Second, we make each of the closing brackets "]" in the original data explicit (*e.g.*, `in:get_distance]`, `sl:destination]`). This transformation provides the model explicit infor-

```
Source: [in:get_distance [mask] [sl:destination [in:get_location [sl:category_location
        [mask] sl:category_location] in:get_location] sl:destination] in:get_distance]
Target: [in:get_distance How far is [sl:destination [in:get_location [sl:category_location
        the coffee shop sl:category_location] in:get_location] sl:destination] in:get_distance]
```

Figure 4: Data for fine-tuning BART.

mation of the scope of the intents and slots.

Fine-tuning and generation: We fine-tune BART generator using the (*template, annotation*) pairs. After fine-tuning, we use the generator to generate full parse trees given templates. To increase the diversity of generated samples, we use top-p sampling (Holtzman et al., 2020) instead of beam search. The generator is trained to generate the tokenized labels together with the words. We remove generated annotations with invalid labels and convert the tokenized labels into the original tags in a post-processing step.

Auxiliary parser (AP) for filtering: In our preliminary experiments, we found that the generated samples are noisy. When we train our parser on the concatenation of both real and generated samples, the test accuracy degrades by 1.13% compared with a parser trained purely on real data. We therefore use an auxiliary parser (AP) to select robust samples. The filtering step is straightforward. First, we train an auxiliary semantic parser $f_\theta(x)$ on the original Facebook TOP dataset. We then use this trained AP to parse synthetic data $(\widetilde{x}_i, \widetilde{y}_i)$ and keep those samples where the outputs of the parser $f_\theta(\widetilde{x}_i)$ match the synthetic labels $\widetilde{y}_i$ (i.e., $f_\theta(\widetilde{x}_i) = \widetilde{y}_i$). The AP for filtering can be different from the target parser we train for semantic parsing. Therefore, we propose three settings: (1) BART as AP and a sequence-to-sequence model with pointer networks (s2s-pointer; Rongali et al., 2020) as the target parser. (2) BART models for both AP and target parser. (3) s2s-pointer models for both AP and target parser. The comparisons and analysis are detailed in Section §3.

3   Experiments

We use Facebook TOP dataset in our experiments. Statistics of the dataset are shown in Table 1. While there are more than 31K annotated utterances in training data, the number of unique templates is about 6K. As we have shown in Section 1, the distribution of the templates is highly unbalanced. In training data, there are 1,511 annotations with the template [IN:UNSUPPORTED_NAVIGATION [mask]] and 1,046 annotations with template

[IN:UNSUPPORTED [mask]]. In the case of no UNSUPPORTED setting (− UNSUPPORTED in Table 2), we exclude those annotations with UNSUPPORTED templates from train, valid, and test data. This results in 28,414 (template, annotation) pairs for training and 4,032 pairs for validation.

Condition	train	valid	test
+ UNSUPPORTED	31,279	4,462	9,042
− UNSUPPORTED	28,414	4,032	8,241

Table 1: Number of samples in Facebook TOP dataset with (+) and without (−) UNSUPPORTED utterances.

We fine-tune our BART generator using Adam optimizer (Kingma and Ba, 2015) with a linear warmup of 4,000 steps at the peak learning rate of 2e−5. We pick the best model based on validation perplexity. After fine-tuning, we use the generator to sample 5 full parse trees per template.

The exact-match results for the three settings of using BART/s2s-pointer as auxiliary and target parser are given in Table 2. We first notice that the BART-based parser performs on-par with SOTA model based on pointer network and RoBERTa (Liu et al., 2019) feature extractor in the work of Rongali et al. (2020). This suggests that pretraining a general purpose seq2seq model is beneficial for downstream conditional generation task. We also see that using synthetic data brings additional 0.89% for BART-parser and 0.88% for s2s-pointer parser on the exact-match accuracy. The gain of using synthetic data is smaller when UNSUPPORTED utterances are present in training and testing data.

Table 3 shows the exact match accuracy of BART-based parser on testset with respect to template frequency f in training data. We see that synthetic data helps low-frequency templates ($f < 5$) the most (+1.36%). The gain of 0.67% for unseen templates ($f = 0$) suggests that there is a room for further improvement by generating new templates.

In order to support new domains (with new intents and slots) for the virtual assistants, we investigate the role of synthetic data when there is a little data available for the new domains. We sim-

```
Template:
[in:get_info_road_condition [mask] [sl:road_condition [mask] ] [mask] [sl:path [mask] ] ]
Generate:
[in:get_info_road_condition is the road [sl:road_condition icy ] on [sl:path I - 5 ] ]
[in:get_info_road_condition Are the roads [sl:road_condition slick ] on [sl:path I90 ] ]
[in:get_info_road_condition Is there [sl:road_condition snow ] on [sl:path the commute ] ]
[in:get_info_road_condition will the roads be [sl:road_condition slippery ] on [sl:path my commute ] ]
[in:get_info_road_condition Are there any [sl:road_condition flooding ] on [sl:path Route 66 ] ]
```

Figure 5: Sample of five synthetic parse trees generated given a template. Colors indicate the corresponding generated spans per [mask] token. The data is reformatted for readability.

Data	AP filter	Target parser	− UNSUPPORTED		+ UNSUPPORTED	
			#Samples	Acc (%)	#Samples	Acc (%)
Real		BART	28,414	83.37	31,279	81.01
+ syn	BART	BART	53,679	84.26 (+0.89)	56,547	81.74 (+0.73)
Real		s2s-pointer	28,414	84.80	31,279	82.10
+syn	BART	s2s-pointer	53,679	85.31 (+0.51)	56,355	82.71 (+0.61)
+syn	s2s-pointer	s2s-pointer	89,629	85.68 (+0.88)	92,264	82.77 (+0.67)

Table 2: Exact-match results of our experiments. The AP filter can be a fine-tuned BART for parsing or a s2s-pointer model of Rongali et al. (2020)

Training data	$f \geq 5$	$f < 5$	$f = 0$
Real	89.46	74.70	61.90
+syn	90.30	76.06	62.57
Δ	0.84	1.36	0.67

Table 3: Exact-match accuracy on testset with respect to template frequency f in training data.

ulate this scenario by sub-sampling 6K utterances in the training data as follows: for each template in the training data, we randomly choose one utterance. We use this sub-sampled data for training our parser, generator, and AP. Table 4 shows the mean and variance of the accuracy on five random sub-sampled portions of the train data. We see that in this low resource setting, our approach boosts the accuracy by more than 2% absolute.

Training data	#Samples	Acc (%)
Real	6,000	72.24 ± 0.05
+syn	30,000	**74.31 ± 0.05**

Table 4: Average accuracy of five different runs for 6K training examples. The synthetic data is filtered by BART parser, which is trained on 6K samples.

4 Related Work

Using pretrained models to generate synthetic data has been studied recently (Amin-Nejad et al., 2020; Kumar et al., 2020). Their work however focuses on multi-class classification problems. Taking a step further, our work shows a viable path for structured output (*i.e.*, parse trees) problems.

5 Conclusions

We have proposed a novel approach for generating synthetic data for hierarchical semantic parsing. Our initial experiments show promising results of this approach and open up possibility for applying it to other problems with highly structured outputs in Natural Language Processing.

Acknowledgments

We thank reviewers for their constructive comments and suggestions. We also thank Raquel G. Alhama for proofreading this paper.

References

Ali Amin-Nejad, Julia Ive, and Sumithra Velupillai. 2020. Exploring transformer text generation for medical dataset augmentation. In *Proceedings of the 12th Language Resources and Evaluation Conference*, pages 4699–4708, Marseille, France. European Language Resources Association.

Sergey Edunov, Myle Ott, Michael Auli, and David Grangier. 2018. Understanding back-translation at scale. In *Proceedings of the 2018 Conference on Empirical Methods in Natural Language Processing*, pages 489–500, Brussels, Belgium. Association for Computational Linguistics.

Sonal Gupta, Rushin Shah, Mrinal Mohit, Anuj Kumar, and Mike Lewis. 2018. Semantic parsing for task oriented dialog using hierarchical representations. In *Proceedings of the 2018 Conference on Empirical Methods in Natural Language Processing*, pages 2787–2792, Brussels, Belgium. Association for Computational Linguistics.

Ari Holtzman, Jan Buys, Li Du, Maxwell Forbes, and Yejin Choi. 2020. The curious case of neural text degeneration. In *International Conference on Learning Representations*.

Mark Johnson. 1998. Pcfg models of linguistic tree representations. *Comput. Linguist.*, 24(4):613–632.

Diederik P. Kingma and Jimmy Ba. 2015. Adam: A method for stochastic optimization. *ICLR*.

Varun Kumar, Ashutosh Choudhary, and Eunah Cho. 2020. Data augmentation using pre-trained transformer models.

Mike Lewis, Yinhan Liu, Naman Goyal, Marjan Ghazvininejad, Abdelrahman Mohamed, Omer Levy, Veselin Stoyanov, and Luke Zettlemoyer. 2020. BART: Denoising sequence-to-sequence pretraining for natural language generation, translation, and comprehension. In *Proceedings of the 58th Annual Meeting of the Association for Computational Linguistics*, pages 7871–7880, Online. Association for Computational Linguistics.

Y. Liu, Myle Ott, Naman Goyal, Jingfei Du, Mandar Joshi, Danqi Chen, Omer Levy, M. Lewis, Luke Zettlemoyer, and Veselin Stoyanov. 2019. Roberta: A robustly optimized bert pretraining approach. *ArXiv*, abs/1907.11692.

Subendhu Rongali, Luca Soldaini, Emilio Monti, and Wael Hamza. 2020. Don't parse, generate! a sequence to sequence architecture for task-oriented semantic parsing. In *Proceedings of The Web Conference 2020*, WWW '20, page 2962–2968, New York, NY, USA. Association for Computing Machinery.

Rico Sennrich, Barry Haddow, and Alexandra Birch. 2016. Improving neural machine translation models with monolingual data. In *Proceedings of the 54th Annual Meeting of the Association for Computational Linguistics (Volume 1: Long Papers)*, pages 86–96, Berlin, Germany. Association for Computational Linguistics.

Luke S. Zettlemoyer and Michael Collins. 2005. Learning to map sentences to logical form: Structured classification with probabilistic categorial grammars. In *Proceedings of the Twenty-First Conference on Uncertainty in Artificial Intelligence*, UAI'05, page 658–666, Arlington, Virginia, USA. AUAI Press.

Structured Prediction for Joint Class Cardinality and Entity Property Inference in Model-Complete Text Comprehension

Hendrik ter Horst and **Philipp Cimiano**
Semantic Computing Group
Bielefeld University, Germany
{hterhors,cimiano}@techfak.uni-bielefeld.de

Abstract

Model-complete text comprehension aims at interpreting a natural language text with respect to a semantic domain model describing the classes and their properties relevant for the domain in question. Solving this task can be approached as a structured prediction problem, consisting in inferring the most probable instance of the semantic model given the text. In this work, we focus on the challenging sub-problem of *cardinality prediction* that consists in predicting the number of distinct individuals of each class in the semantic model. We show that cardinality prediction can successfully be approached by modeling the overall task as a joint inference problem, predicting the number of individuals of certain classes while at the same time extracting their properties. We approach this task with probabilistic graphical models computing the maximum-a-posteriori instance of the semantic model. Our main contribution lies on the empirical investigation and analysis of different approximative inference strategies based on Gibbs sampling. We present and evaluate our models on the task of extracting key parameters from scientific full text articles describing pre-clinical studies in the domain of spinal cord injury.

1 Introduction

While there has been significant progress on information extraction tasks with a comparably low level of structural complexity such as entity recognition (Goulart et al., 2011; Nadeau and Sekine, 2007), relation extraction (Zhou et al., 2014; Kumar, 2017), and co-reference resolution (Soon et al., 2001; Ferracane et al., 2016), there is not much progress on capturing the comprehensive meaning of a text with respect to a given semantic model in terms of a given vocabulary of classes and properties. We refer to this task as *model-complete text comprehension* (MCTC) which requires to put all the above mentioned classical NLP-tasks into a larger context. The goal of MCTC is to capture all the information in the text that is expressible with respect to the semantic model, while ignoring those meaning aspects which are not. This can be framed as a structured prediction problem consisting in inferring the most plausible instance of the semantic model.

One challenging problem in MCTC lies in the prediction of the correct number of individuals for each class, hereinafter referred to as *cardinality prediction*, that is answering the question(s): *"How many (and which) individuals of a class are mentioned in the text?"*. In essence, this can be approached by grouping mentions of known real-world entities into equivalence classes, which has widely been addressed under the heading of *co-reference resolution* (He, 2007; Singh et al., 2013). However, in many problem domains, we need to identify equivalence classes of entities that are priorly unknown (in terms of not referring to a specific real-world entity). Thus, explicit mentions in text such as naming variations etc. can not be directly mapped to a set of existing entities. To the contrary, such entities are only distinguishable on the basis of their describing properties. Take the case of scientific publications concerning pre-clinical studies containing a variable number of experimental groups each of which is described by an injury model, an animal species, treatments etc. Here, mentions of experimental groups do not refer to existing real-world entities and they need to be inferred/grouped on the basis of their identifying properties that are mentioned in the text. We refer to the prediction of how many *distinct* individuals[1] of a particular class are (indirectly) mentioned in a text as cardinality prediction and solve it jointly

---

[1] We refer to mentions of entities in a text as *entities* and to the denotation of such entities in a given model of the text as *individuals*

Proceedings of 4th Workshop on Structured Prediction for NLP, pages 22–32
November 20, 2020. ©2020 Association for Computational Linguistics

with the prediction of the properties of each individual. We model this joint task as the task of predicting a (logical) model of the text, which involves making choices as to which individuals exist for each class.

Towards capturing the dependence of class cardinalities and properties, we propose a joint inference approach that infers equivalence classes of entities in a text while at the same time predicting the properties of each equivalence class. We model this task as a statistical inference problem, relying on a factorized posterior conditional distribution $p(\vec{y} \mid \vec{x})$ as implemented in CRFs to approximate the true distribution over possible instantiations $\vec{y} \in Y$ of the semantic model given a text $\vec{x}$. Applying maximum-a-posteriori inference, we infer the most likely instance of the model that captures the whole meaning of the text as expressible by the semantic model. This includes the determination of the number of distinct equivalence classes (thus solving cardinality prediction) as well as predicting the properties for each equivalence class. Our approach is evaluated on text comprehension of research articles describing pre-clinical studies in the domain of spinal cord injury. Capturing correct key-parameters of the study protocol can be modeled as an MCTC problem as it requires a comprehensive understanding of the text rather than extracting single binary relations only. In this domain, we focus in particular on the extraction of experimental groups and their properties as described in Section 4.1. The data set[2] and the source code [3] are public available.

In this work, we answer the following research questions:

1) What is the advantage of jointly predicting the cardinality of classes and their properties over an isolated approach and how much does the prediction of the cardinality profit from the joint modelling?

2) What approximative inference strategies work best on this complex inference problem? We examine i) a vanilla Gibbs-based inference strategy ii) an inference strategy that is seeded with cardinality values based on a preceding clustering step., and iii) a parallel multi-chain

inference strategy in which one chain is constructed for each potential cardinality value.

2 Related Work

There are a number of traditional natural language processing tasks related to *model-complete text comprehension*. In this section, we briefly discuss each task and provide some pointers to systems addressing the corresponding task, focusing on the bio-medical domain.

Entity Recognition and Linking (NER+L) describes the task of finding entity mentions in a text and linking them to unique concepts in some knowledge base. The task originated in the context of information extraction, consisting of identifying persons, company names etc. (Nadeau and Sekine, 2007) but has also received prominent attention in the biomedical field focusing on entities such as genes, diseases, treatments, etc. (Goulart et al., 2011). NER+L is an important preliminary step in many downstream applications as it identifies core informational units that are needed for more complex analysis levels including relation extraction, slot filling, and MCTC.

Relation Extraction (RE) describes the task of detecting relations between entities mentioned in a text (Giuliano et al., 2007). While many models rely on a pipeline architecture predicting entities first and then predicting relations, more recent works model both tasks jointly (Luo et al., 2015). Although there has been notable progress on RE in the last years, the task has been typically restricted to extracting binary relations within single sentence boundaries only (Zhou et al., 2014). With our work, we strive to go beyond such simplifications towards document-level text interpretation with respect to a more complex model.

Co-reference resolution (CRR) describes originally the task of finding nouns and pronouns that refer to the same underlying entity (Soon et al., 2001). When applying CRR to the medical field, the task shifts towards the resolution of mentions of diseases, tests, compounds, groups, treatments, etc. (He, 2007). Cardinality prediction in isolation can be modeled as a CRR problem, where the number of distinct non co-referring entities need to be found. With regard to the goal of comprehensive text understanding, classical co-reference resolution is clearly not enough, as also the properties of each entity need to be extracted. While Singh et al. (Singh et al., 2013) have attempted to model the tasks of entity recognition, relation extraction and co-reference resolution jointly, in their approach the interaction between relation extraction and co-reference resolution is not modelled directly, only via entity tags. In our approach we model the joint interaction between inducing equivalence classes (resolving co-references) while extracting the properties of entities/individuals as a basis to inform the decision about whether two individuals are the same (thus co-refer) given their properties. Durret et al. (Durrett et al., 2013) propose a global inference entity-level modeling for classical co-reference resolution based on a rich factor graph. In the unrolled factor graph, each factor refers to one entity property defined on a semantic or syntactic linguistic basis. In contrast to this work where properties of an individual/entity are pre-defined by the semantic model. Thus, our focus lies in their joint exploration while learning their interplay during inference in order to decide whether the properties belong to the same individual or not. Haghighi et al. (Haghighi and Klein, 2010) propose an unsupervised generative model incorporating several linguistic properties of the entity and its mention. In contrast, our work does not rely on entities that are explicitly mentioned in text. Instead, our model follows the schema of a semantic model to reason about the existence of individuals that can be inferred from the text and groups these individuals into groups by way of inferring the properties of these individuals.

The task of *slot-filling* (SF) was first introduced in the Message Understanding Conference (Grishman and Sundheim, 1996). It is concerned with predicting an entity-centric structure having a set of relations to other entities as it can be found e.g. in ontology-based information extraction (Sanchez-Cisneros and Aparicio Gali, 2013; Buitelaar et al., 2006) or extracting info-boxes from Wikipedia articles (Lange et al., 2010). Contrary to MCTC, classical slot-filling requires the prediction of a single structure per document only, which heavily reduces relational complexity and does not include nested individuals. There are many approaches to SF ranging from relying on distant supervision as described by Surdeanu et al. (Surdeanu et al., 2010) to, more recently, neural approaches as described by Zhang et al. (Zhang et al., 2017). Finally, SF can be seen as an upstream process for (cold-start) knowledge base population as described by ter Horst et al. (ter Horst et al., 2018).

Our work is highly related to information extraction systems in the (bio-) medical field. When it comes e.g. to the prediction of key parameters of clinical studies, most work focuses on the extraction of PICO-concepts: Patient/Problem (P), Intervention (I), Comparison (C) and Outcome (O). Summerscales et al. (Summerscales et al., 2009) have applied conditional random fields to extract key parameters from abstracts of clinical studies including treatments, experimental groups, and outcomes. Contrary to our approach, the task is defined as an NER+L problem, not aiming at capturing the semantic relations and concepts. Trenta et al. (Trenta et al., 2015) have proposed to rely on a maximum entropy classifier jointly extracting fine grained PICO elements from abstracts. Brujin et al. (De Bruijn et al., 2008) combined an SVM-based text classifier with regular expressions to extract PICO elements. Further, Ferracane et al. (Ferracane et al., 2016) aim to leverage co-reference resolution to identify experimental groups (patients) from medical abstracts. However, none of these works aims at deeper extraction of arms/experimental groups and their properties. In general, most approaches in the literature focus on sentence extraction and classification only (Mayer et al., 2018; Zhao et al., 2012; Wallace et al., 2016) rather than on predicting a semantic structure.

3 Method

Structured prediction describes a variety of tasks with the goal of predicting a pre-defined target structure that is extracted from an unstructured input text (Smith, 2011). We formulate the MCTC problem as a structured prediction task, where the structure to be predicted is an instance of the semantic model capturing the meaning of a text. This involves the task of predicting the number of individuals of each class (cardinality prediction) as well as predicting the values of the key properties of each individual. Our proposed method relies on probabilistic graphical models i.e. conditional random fields (CRFs; (Lafferty et al., 2001; Sutton et al., 2012)) as their application is well established in many structured prediction tasks in the context of NLP.

Encoding Semantic Models: An instance of the semantic model is encoded as a nested vector $\vec{y}$ containing as many elements as there are classes and properties in the model. Thus, given a set of classes $\{C_1, \ldots, C_n\}$ and a set of properties $\mathcal{P} =$

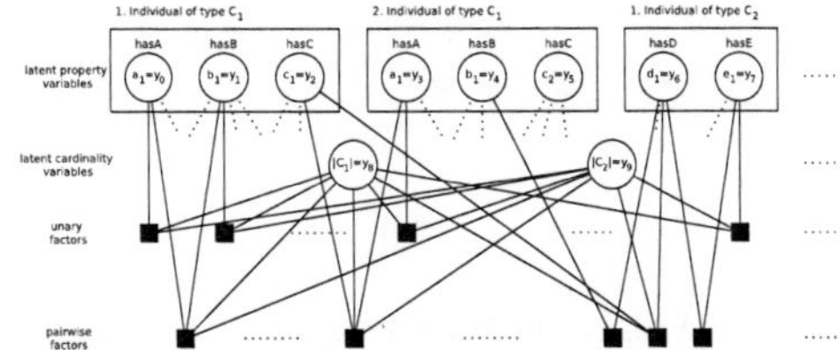

Figure 1: Schematized factor graph unrolled over the previously shown example. We introduce unary property factors connected to a single property of a single individual and pairwise property factors, connected to two properties of one or two individuals. Both factors are additionally connected to the cardinality variables jointly modelling the properties and cardinalities. For clarity, we omit the observed variables in this example.

$\{P_1, \ldots, P_m\}$, $\vec{y}$ can be written as $\{\vec{v}_{C_1}, \ldots, \vec{v}_{C_n}\}$ where each $\vec{v}_{C_i}$ has the form $[|C_i|, \vec{I_1^i}, \ldots, \vec{I_m^i}]$. $|C_i|$ represents the cardinality of class C_i, i.e. the number of individuals of class C_i mentioned in the text. $I_j^i \subseteq \mathcal{P}$ is a vector describing an individual of class C_i in terms of its properties.

Example: Consider a semantic model consisting of two classes C_1 and C_2 where individuals of class C_1 have properties $hasA, hasB, hasC$, and individuals of class C_2 have properties $hasD, hasE$. One specific instance of the semantic model would be represented as: $[[2, [a_1, b_1, c_1], [a_1, b_1, c_2]], [1, [d_1, e_2]]]$. The first component of the first tuple shows that there are two individuals of class C_1. The first individual has the property values a_1, b_1, c_1 for properties $hasA, hasB, hasC$, respectively. The second individual of class C_1 has property values a_1, b_1, c_2 for the above mentioned properties. The second tuple shows that there is one individual of class C_2 which has property values d_1, e_2 for properties $hasD, hasE$, respectively.

3.1 CRF-based Modelling

Let Y be the set of all possible (nested) vectors over a given vocabulary of classes and properties as exemplified above. Intuitively, this is the set of all possible instantiations of the semantic model. With $\vec{x}$ being the set of observed input variables corresponding to the list of tokens of the input text, the conditional probability of a specific instance of the semantic model $\vec{y} \in Y$ is $p(\vec{y}|\vec{x}; \theta)$, with θ being a learned model parameter vector. The best value assignment to the set of target variables, denoted as $\hat{\vec{y}}$, is found by maximum a-posteriori

(MAP) inference as shown in Equation (1):

$$\hat{\vec{y}} = \operatorname*{argmax}_{\vec{y} \in Y} p(\vec{y}|\vec{x}; \theta) \qquad (1)$$

As inference in high dimensional vector spaces is often intractable, conditional random fields decompose the joint probability into individual factors. The set of factors and their operating scope is defined by a factor graph (Kschischang et al., 2001; Koller and Friedman, 2009). A factor graph is a bipartite undirected graph $\mathcal{G} = (V, F)$ consisting of a set of factors F and a set of variables V defined as the union of the observed input and the target output variables $V = \vec{y} \cup \vec{x}$. A factor $\Psi \in F$ is a non-negative real-valued exponential function $\Psi : V \to \mathbb{R}_{\geq 0}$ that computes a scalar score based on a subset $\omega \subseteq V$ of random variables defining its operating scope $\Psi(\omega) = \exp(\langle f(\omega), \theta_\Psi \rangle)$, with $f(\cdot)$ representing a feature vector based on a set of indicator functions, and θ_Ψ referring to the set of model weights that are shared between factors of the same type.

In our approach, it is crucial to capture dependencies between multiple target variables, in particular between the variables representing the cardinalities of classes and variables representing the individuals' properties. For this reason, we introduce factors that model the interaction between all pairs of property variables while having access to the cardinalities. We schematize our factor graph in Figure 1, unrolled over the previously given example. Let $\vec{\mathcal{C}}$ denote the vector of the cardinalities of all classes and $|C_i| \in \vec{\mathcal{C}}$ the cardinality of class C_i. The decomposition of the conditional probability $p(\vec{y} \mid \vec{x}; \theta)$ can be written as shown in Equation (2):

$$\frac{1}{Z} \prod_{y_i \in \vec{y}} \left[\Psi'(\vec{\mathcal{C}}, y_i, \vec{x}) \prod_{y_j \in \vec{y} \setminus \{y_i\}} \Psi''(\vec{\mathcal{C}}, y_i, y_j, \vec{x}) \right]$$

$$(2)$$

where Z denotes the partition function and $\Psi'(\cdot)$, $\Psi''(\cdot)$ denote factors defined for single and pairs of output variables while having access to the cardinalities $\vec{\mathcal{C}}$.

The unrolling of factors over the input is performed using imperatively defined factor graphs as proposed by McCallum et al. (McCallum et al., 2009). For approximative inference of the posterior distribution, we rely on the state-based Markov Chain Monte Carlo sampling paradigm. Proposal states are computed and sampled via Gibbs sampling (Casella and George, 1992). While training, the model parameters θ are updated with SampleR-ank (Wick et al., 2009) that is computing parameter update gradients based on an objective comparison of two states, usually between the current state and the selected successor state (cf. next sections for proposed variations). In our approach the objective is to maximize the F_1 score to the ground truth.

3.2 State-based Inference Strategies

In the following, we propose our inference strategies to MCTC with a focus towards cardinality prediction. In state-based inference, a state s^t is defined as one specific variable assignment to the target structure $\vec{y}$ at a specific time point t. While inference proceeds, in each step a set of proposal states $\mathcal{S}^{t+1}$ is computed based on a list of predefined atomic change rules that are applied to the current state, e.g. changing cardinalities of classes or the properties of individuals. The successor state $s^{t+1} \in \mathcal{S}^{t+1}$ is sampled from the generated set of proposal states.

Vanilla Inference: The *vanilla inference* is based on traditional Gibbs sampling. The inference procedure is initialized with one empty state s^0 that is $\vec{y} = \emptyset$ (no values are assigned) and it-eratively updated with atomic change rules. Mod-ifying the cardinality for a class C_i is defined as either deleting an existing individual of index j ($\vec{y} \leftarrow \vec{y} \setminus \vec{I}_j^i;\ |C_i| \leftarrow (|C_i| - 1)$) or adding a new individual with leading index $|C_i|$ ($\vec{y} \leftarrow \vec{y} \cup \vec{I}_{|C_i|}^i;\ |C_i| \leftarrow (|C_i| + 1)$). On the level of individuals, an atomic change is defined as deleting, adding, or changing a property value. The inference pro-cedure terminates if the model parameter update converges. The final state represents the most likely instance of the semantic model.

Cardinality Seeded$^+$ Inference: In the *seeded$^+$ inference* (c.f. Figure 2), the first state s^0 is initial-ized with an a priori predicted cardinality value λ_{C_i} for each class C_i, which is re-sampled as inference proceeds. For this, the system relies on the same atomic change and termination rules as defined for the vanilla inference.

Parallel Multi Chain Inference: The *parallel multi chain inference* procedure (c.f. Figure 3) is initialized with n independent Markov chains $S^0 = [s_1^0, s_2^0, \ldots, s_n^0]$ that are explored in paral-lel but independently from each other. Each state $s_i^0 \in S^0$ is initialized with a fixed number of in-dividuals for each class type ranging between a

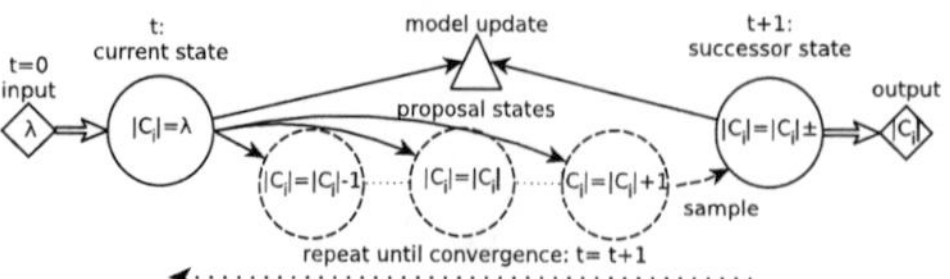

Figure 2: Schematized *seeded$^+$* inference. The input is the seed parameter λ which is used to initialize the cardinality of the first state. Within the proposal states, λ can be altered. In each time step the model is updated based on the current state and successor state.

pre-defined minimum α_{C_i} and maximum β_{C_i}. Con-trary to the previous inference strategies, the car-dinalities in each chain are not sampled over but remain fixed. Only the property values of the in-dividuals are sampled. The parallel sampling is independent in the sense that for each chain the computation of the set of proposal states and the selection of the successor states is independent of the other chains. The model parameters θ however are shared throughout all chains and are thus up-dated n times every time step; once for each pair of current–successor state. This inference procedure terminates if all chains converge. The final output is selected based on the highest model probability among the final states of all chains.

Parallel Multi Chain Inference$^+$: The *parallel multi chain inference with cross-chain model up-dates* strategy builds on the previous inference strat-egy in that it includes parallel inference chains with fixed cardinality but integrates cross-chain model update operations after each time step (bold trian-gle in Figure 3). That is, in addition to the n model updates, a set of state-pairs is computed by pair-wise combining the selected successor states of the chains for cross-over model updates. This gener-ates $\frac{n^2+n}{2}$ model parameter updates in each time step. The motivation for this cross-chain model updates is to force the model to learn to prefer the correct cardinality values.

3.3 Features

Factors are defined in terms of indicator functions that measure the compatibility of variable assign-ments to the output structure $\vec{y}$ given the input doc-ument $\vec{x}$. In the following, we explain four types of feature groups that we consider in our model. The proposed features are intuitively designed to cap-ture document-level semantics and finally selected empirically based on an evaluation of a subset of the training data.

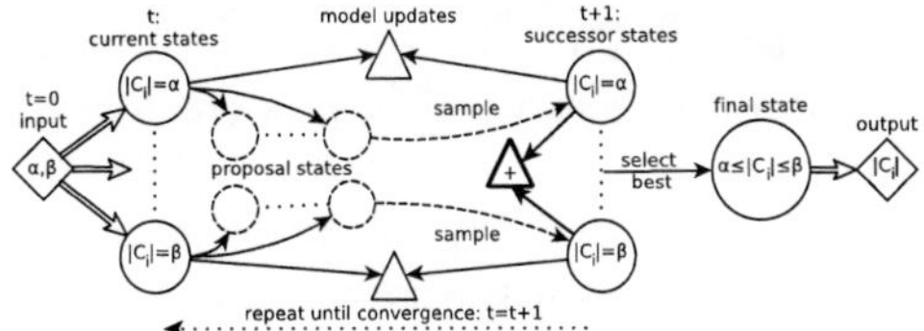

Figure 3: Schematized *parallel multi chain$^+$ inference*. For each value between the input α and β a Markov chain is instantiated. In each time step the model is updated between the current and successor states for each chain. In the advanced version, additional model update operations based on the successor states are added (bold triangle).

Document-level: Document-level features measure the compatibility of property assignments of individuals based on the textual content of the document represented as 3-grams. For this, triples are considered for plausibility, containing the property type, the entity type of the property value, and its textual representation as 3-grams. We further measure the compatibility of pairwise assignments of property values considering their sentential distance, assuming that values within the same property (in case of multi value properties) or individual (throughout multiple properties) are more likely to appear closer together rather than being spread across the document.

Document-structure: Document structure features rely on a heuristic segmentation of the document into the standard sections of a scientific article: *abstract, introduction, method, results, discussion, references,* and *unknown.* We compute features that capture 3-grams mentioned in specific sections of the article as indicators for the assignment of certain values to properties. By this, we can model that certain content is expected in certain sections and should override inconsistent information appearing in other sections.

Cardinality: Aiming at cardinality prediction, we measure the compatibility of cardinality values in dependence of other random variables in $\vec{y}$. For this, we make the choice of a cardinality dependent on n-grams appearing in the surface forms of property values.

In addition, we also consider features implementing a prior for the cardinalities of classes as well as for the number of different values for multi-value properties. By this, the model is able to learn a class/property-specific distribution of cardinality values. For example, assuming that the cardinality

of a class $\hat{C}$ has a very high a priori likelihood for a specific value $\lambda_{\hat{C}}$ throughout the training data, this puts pressure on the model during inference to prefer model instances where there are $\lambda_{\hat{C}}$ individuals for the respective class, unless other features provide strong evidence for the contrary.

Within- and Across-Individual Coherence: Sometimes values of properties are shared across individuals within the same class. Thus, we measure the compatibility of value assignments across properties within one individual, but also how plausible it is that a certain value is shared across individuals.

4 Experiments

Model-complete text comprehension aims at the automatic instantiation of a semantic model based on information extracted from a natural language text. Such an instance contains information about individuals of equivalence classes, their cardinality and their properties. Thus the overall task of MCTC can be evaluated towards i) the correct prediction of the number of individuals, and ii) the prediction of properties for each individual. In the following, we describe our use case application, the experimental procedure and results.

4.1 Semantic Model and Data Set

We apply our approach to full text articles describing pre-clinical studies in the domain of spinal cord injury. Our semantic model is an excerpt of the Spinal Cord Injury Ontology (SCIO) (Brazda et al., 2017) centered on the key concept of an experimental group. An experimental group represent an animal model to which a certain injury and treatment is applied and is described by four key properties: i) *hasSpecies* specifying the species that the animal model belongs to, ii) *hasInjury* specifying the experimentally inflicted injury, ii) *hasTreatment* is the list of treatments that were applied, and iv) *hasName* is a list of naming variations for that animal group that are used throughout the document. Note that, in accordance with domain experts, only the first three properties are considered to be relevant to describe the experimental group semantically and thus are evaluated. However, the property *hasName* can be seen as an auxiliary property that is not necessary to understand the study but provides useful information, e.g. to detect co-references.

The data set contains full text articles that have been annotated by three domain experts using the

SANTO framework (Hartung et al., 2018). Annotations are available on the full level of relevant concepts of SCIO. Each document can be seen as a data point that is annotated with an instance of the semantic model containing a list of experimental groups and their properties. While annotations for the *hasName* property are linked to specific textual phrases in the document, all other properties are annotated in a distantly supervised fashion. In a preliminary step, we apply a named entity recognition heuristic based on automatically generated regular expressions to compute a set of document-based annotations for all classes and property values that exist in the semantic model. The names of groups are additionally extracted with a standard CRF using standard token-level features. The final data set contains 96 data points with an average length of approx. 273 sentences per document and a total number of 345 experimental groups ($\mu = 3.3$, $\sigma = 1.3$, $min = 2$, $max = 7$).

4.2 Inference Parameter Estimation

Our proposed inference strategies rely on a prior estimation of the number of individuals for initialization. As described in Section 3.2 the seeded inference strategy requires the seed variable λ. The parallel multi chain inference requires a range of cardinality values $0 \leq \alpha \leq \beta$. Details about their estimation are briefly described below.

Seed Prior Cardinality Estimation λ The cardinality seeded[(+)] inference procedure requires the estimation of the seed parameter λ for each class determining the number of individuals (experimental groups) the initial state begins with. λ is computed by relying on the k-Means algorithm by clustering group names based on textual features. The cluster quality of k-Means depends on two main parameters. First, the determination of the number of clusters, for which we rely on the residual sum of squares (RSS) algorithm with an empirically determined penalization factor for large number of clusters. Second, we rely on a function measuring the distance between two data points, i.e. between two group names. We compare three distance functions: i) Levenshtein distance with a k-Medoid implementation of k-Means, ii) cosine distance of the averaged sum of pre-trained Pubmed-based word embeddings induced with Word2vec (Mikolov et al., 2013), and iii) a random forest classifier (Liaw et al., 2002) with a correlation based feature selection (resulting in Smith-Waterman and 3-gram

based Jaccard similarity as features).We evaluate the performances based on the F_1 score using a reference clustering as ground truth obtained from our annotated data set. We define a true positive as a group name that is in the correct cluster, a false positive if it is in a wrong cluster, and a false negative if it is missing in its respective cluster. The Levenshtein distance performed with $F_1 = 0.41$, the Word2Vec-based cosine distance performs slightly better with $F_1 = 0.45$, while the random forest classifier reaches a value of $F_1 = 0.56$. With the random forest outperforming both other models, we rely on this distance function in a k-Means clustering for estimating λ.

Parallel Multi Chain[(+)] Parameters α and β The parallel multi chain[(+)] inference strategies require the estimation of a minimum (α) and a maximum (β) number of individuals assuming that the correct cardinality lies between α and β. We estimate both parameters in dependence of the average cardinality of individuals in the training set. With μ being the average cardinality and σ its standard deviation, we set $\alpha = \mu - \sigma$ and $\beta = \mu + \sigma$.

4.3 Evaluation Setting

Our experiments follow a randomized cross validation regime as usual for experiments on relatively small data sets. We ran each experiment 10 times with a random split into 80% training data (76 in number) and 20% test data (20 in number). We provide evaluation results in terms of precision, recall, and F_1 macro averaged over all documents in three configurations:

Cardinality Prediction (CP): We compare the predicted cardinality p_c to the ground truth cardinality g_c where $tp = min(p_c, g_c)$, $fp = max(0, (p_c - g_c))$, and $fn = max(0, (g_c - p_c))$

Property Prediction (PP): We compare the predicted property values to the ground truth property values where a true positive is a correctly assigned property value, a false positive is a wrongly assigned property value and a false negative as a missing property value of an individual.

Combined (Comb): We compute the harmonic mean between the cardinality and property prediction scores.

4.4 Experimental Results

Our experiments comprise the evaluation of four models each of which is based on one of the described joint inference strategies predicting cardinality and properties at the same time, as well as a pure cardinality prediction baseline ignoring property prediction. The joint inference models are: *RSS*: the seeded inference with a fixed cardinality, RSS^+: the seeded inference that allows further sampling of the cardinality as described in Section 3.2, *PAR*: the parallel multi chain inference, and PAR^+: the parallel multi chain inference with chain-cross over model updates. As cardinality baseline(s), we provide *Co-ref CRF*, a CRF based method for clustering group names without a joint prediction of properties, relying on linguistic features only, and *RSS*, the cardinality as predicted by the RSS based k-Means as reported in the RSS-model. Note that the cardinality in RSS is fixed and does not change during inference so that it can be seen as a baseline for predicting the cardinalities. The experimental results of those models are reported in Table 1. In Table 2, we compare the run time and the number of generated states for the four inference methods.

4.5 Discussion

We analyze the results with respect to three different aspects: i) performance of the cardinality prediction, ii) overall performance as measured by the combined harmonic mean, and iii) performance with respect to the run time and complexity.

Cardinality Prediction The performances of the cardinality prediction can be seen in the first row of Table 1. The CRF-based baseline already yields a very strong F_1-score of 0.79 which shows that cardinality prediction with linguistic features ignoring property prediction provides already decent results. The k-Means approach with an unsupervised RSS cluster estimation yields a cardinality F_1-score of 0.64, performing worse than the CRF baseline. When seeding our approximate inference approach with prior cardinality values (RSS^+), the F_1-score considerably improves by 19 %-points up to 0.83, even outperforming the CRF baseline. The cardinality prediction in PAR performs comparably strong with an F_1-score of 0.81. This score is further outperformed when integrating the cross-chain model update operation. PAR+ archives performs best in predicting the cardinalities with an F_1-score of 0.84.

Overall Score The performances of the overall prediction can be seen in the second to last rows in Table 1. With respect to the property prediction, RSS performs best with a score of 0.57, mainly due to the correct detection of TREATMENTS (0.67) and SPECIES (0.62). With a low cardinality performance, the overall score sums up to 0.63 in F_1. The strong increase in the performance of cardinality prediction in RSS^+, compared to the RSS model comes at the cost of an inferior property prediction quality. The combined score for RSS^+ however shows slightly better results with an F_1-score of 0.65. The property prediction in PAR shows similar results to the RSS^+ for INJURY, a slight decrease for TREATMENTS, and a huge increase (10% points) for SPECIES. The PAR model yields an overall score of 0.66. Activating cross-chain model updates (PAR^+), the property prediction shows a performance increase by 8% points for *hasTreatment* while for both other properties the value is similar to PAR. The PAR^+ model outperforms all other models in the overall score, but lacks 4%-points for property prediction in comparison to RSS. The results show that property prediction works best when fixing the number of individuals. With PAR^+ model working best for cardinality prediction, an interesting model combination could be to use the cardinality output of PAR^+ as initialization to RSS. This however, is left for future work.

Run Time Performance The run time as well as the number of states for each inference method is shown in Table 2. We report statistics on the average time in seconds (s) that is needed to process a document and depict the search space complexity by providing the average number of generated and evaluated states in thousands (k). All experiments ran on an Intel(R) Xeon(R) CPU E5-2630 v3 @ 2.40GHz with 16 cores and 120 GB of available RAM. No GPU or further hardware acceleration was used. The table shows that RSS has the lowest complexity in terms of state generation, which is due to the fixed cardinality and in consequence a significantly reduced search space. In RSS^+, we notice a huge increase in the number of generated states by a factor of around 7. At the same time, we observe that the run time factor rises only by a factor of 2.2 in training and 2.8 in test. It is noticeable that the number of generated states and the run time at test time decreases from PAR to PAR^+ which is probably due to a faster model convergence, however training run time increases.

Approach	Co-ref CRF			RSS			RSS$^+$			PAR			PAR$^+$		
	F_1	P	R	F_1	P	R	F_1	P	R	F_1	P	R	F_1	P	R
CP	0.79	0.99	0.65	0.64	0.48	0.97	0.83	0.89	0.78	0.81	0.70	0.96	**0.84**	0.75	0.96
Comb				0.63	0.53	0.77	0.65	0.68	0.63	0.66	0.60	0.73	**0.69**	0.64	0.75
PP				**0.57**	0.58	0.57	0.48	0.47	0.48	0.50	0.50	0.49	0.53	0.53	0.53
→Injury				0.35	0.35	0.35	0.46	0.46	0.46	0.47	0.47	0.47	**0.48**	0.48	0.48
→Species				**0.62**	0.62	0.62	0.50	0.50	0.50	0.60	0.60	0.60	0.61	0.61	0.61
→Treatments				**0.67**	0.68	0.66	0.46	0.45	0.48	0.42	0.44	0.41	0.50	0.51	0.49

Table 1: Results of the cardinality baseline(s) and of the inference strategies for joint cardinality and property prediction. We provide macro-F_1, precision, and recall averaged over 10 runs with random 80/20 splits.

Approach	RSS	RSS$^+$	PAR	PAR$^+$
Avg. # states (k)	**46**	324	150	119
Avg. train time (s)	**28.11**	63.87	54.71	60.73
Avg. test time (s)	**8.95**	25.21	38.67	32.87

Table 2: Run time and complexity statistics of the inference strategies. We provide the average number of evaluated states in thousands (k), averaged training and test time per document in seconds (s).

5 Conclusion

We have proposed an approach to the task of *model-complete text comprehension* (MCTC) that relies on a learned model of the posterior distribution of instances of a semantic model given a text to infer the most likely instance of a semantic model that captures the meaning of the text best. We have relied on CRFs to model the conditional distribution in a factorized way and empirically investigated the impact of different approximate inferences strategies on our problem. Our experiments on the task of predicting the structure of experimental groups from scientific full text articles describing pre-clinical studies in the field of spinal cord injury show that modeling the MCTC task as a joint inference problem, extracting the cardinality in combination with predicting the properties of the individuals, outperforms a number of reasonable baselines predicting the cardinality alone. In future work, we intend to investigate combinations of our inference strategies, relying on the result state produced by our PAR$^+$ inference strategy to seed the RSS inference method to re-sample the property values, expecting to see an overall gain in both cardinality prediction and entity property prediction over both inference strategies.

Acknowledgements

This work has been funded by the Federal Ministry of Education and Research (BMBF, Germany) in the PSINK project (project number 031L0028A).

References

Nicole Brazda, Hendrik ter Horst, Matthias Hartung, Cord Wiljes, Veronica Estrada, Roman Klinger, Wolfgang Kuchinke, Hans Werner Müller, and Philipp Cimiano. 2017. Scio: an ontology to support the formalization of pre-clinical spinal cord injury experiments. In *Proc. of the 3rd Joint Ontology Workshops (JOWO): Ontologies and Data in the Life Sciences*, volume 2050.

Paul Buitelaar, Philipp Cimiano, Stefania Racioppa, and Melanie Siegel. 2006. Ontology-based information extraction with soba. In *Proc. of the International Conference on Language Resources and Evaluation (LREC)*.

George Casella and Edward I George. 1992. Explaining the gibbs sampler. *The American Statistician*, 46(3):167–174.

Berry De Bruijn, Simona Carini, Svetlana Kiritchenko, Joel Martin, and Ida Sim. 2008. Automated information extraction of key trial design elements from clinical trial publications. In *Proc. of the AMIA Annual Symposium*, volume 2008, page 141. American Medical Informatics Association.

Greg Durrett, David Hall, and Dan Klein. 2013. Decentralized entity-level modeling for coreference resolution. In *Proceedings of the 51st Annual Meeting of the Association for Computational Linguistics (Volume 1: Long Papers)*, pages 114–124.

Elisa Ferracane, Iain Marshall, Byron C Wallace, and Katrin Erk. 2016. Leveraging coreference to identify arms in medical abstracts: An experimental study. In *Proc. of the Seventh International Workshop on Health Text Mining and Information Analysis*, pages 86–95.

Claudio Giuliano, Alberto Lavelli, and Lorenza Romano. 2007. Relation extraction and the influence of automatic named-entity recognition. *ACM Transactions on Speech and Language Processing (TSLP)*, 5(1):1–26.

Rodrigo Rafael Villarreal Goulart, Vera Lúcia Strube de Lima, and Clarissa Castellã Xavier. 2011. A systematic review of named entity recognition in biomedical texts. *Journal of the Brazilian Computer Society*, 17(2):103–116.

Ralph Grishman and Beth M Sundheim. 1996. Message understanding conference-6: A brief history. In *Proc. of the 16th International Conference on Computational Linguistics (COLING)*.

Aria Haghighi and Dan Klein. 2010. Coreference resolution in a modular, entity-centered model. In *Human Language Technologies: The 2010 Annual Conference of the North American Chapter of the Association for Computational Linguistics*, pages 385–393.

Matthias Hartung, Hendrik ter Horst, Frank Grimm, Tim Diekmann, Roman Klinger, and Philipp Cimiano. 2018. Santo: a web-based annotation tool for ontology-driven slot filling. In *Proceedings of ACL 2018, System Demonstrations*, pages 68–73.

Tian Ye He. 2007. *Coreference resolution on entities and events for hospital discharge summaries*. Ph.D. thesis, Massachusetts Institute of Technology.

Hendrik ter Horst, Matthias Hartung, and Philipp Cimiano. 2018. Cold-start knowledge base population using ontology-based information extraction with conditional random fields. In *Proc. of the Reasoning Web International Summer School (RW)*, pages 78–109. Springer.

Daphne Koller and Nir Friedman. 2009. *Probabilistic Graphical Models. Principles and Techniques*. MIT Press.

Frank R. Kschischang, Brendan J. Frey, and Hans-Andrea Loeliger. 2001. Factor Graphs and Sum Product Algorithm. *IEEE Transactions on Information Theory*, 47(2):498–519.

Shantanu Kumar. 2017. A survey of deep learning methods for relation extraction. *CoRR*, abs/1705.03645.

John Lafferty, Andrew McCallum, and Fernando Pereira. 2001. Conditional Random Fields. Probabilistic Models for Segmenting and Labeling Sequence Data. In *Proc. of the International Conference on Machine Learning (ICML)*, pages 282–289.

Dustin Lange, Christoph Böhm, and Felix Naumann. 2010. Extracting structured information from wikipedia articles to populate infoboxes. In *Proc. of the ACM International Conference on Information and Knowledge Management (CIKM)*, pages 1661–1664.

Andy Liaw, Matthew Wiener, et al. 2002. Classification and regression by randomforest. *R news*, 2(3):18–22.

Gang Luo, Xiaojiang Huang, Chin-Yew Lin, and Zaiqing Nie. 2015. Joint entity recognition and disambiguation. In *Proc. of the 2015 Conference on Empirical Methods in Natural Language Processing (EMNLP)*, pages 879–888.

Tobias Mayer, Elena Cabrio, and Serena Villata. 2018. Evidence type classification in randomized controlled trials. In *Proc. of the 5th Workshop on Argument Mining*, pages 29–34. Association for Computational Linguistics.

Andrew McCallum, Karl Schultz, and Sameer Singh. 2009. Factorie: Probabilistic programming via imperatively defined factor graphs. In *Proc. of Advances in Neural Information Processing Systems (NIPS)*, pages 1249–1257.

Tomas Mikolov, Ilya Sutskever, Kai Chen, Greg S Corrado, and Jeff Dean. 2013. Distributed representations of words and phrases and their compositionality. In *Proc. of the Advances in Neural Information Processing Systems (NIPS)*, pages 3111–3119.

David Nadeau and Satoshi Sekine. 2007. A survey of named entity recognition and classification. *Lingvisticae Investigationes*, 30(1):3–26.

Daniel Sanchez-Cisneros and Fernando Aparicio Gali. 2013. UEM-UC3M: An ontology-based named entity recognition system for biomedical texts. In *Proc. of the Seventh International Workshop on Semantic Evaluation (SemEval)*, pages 622–627. Association for Computational Linguistics.

Sameer Singh, Sebastian Riedel, Brian Martin, Jiaping Zheng, and Andrew McCallum. 2013. Joint inference of entities, relations, and coreference. In *Proc. of the 2013 workshop on Automated knowledge base construction (AKBC)*, pages 1–6.

Noah A. Smith. 2011. *Linguistic Structure Prediction*. Morgan and Claypool.

Wee Meng Soon, Hwee Tou Ng, and Daniel Chung Yong Lim. 2001. A machine learning approach to coreference resolution of noun phrases. *Computational linguistics*, 27(4):521–544.

Rodney Summerscales, Shlomo Argamon, Jordan Hupert, and Alan Schwartz. 2009. Identifying treatments, groups, and outcomes in medical abstracts. In *Proc. of the Sixth Midwest Computational Linguistics Colloquium (MCLC)*. Indiana University.

Mihai Surdeanu, David McClosky, Julie Tibshirani, John Bauer, Angel X Chang, Valentin I Spitkovsky, and Christopher D Manning. 2010. A simple distant supervision approach for the tac-kbp slot filling task.

Charles Sutton, Andrew McCallum, et al. 2012. An introduction to conditional random fields. *Foundations and Trends® in Machine Learning*, 4(4):267–373.

Antonio Trenta, Anthony Hunter, and Sebastian Riedel. 2015. Extraction of evidence tables from abstracts of randomized clinical trials using a maximum entropy classifier and global constraints. *CoRR*, abs/1509.05209.

Byron C Wallace, Joël Kuiper, Aakash Sharma, Mingxi
Zhu, and Iain J Marshall. 2016. Extracting pico sentences from clinical trial reports using supervised
distant supervision. *The Journal of Machine Learning Research*, 17(1):4572–4596.

M. Wick, K. Rohanimanesh, A. Culotta, and A. Mc-
Callum. 2009. SampleRank. Learning Preferences
from Atomic Gradients. In *Proc. of the NIPS Workshop on Advances in Ranking*, pages 1–5.

Yuhao Zhang, Victor Zhong, Danqi Chen, Gabor An-
geli, and Christopher D Manning. 2017. Position-
aware attention and supervised data improve slot filling. In *Proc. of the 2017 Conference on Empirical
Methods in Natural Language Processing (EMNLP)*,
pages 35–45.

Jin Zhao, Praveen Bysani, and Min-Yen Kan. 2012. Exploiting classification correlations for the extraction
of evidence-based practice information. In *Proc. of
the AMIA Annual Symposium*, volume 2012, page
1070. American Medical Informatics Association.

Deyu Zhou, Dayou Zhong, and Yulan He. 2014.
Biomedical relation extraction: from binary to com-
plex. *Computational and Mathematical Methods in
Medicine*, 2014.

Energy-based Neural Modelling for Large-Scale Multiple Domain Dialogue State Tracking

Anh Duong Trinh [†]**, Robert J. Ross** [†]**, John D. Kelleher** [‡]
ADAPT Centre
[†] School of Computer Science
[‡] Information, Communications & Entertainment Institute
Technological University Dublin, Ireland
{anhduong.trinh, robert.ross, john.d.kelleher}@tudublin.ie

Abstract

Scaling up dialogue state tracking to multiple domains is challenging due to the growth in the number of variables being tracked. Furthermore, dialog state tracking models do not yet explicitly make use of relationships between dialogue variables, such as slots across domains. We propose using energy-based structure prediction methods for large-scale dialogue state tracking task in two multiple domain dialogue datasets. Our results indicate that: (i) modelling variable dependencies yields better results; and (ii) the structured prediction output aligns with the dialogue slot-value constraint principles. This leads to promising directions to improve state-of-the-art models by incorporating variable dependencies into their prediction process.

1 Introduction

Task-oriented dialogue systems have been developed to assist users in many fields (Brixey et al., 2017; Zhao et al., 2019). In recent years it is a rising trend to scale-up task-oriented dialogue systems from single domain to multiple domains to improve the generalisability of models and support transfer of knowledge across domains. This leads to a new challenge in handling dialogues in the multi-domain context, that in turns increases the work load of the dialogue manager, and in particular the dialogue state tracking component. On the other hand, a number of works have demonstrated the benefit of processing multiple domains, for example it has been shown that such models yield better performances across domains in comparison with single domain trackers constructed and trained with the same approach (Mrksic et al., 2015).

Dialogue state tracking in task-oriented dialogue systems frequently uses a multi-slot representation for the dialogue state, thus casting the task as a multi-task classification problem. In these scenar-

ios, an increase in the number of domains is equivalent to an increase in the number of slots, this in turn enlarges the models and makes the task more challenging. While traditionally one can develop a number of models to track dialogue states in each domain separately, recent advanced techniques tend to train dialogue state trackers in the multi-domain environment. Such multi-domain trackers produce state-of-the-art results (Kim et al., 2020; Heck et al., 2020).

To date state-of-the-art dialogue state trackers have treated the task as a set of individual domain-dependent classification problems (Heck et al., 2020; Wu et al., 2019; Zhou and Small, 2019). However, we argue that such approaches leave room for improvement; particularly with the consideration of the nature of human-machine interactions (Landragin, 2013). Specially, we argue that the multi-task classification methodology usually does not take into account the relationships between dialogue slot variables, despite the fact that these factors can play an essential part in the dialogue state prediction (Trinh et al., 2019a). Therefore, we propose to explicitly incorporate dialogue variable associations into the prediction process in a multi-domain dialogue environment, thus casting the dialogue state tracking task a structured prediction problem.

In this paper we demonstrate the manner, in which dialogue variable dependencies make an impact on the dialogue state tracking process in a multiple domain context. We choose two newly published multiple domain datasets, MultiWOZ 2.0 (Budzianowski et al., 2018) and MultiWOZ 2.1 (Eric et al., 2019), to conduct our study. These datasets contain a large number of dialogues across several different domains, thus they are practical for our study. Our investigation is detailed in three stages:

Proceedings of 4th Workshop on Structured Prediction for NLP, pages 33–42
November 20, 2020. ©2020 Association for Computational Linguistics

- **Data analysis** – It is important to clearly determine whether variable dependencies exist in dialogue data, and to what extent they present in dialogue states. These questions can be solved by performing statistical tests on dialogue data (Trinh et al., 2019c).

- **Model development** – Since we treat the dialogue state tracking task as a structured prediction problem, we develop an energy-based tracking model for the task, where the energy-based learning methodology has been found effective in handling variable dependencies (Trinh et al., 2019b).

- **Evaluation & Analysis** – We evaluate the performance of our energy-based model and benchmark it against state-of-the-art trackers. Furthermore, we conduct an analysis study on the effectiveness of dialogue variable dependencies on the dialogue state tracking process in comparison with a multi-task deep learning method.

To the best of our knowledge, there have been structured prediction models developed for dialogue state tracking in single domains, but no work has been performed for multiple domains. On the other hand, several multi-domain dialogue state trackers study the topic of variable dependencies to some extent, but do not provide a detailed analysis on this phenomenon. Therefore, the contributions of our work are two-fold: (i) a large-scale structured prediction model for multi-domain dialogue state tracking; and (ii) a systematic analysis of variable dependencies across dialogue slots and domains.

The work presented in this paper is an empirical research of our previous work on capturing variable dependencies in dialogue states within single dialogue domains (Trinh et al., 2019a,b). We demonstrate that the energy-based method has good generalisability when applied to track dialogue states in multiple domain settings.

2 Variable Associations in Multi-Domain Dialogue

There are a number of works that to some extent have studied the variable associations in dialogue data in both single and multiple domain contexts. Single-domain dialogue variable dependencies were explicitly studied in the work by Trinh et al. (2019c,a). The associations between slots in single domain dialogue data are demonstrated to be beneficial factors for dialogue state tracking, and structured prediction approaches such as energy-based learning are effective in studying this phenomenon. On the other hand, although there has been no explicit study on variable dependencies in multiple domain dialogue data, we can indirectly infer the benefit of modelling such dependencies. Mrksic et al. (2015) show that shared models across dialogue domains yield better results than their domain-specific counterparts. Similarly in the TRADE model, Wu et al. (2019) highlighted the correlations between domains by training the base model on all of the domains except one, then fine-tuning on the remaining domain.

Since we focus on multiple domain dialogue state tracking, we conduct our study on MultiWOZ 2.0 (Budzianowski et al., 2018) and MultiWOZ 2.1 (Eric et al., 2019), two novel chat-based multi-domain dialogue datasets. We perform statistical tests on the dialogue data, and present the data analysis results in Figure 1. The statistical tests are Pearson's chi-squared test, which is useful for detecting pairwise dependencies between variables, and the chi-square test-based Cramer's V measurement, that measures the dependency strength once confirmed (Trinh et al., 2019c). In Figure 1 we present the heatmap of measured Cramer's V between all slot pairs in MultiWOZ 2.1 dataset, since this dataset contains manually fixed labels based on MultiWOZ 2.0 data.

The analysis explicitly confirms the variable dependencies in the multiple domain dialogue data, where pairwise statistical significance coefficient **p** $< \mathbf{0.05}$ for all slot pairs. These dependencies exist on both slot and domain levels. Our analysis results also align to some extent with the cosine similarity of slot embedding presented in the TRADE model (Wu et al., 2019).

3 Energy-based Learning Dialogue State Tracking

Energy-based learning (LeCun et al., 2006) is an approach to structured prediction that can be used to account for variable dependencies in a supervised learning process. The core concept of the approach is to represent the associations of all variables in the system with a scalar value called *energy*, and to train an *energy function* that assigns low energy values to valid combinations of variables. There

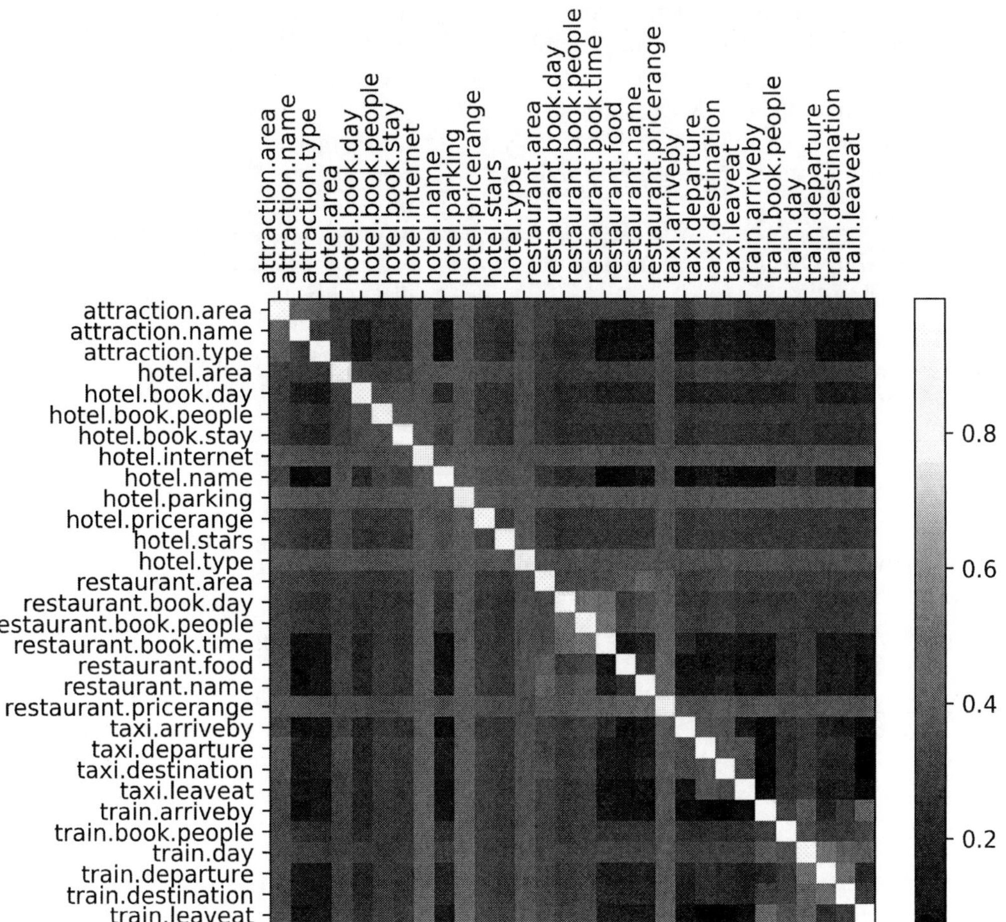

Figure 1: Cramer's V assessment of variable dependencies in MultiWOZ 2.1 data

are two key functions in the energy-based dialogue state tracker that we have developed:

- **Feature function** $F(X)$ – As a first step, we transform raw data into a distributed representation; this can be done with advanced techniques such as combinations of embedding and recurrent neural networks (Kelleher, 2019). The feature function can be either pretrained separately as an auxiliary task or jointly trained with the energy function.

- **Energy function** $E(F(X), Y)$ – The energy function is designed to capture variable dependencies and present them via a scalar value called *energy*. In our work, we develop the energy function with a deep learning architecture called Structured Prediction Energy Networks (SPEN) (Belanger and McCallum, 2016) to capture the dependencies between

input and output variables, as well as among output variables.

The working mechanism of an energy-based model is different from a standard feedforward deep learning model:

- **Learning process** – During the learning process the energy function is typically trained to assign lower energy values to correct variable configurations, i.e. the desired output can be predicted with the minimal energy value with respect to our input. In our work we adopt a variant of the learning strategy detailed for the Deep Value Networks (DVN) architecture (Gygli et al., 2017) for this task.

- **Inference process** – Since in the energy-based learning methodology the energy function is trained to be an estimator for the good-

35

ness of fit between variables in the system, the output variables cannot be predicted in a straight forward manner. Therefore, we perform multiple inference loops guided by the gradient of the energy surface to find a set of labels for a given input using the trained energy function.

3.1 Hierarchical Recurrent Neural Feature Network

Task-oriented dialogues consist of multiple turns, where each turn contains machine and user actions. In the MultiWOZ datasets these actions are presented in a sentence format instead of dialogue act semantic representations. To accommodate the structure of multiple domain dialogue data, we make use of a multi-task LSTM-based dialogue state encoder (Trinh et al., 2018). In the description below we denote dialogue input data X, and the multi-task LSTM network $F(X)$. The architecture of our feature network is visualised in Figure 2.

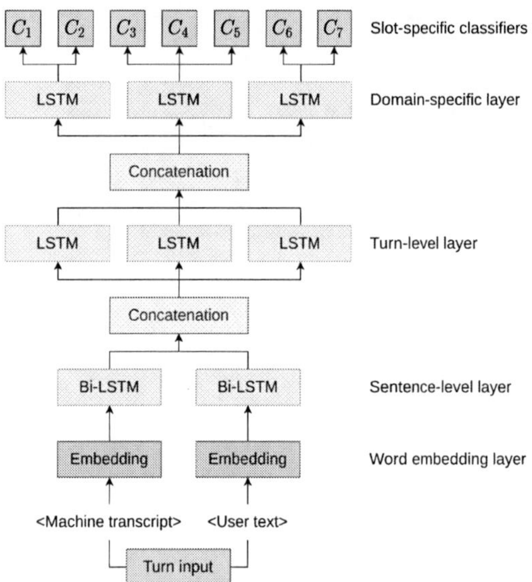

Figure 2: Multi-task Recurrent Neural Feature Network for MultiWOZ datasets. All recurrent units are LSTM (Hochreiter and Schmidhuber, 1997).

Our LSTM-based feature network consists of 5 layers:

- Word embedding layer – The word embedding layer is trained from scratch due to the small vocabulary present in the data.

- Sentence-level LSTM layer – To transform the sentence into vector representations, we make use of bidirectional LSTM structure (Bi-LSTM) (Schuster and Paliwal, 1997). In this layer machine and user transcripts are processed with separate Bi-LSTM cells, then their output vectors are concatenated before being fed into the next layer.

- Turn-level LSTM layer – A number of unidirectional LSTM cells are used to roll out the dialogue by turns. As highlighted in an earlier multi-task LSTM-based model (Trinh et al., 2018), using a number of LSTM cells can extract more useful information. The output of all the LSTM cells is concatenated into joint vectors, and treated as dialogue turn representations.

- Domain-specific LSTM layer – For each domain in the data we assign one LSTM cell to specialise the information downstream from the overall dialogue to the domain level.

- Slot-specific classifiers – The output layer consists of a number of slot-specific classifiers. Each classifier produces the prediction of the slot it corresponds to with a *softmax* activation function.

We pretrain this feature network $F(X)$ following the method as highlighted in a number of works on energy-based learning (Belanger and McCallum, 2016; Trinh et al., 2019b). It should be noted that the dialogue features can be extracted as the output of either the turn-level layer or the domain-specific layer. From our experiments, we have observed that the domain-specific LSTM layer produces more meaningful representations, thus it is more beneficial to pass on the energy function.

3.2 Deep Learning Energy Network

Since we focus on studying the variable dependencies between slots, our energy function must include the term for this phenomenon explicitly. We base the design of our energy network on the concept of Structured Prediction Energy Networks (SPEN) (Belanger and McCallum, 2016). The SPEN network is developed as a deep learning architecture to define an energy function that includes two individual energy terms, *local energy* and *global energy*:

$$E(F(X), Y) = E_{local}(F(X), Y) + E_{global}(Y) \tag{1}$$

Local energy is computed between input and output (label) variables, and is intended to capture the agreement between feature representations and labels:

$$E_{local}(F(X), Y) = \sum_{i=1}^{L} y_i W_i^\top X \qquad (2)$$

where W is the set of trainable parameters, $Y = \{y_i\}^L$ is a label vector, and L is the number of label classes.

Global energy meanwhile is the energy term that captures the relationship between labels independently of the input features:

$$E_{global}(Y) = W_{g2}^\top f(W_{g1}^\top Y) \qquad (3)$$

where weights W_{g1} and W_{g2} are trainable parameters, and $f(\cdot)$ is a non-linear function.

3.3 Learning Process

The purpose of the learning process is to train the energy function to measure the goodness of fit between variables correctly. It is important to design a suitable objective function to ensure that the energy function is well trained (Trinh et al., 2020).

For multi-label classification tasks, F_1 measurement is a common evaluation metric. In our structured dialogue state tracking task we make use of the F_1 metric for continuous variables, and interpret it as the ground truth energy:

$$E_{F_1}^*(Y, Y^*) = \frac{2 \sum_i y_i y_i^*}{\sum_i y_i + \sum_i y_i^*} \qquad (4)$$

where Y is the predicted labels, and Y^* is the ground truth labels.

Since the ground truth energy is calculated with our F_1 measurement, its value can only fall into the range $[0, 1]$. Therefore, it is appropriate to use a cross entropy function as the loss function between predicted and ground truth energies:

$$L(E, E_{F_1}^*) = -E_{F_1}^* \log E - (1 - E_{F_1}^*) \log(1 - E) \qquad (5)$$

where $E = E(F(X), Y)$ is the predicted energy, and $E_{F_1}^* = E_{F_1}^*(Y, Y^*)$ is the ground truth energy.

There exist slot-value constraint rules in the task-oriented dialogue state tracking task such that at any time in the conversation each slot can be classified with not more than one value. However, multi-label classification methods do not include a

mechanism to control the output prediction following these rules. Therefore we introduce a regularisation term to encourage our energy-based tracker to shape the output into the desired format:

$$R(Y, Y^*) = \left(\frac{\sum_i y_i - \sum_i y_i^*}{\sum_i y_i^*} \right)^2 \qquad (6)$$

where Y is the predicted output, and Y^* is the ground truth labels.

Our final objective function including the label regularisation term for the learning process of the energy network is formulated as follow:

$$\mathcal{L} = L(E, E_{F_1}^*) + \alpha R(Y, Y^*) \qquad (7)$$

where α is a regularisation coefficient.

This learning process is visualised in Fig. 3.

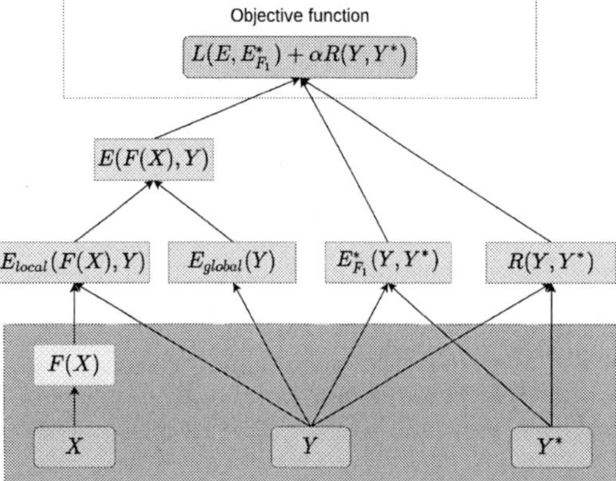

Figure 3: The learning process of our energy-based dialogue state tracker. The grey area denotes a frozen network where the parameters have been pretrained.

3.4 Inference Process

The energy function, as described above, can be interpreted as an estimator of the goodness of fit of the variables in the system. However, at prediction time we do not have the output variables that are an essential part of the energy formulation. Instead, to determine these values we perform a loopy inference process guided by the gradient of the energy surface.

We start with a random hypothesis and use gradient ascent to update the output hypothesis:

$$Y^{(0)} = \{random(y_i)\}^L$$
$$Y^{(t+1)} = \mathcal{P}_Y\left(Y^{(t)} + \eta \nabla_Y E(F(X), Y^{(t)})\right) \qquad (8)$$

where $\mathcal{P}_y$ is the projection operation to shape the predicted output to the output variable space $Y =$

$\{y_i\}^M \in \{[0,1]\}^M$, and η is the learning rate for gradient ascent.

Here, it should be noted that the energy function is an estimator for our F_1 measurement of the predicted output; thus, we aim to maximise the F_1 score to achieve the desired prediction:

$$E(F(X), Y^{(t)}) \sim E^*_{F_1}(Y^{(t)}, Y^*) \qquad (9)$$

4 Experiments

As indicated earlier, we have selected the multiple domain dialogue datasets, MultiWOZ 2.0 (Budzianowski et al., 2018) and MultiWOZ 2.1 (Eric et al., 2019), to conduct our study of variable dependencies. Since the MultiWOZ 2.0 dataset was known to contain a lot of labelling errors, the latter version MultiWOZ 2.1 was manually annotated to correct them. Each dataset contains more than 10000 dialogues across 7 domains, split into three subsets: train, development and test for training, validation and test purposes respectively.

However, following the common practice of other previous works we excluded two domains that rarely appear in the datasets. We followed the data processing and scoring scripts from the TRADE model (Wu et al., 2019) for our dialogue state tracking task.

Our experiments were conducted in two stages: first, we trained a multi-task learning network to extract dialogue features; then, we experimented on the energy-based learning level to explore inter-label dependencies.

Our model's hyperparameters are presented in Table 1.

We train both feature network and energy-based models with Adam optimiser (Kingma and Ba, 2015) for 300 epochs. To avoid the overfitting problem, we apply the early stopping technique and find that our models converge shortly after 200 epochs. We trained the feature network 3 times for each dataset, and selected the best model to extract features. The energy-based network was trained 5 times and the predictions were ensembled into the ultimate dialogue states for evaluation.

5 Results & Discussion

We evaluate the performance of both our multi-task feature system and the energy-based tracker with an *Accuracy* metric as is common in dialogue state tracking. The results are reported in Table 2 alongside results of a number of state-of-the-art systems to our knowledge.

Hyper parameter	Value
Energy-based Network	
Word embedding size	300
LSTM number of turn-level cells	5
LSTM number of units	128
LSTM drop out	0.2
LSTM output activation	tanh
Energy non-linearity function $f(\cdot)$	tanh
Inference process	
Number of iterations	50
Inference learning rate	0.001
Learning process	
Objective function	Equation 7
Regularisation coefficient	0.01
Optimiser	Adam
Learning rate	0.001
Maximal global gradient norm	5.0

Table 1: Basic hyper parameters used in experiments constructing the energy-based dialogue state tracker.

Overall, our energy-based dialogue state tracker yields competitive results in comparison to models that account for variable relationships using techniques such as attention mechanism (Kumar et al., 2020; Zhong et al., 2018) and transfer learning (Wu et al., 2019). When accounting for the variable dependencies with the energy-based method, we improve the belief state tracking results by large margins, i.e., 13.9% for MultiWOZ 2.0 and 18.1% for MultiWOZ 2.1. We believe that there are at least two reasons for this large improvement:

- High quality features are extracted from dialogue data due to the architecture of a hierarchical multi-task LSTM network. As we extract input features from domain-specific LSTM cells, the features contain both dialogue information up to current turns as well as domain information.

- The associations between variables, in particular label dependencies, are accounted for explicitly; hence more information is available for the classification of each slot than would be available in a straightforward multi-task classification process.

While the energy-based system does not achieve the state-of-the-art performance, it should be noted that state-of-the-art systems currently employ a

Model	MultiWOZ 2.0	MultiWOZ 2.1
TripPy (Heck et al., 2020)	-	**0.553**
Schema-guided (Chen et al., 2020)	0.512	0.552
DST-Picklist (Zhang et al., 2019)	-	0.533
SOM-DST (Kim et al., 2020)	**0.517**	0.530
MA-DST (Kumar et al., 2020)	-	0.519
DSTQA (Zhou and Small, 2019)	0.514	0.512
COMER (Ren et al., 2019)	0.488	-
TRADE (Wu et al., 2019)	0.486	0.456
HyST (Goel et al., 2019)	0.442	-
Neural reading (Gao et al., 2019)	0.411	-
GCE (Nouri and Hosseini-Asl, 2018)	0.363	-
GLAD (Zhong et al., 2018)	0.356	-
Our work		
Energy-based system	0.488	0.547
Multi-task feature system	0.349	0.366

Table 2: Performances of state-of-the-art and presented dialogue state tracking systems on MultiWOZ 2.0 & 2.1 data. The results for belief states are reported with the Accuracy metric.

very wide variety of modelling techniques while the currently presented work focuses on the addition of a mechanism to guide final labelling. For example, TripPy (Heck et al., 2020), which achieves the highest accuracy in MultiWOZ 2.1 data, is based on span-prediction and a number of memory mechanisms. Meanwhile, SOM-DST (Kim et al., 2020) improves the dialogue state tracking efficiency with a selectively overwriting memory mechanism. Both of these however do not explicitly look at the variable dependencies as potentially useful factors of dialogue states. The practical use of the energy-based learning method may lie in its use to fine tune results to take into account variable dependencies. Given the fact that the energy-based model is developed separately from the feature network, we can apply it to state-of-the-art models to investigate the effectiveness of variable dependencies in different situations.

One final observation with respect to the results is differences in performance across MultiWOZ 2.0 and 2.1 datasets. Even though the labels in MultiWOZ 2.1 dataset are corrected with manual labour, meaning the data is less noisy than the MultiWOZ 2.0 data, not all systems yield better results in MultiWOZ 2.1 than in MultiWOZ 2.0, e.g., models such as TRADE (Wu et al., 2019) and DSTQA (Zhou and Small, 2019) perform better with the original noisy data. In contrast, we observe that other state-of-the-art systems includ-

ing our energy-based tracker perform better with cleaner data (MultiWOZ 2.1); this is of course a common phenomenon in supervised learning.

5.1 Variable Dependencies Analysis

In term of accuracy score our energy-based tracker outperforms the multi-task feature system by a large margins. However, the accuracy metric does not in itself verify the system's ability to capture variable dependencies. In order to evaluate the effectiveness of the energy-based learning method in capturing variable dependencies, we conduct an analysis on the performance of our trackers on the MultiWOZ 2.1 test set. Specifically, we analyse pairwise variable dependencies with Pearson's chi-squared test and measure their strength with Cramer's V coefficient as detailed earlier in Section 2. We present the results of variable association analysis between a number of slots in Table 3 with respect to test labels, labels produced by the Energy-based Tracker and labels produced by our Multi-Task Learning tracker. Here, we only show the dependencies between a subset of the slots purely for space reasons. If we were to show more or all of them, the table wouldn't fit in the template. We have, however, done the analysis of the dependencies for other slots and the results indicate that the other slots have similar tendencies, and more importantly that the data we present is representative of this more general pattern.

		hotel price range	restaurant price range	taxi		train	
				departure	destination	departure	destination
Test label							
attraction	area	0.200	0.236	0.272	0.276	0.107	0.089
hotel	area	0.225	0.315	0.218	0.218	0.094	0.078
restaurant	area	0.214	0.411	0.254	0.286	0.093	0.107
Energy-based tracker							
attraction	area	0.182	0.173	0.193	0.194	0.095	0.096
hotel	area	0.236	0.336	0.199	0.199	0.075	0.078
restaurant	area	0.256	0.419	0.254	0.321	0.120	0.109
Multi-task feature system							
attraction	area	0.291	0.194	0.153	0.151	0.086	0.084
hotel	area	0.147	0.232	0.149	0.160	0.055	0.056
restaurant	area	0.287	0.213	0.137	0.137	0.124	0.126

Table 3: Data analysis on variable dependencies in the performance of multi-task and energy-based trackers in MultiWOZ 2.1 data. The variable dependencies are reported with Cramer's V coefficient. In the table, the first block is variable dependencies in labels of the test set, while the second block is variable dependencies detected by our energy-based model, and the last block is the performance of the multi-task feature system.

The analysis results demonstrate that the energy-based tracker more consistently mirrors the association strengths seen in the test labels then does our baseline Multi-Task Learning approach. It is evidenced by smaller margins in Cramer's V coefficients between the *Energy-based tracker* and the *Test label* results than seen between the *Multi-task system* results and the *Test label* results[1]. There are, however, very few exceptions to this trend, namely the *attraction.area – restaurant.price range* and *attraction.area – train.destination* pairs where the multi-task based system has produced associations closer to the test label case than does the energy-based model.

Overall, we argue that the ability to capture variable dependencies between slots across dialogue domains explains the reason why the energy-based method outperforms the multi-task learning approach.

5.2 Slot-Value Constraint Analysis

Dialogue states of many task-oriented dialogue systems must satisfy a slot-value constraint principle that each slot must not have more than one value in the belief state of any turn. Specifically, the value of each informable slot can be either *none* if it is not mentioned by users, or a specific value, for example *Chinese* for the slot *food* in domain *restaurant* if information is provided by the user. While the underlying multi-task feature system follows this rule strictly due to the use of the output *softmax* activation function in slot-specific classifiers, the energy-based tracking model is not guaranteed to maintain this strict constraint.

To overcome this challenge, we proposed a label regularisation term (Equation 6) in the objective function detailed in Section 3.3. To evaluate the effectiveness of this mechanism, we conduct an additional analysis to determine the behaviours of our energy-based system based on this regularisation. This analysis is conducted in two stages:

- First, we train and evaluate our energy-based method on the dialogue data without the label regularisation term. Thus, the loss function (Equation 5) becomes our learning objective in this baseline case.

- Second, we set different threshold values, and calculate the proportion of correct predictions over the total number of dialogue turns that follow slot-value constraint rules with different thresholds. A value is considered activated if the predicted belief score of this value exceeds the threshold. This stage is conducted for our energy-based method both with and without the regularisation term.

---

[1]It should be noted that stronger associations do not necessarily indicate better tracking performance – our goal is to capture valid associations not to arbitrarily increase the number of associations seen in label outputs.

The slot-value constraint analysis is presented in Table 4.

Threshold	MultiWOZ 2.0		MultiWOZ 2.1	
	+Reg	–Reg	+Reg	–Reg
0.5	45.7	36.8	52.4	48.3
0.7	29.7	26.3	39.4	35.1
0.9	16.8	15.5	18.3	18.1

Table 4: Analysis of the impact of label regularisation on the energy-based dialogue state tracking on the MultiWOZ 2.0 & 2.1 data. The results are reported with the proportion (%) of correct predictions over the total number of dialogue turns that follow the slot-value constraint rules. +Reg/–Reg denotes the presence/absence of the label regularisation in the learning process.

The analysis result demonstrates that our energy-based systems with the label regularisation consistently outperforms those that do not include this term in the learning process with different belief score thresholds. Here, the label regularisation helps guide the system's prediction behaviour towards the requirement of the task-oriented domains. We can conclude that the impact of label regularisation on dialogue state tracking is systematic.

6   Conclusion

In this paper we demonstrated the effectiveness of applying the energy-based learning method to a large-scale dialogue state tracking task in multiple domains. We showed that the energy-based method is capable of capturing the dependencies between dialogue variables such as slots across domains, thus it improves the performance over a multi-task deep learning system significantly. Our analyses also showed that the structured prediction method can produce dialogue states that follow dialogue slot-value constraint rules in contrast with a multi-label classification method.

Although the results achieved with the energy-based method are competitive with published dialogue state tracking systems, they are not yet state of the art. There are several directions to investigate the further impact of an energy-based methodology on the dialogue state tracking task. One promising direction is the application of our energy-based method on top of an existing state-of-the-art systems to further improve that system's performance. Another direction is to refine the energy-based structure and investigate various strategies for the learning and inference processes to improve

the ability to integrate captured dependencies into the structured prediction at a higher level. Furthermore our long term goal is to apply the structured learning approach in tracking different aspects of the conversations such as personality and preference as well as user intents.

Acknowledgements

This research was conducted with the financial support of Science Foundation Ireland under Grant Agreement No. 13/RC/2106 at the ADAPT SFI Research Centre at Technological University Dublin. The ADAPT SFI Centre for Digital Media Technology is funded by Science Foundation Ireland through the SFI Research Centres Programme and is co-funded under the European Regional Development Fund (ERDF) through Grant No. 13/RC/2106.

References

David Belanger and Andrew McCallum. 2016. Structured Prediction Energy Networks. In *Proceedings of the 33rd International Conference on Machine Learning*, volume 48.

Jacqueline Brixey, Rens Hoegen, Wei Lan, Joshua Rusow, Karan Singla, Xusen Yin, Ron Artstein, and Anton Leuski. 2017. SHIHbot : A Facebook chatbot for Sexual Health Information on HIV / AIDS. In *Proceedings of the SIGDIAL 2017 Conference*, pages 370–373.

Paweł Budzianowski, Tsung-Hsien Wen, Bo-Hsiang Tseng, Iñigo Casanueva, Stefan Ultes, Osman Ramadan, and Milica Gašić. 2018. MultiWOZ - A Large-Scale Multi-Domain Wizard-of-Oz Dataset for Task-Oriented Dialogue Modelling. In *Proceedings of 2018 Conference on Empirical Methods in Natural Language Processing*.

Lu Chen, Boer Lv, Chi Wang, Su Zhu, Bowen Tan, and Kai Yu. 2020. Schema-Guided Multi-Domain Dialogue State Tracking with Graph Attention Neural Networks. In *Association for the Advancement of Artificial Intelligence*.

Mihail Eric, Rahul Goel, Shachi Paul, Adarsh Kumar, Abhishek Sethi, Anuj Kumar Goyal, Peter Ku, Sanchit Agarwal, Shuyang Gao, and Dilek Hakkani-Tur. 2019. MultiWOZ 2.1: A Consolidated Multi-Domain Dialogue Dataset with State Corrections and State Tracking Baselines.

Shuyang Gao, Abhishek Sethi, Sanchit Agarwal, Tagyoung Chung, and Dilek Hakkani-tur. 2019. Dialog State Tracking: A Neural Reading Comprehension Approach. In *Proceedings of the SIGDial 2019 Conference*, pages 264–273.

Rahul Goel, Shachi Paul, and Dilek Hakkani-Tur. 2019. HyST: A Hybrid Approach for Flexible and Accurate Dialogue State Tracking. In *Proceedings of the INTERSPEECH 2019 Conference*.

Michael Gygli, Mohammad Norouzi, and Anelia Angelova. 2017. Deep Value Networks Learn to Evaluate and Iteratively Refine Structured Outputs. In *Proceedings of the 34th International Conference on Machine Learning*.

Michael Heck, Carel van Niekerk, Nurul Lubis, Christian Geishauser, Hsien-Chin Lin, Marco Moresi, and Milica Gašić. 2020. TripPy: A Triple Copy Strategy for Value Independent Neural Dialog State Tracking. In *Proceedings of the SIGDial 2020 Conference*.

Sepp Hochreiter and Jurgen Schmidhuber. 1997. Long Short-Term Memory. *Neural Computation*, 9(8):1735–1780.

John D Kelleher. 2019. *Deep Learning*. The MIT Press.

Sungdong Kim, Sohee Yang, Gyuwan Kim, and Sang-Woo Lee. 2020. Efficient Dialogue State Tracking by Selectively Overwriting Memory. In *Proceedings of the 58th annual meeting of the Association for Computational Linguistics (ACL)*.

Diederik P. Kingma and Jimmy Ba. 2015. Adam: A Method for Stochastic Optimization. In *Proceedings of the 3rd International Conference for Learning Representations*.

Adarsh Kumar, Peter Ku, Anuj Goyal, Angeliki Metallinou, and Dilek Hakkani-Tur. 2020. MA-DST: Multi-Attention-Based Scalable Dialog State Tracking. In *Proceedings of the 34th AAAI Conference on Artificial Intelligence (AAAI 2020)*.

Frédéric Landragin. 2013. *Man-Machine Dialogue: Design and Challenges*. ISTE Ltd and John Wiley & Sons, Inc.

Yann LeCun, Sumit Chopra, Raia Hadsell, Marc' Aurelio Ranzato, and Fu Jie Huang. 2006. A Tutorial on Energy-Based Learning. *Predicting Structured Data*.

Nikola Mrksic, Diarmuid O'Seaghdha, Blaise Thomson, Milica Gasic, Pei-Hao Su, David Vandyke, Tsung-Hsien Wen, and Steve Young. 2015. Multi-domain Dialog State Tracking using Recurrent Neural Networks. In *Proceedings of the 53rd Annual Meeting of the Association for Computational Linguistics*, pages 794–799.

Elnaz Nouri and Ehsan Hosseini-Asl. 2018. Toward Scalable Neural Dialogue State Tracking Model. In *Proceedings of the 2nd Conversational AI workshop, NeurIPS 2018*.

Liliang Ren, Jianmo Ni, and Julian McAuley. 2019. Scalable and Accurate Dialogue State Tracking via Hierarchical Sequence Generation. In *Proceedings of the 2019 Conference on Empirical Methods in Natural Language Processing and the 9th International Joint Conference on Natural Language Processing*, pages 1876–1885.

Mike Schuster and Kuldip K. Paliwal. 1997. Bidirectional recurrent neural networks. *IEEE Transactions on Signal Processing*, 45(11):2673–2681.

Anh Duong Trinh, Robert J. Ross, and John D. Kelleher. 2018. A Multi-Task Approach to Incremental Dialogue State Tracking. In *Proceedings of The 22nd workshop on the Semantics and Pragmatics of Dialogue, SEMDIAL*, pages 132–145.

Anh Duong Trinh, Robert J. Ross, and John D. Kelleher. 2019a. Capturing Dialogue State Variable Dependencies with an Energy-based Neural Dialogue State Tracker. In *Proceedings of the SIGDial 2019 Conference*, pages 75–84.

Anh Duong Trinh, Robert J. Ross, and John D. Kelleher. 2019b. Energy-Based Modelling for Dialogue State Tracking. In *Proceedings of the 1st Workshop on NLP for Conversational AI*, pages 77–86.

Anh Duong Trinh, Robert J. Ross, and John D. Kelleher. 2019c. Investigating Variable Dependencies in Dialogue States. In *Proceedings of the 23rd Workshop on the Semantics and Pragmatics of Dialogue*, pages 195–197.

Anh Duong Trinh, Robert J. Ross, and John D. Kelleher. 2020. F-Measure Optimisation and Label Regularisation for Energy-Based Neural Dialogue State Tracking Models. In *Artificial Neural Networks and Machine Learning ICANN 2020*.

Chien-Sheng Wu, Andrea Madotto, Ehsan Hosseini-Asl, Caiming Xiong, Richard Socher, and Pascale Fung. 2019. Transferable Multi-Domain State Generator for Task-Oriented Dialogue Systems. In *Proceedings of the 57th Annual Meeting of the Association for Computational Linguistics*.

Jian-Guo Zhang, Kazuma Hashimoto, Chien-Sheng Wu, Yao Wan, Philip S. Yu, Richard Socher, and Caiming Xiong. 2019. Find or Classify? Dual Strategy for Slot-Value Predictions on Multi-Domain Dialog State Tracking.

Guoguang Zhao, Jianyu Zhao, Yang Li, Christoph Alt, Robert Schwarzenberg, Leonhard Hennig, Stefan Schaffer, Sven Schmeier, Changjian Hu, and Feiyu Xu. 2019. MOLI: Smart Conversation Agent for Mobile Customer Service. *Information (Switzerland)*, 10(2).

Victor Zhong, Caiming Xiong, and Richard Socher. 2018. Global-Locally Self-Attentive Dialogue State Tracker. In *Proceedings of the 56th Annual Meeting of the Association for Computational Linguistics*, pages 1458–1467.

Li Zhou and Kevin Small. 2019. Multi-domain Dialogue State Tracking as Dynamic Knowledge Graph Enhanced Question Answering.

End-to-End Extraction of Structured Information from Business Documents with Pointer-Generator Networks

Clément Sage[1,2], Alex Aussem[1], Véronique Eglin[1], Haytham Elghazel[1], Jérémy Espinas[2]

[1]Univ Lyon, CNRS, LIRIS, France
{csage, aaussem, veglin, helghazel}@liris.cnrs.fr
[2]Esker, France
{clement.sage, jeremy.espinas}@esker.fr

Abstract

The predominant approaches for extracting key information from documents resort to classifiers predicting the information type of each word. However, the word level ground truth used for learning is expensive to obtain since it is not naturally produced by the extraction task. In this paper, we discuss a new method for training extraction models directly from the textual value of information. The extracted information of a document is represented as a sequence of tokens in the XML language. We learn to output this representation with a pointer-generator network that alternately copies the document words carrying information and generates the XML tags delimiting the types of information. The ability of our end-to-end method to retrieve structured information is assessed on a large set of business documents. We show that it performs competitively with a standard word classifier without requiring costly word level supervision.

1 Introduction

Companies and public administrations are daily confronted with an amount of incoming documents from which they want to extract key information as efficiently as possible. They often face known types of documents such as invoices or purchase orders, thus knowing what information types to extract. However, layouts are highly variable across document issuers as there are no widely adopted specifications constraining the positioning and textual representation of the information within documents. This makes information extraction a challenging task to automate.

In addition to the incremental approaches based on layout identification (d'Andecy et al., 2018; Dhakal et al., 2019), a number of recent works have proposed deep neural models to extract information in documents with yet unseen layouts. Following Palm et al. (2017), most of these layout-free approaches resort to classifiers that predict the information type of each document word. Yet, the information extraction task does not offer word level ground truth but rather the normalized textual values of each information type (Graliński et al., 2020). The word labels can thus be obtained by matching these textual values with the document words but this process is either time-consuming if manually performed or prone to errors if algorithmically performed. Indeed, extracted information may not appear verbatim in the document as its textual values are normalized. For example, the value "2020-03-30" for the document date field may be derived from the group of words "Mar 30, 2020". This forces the development of domain specific parsers to retrieve the matching words. Also, multiple document words can share the textual value of a extracted field while being semantically distinct, hence imposing additional heuristics for disambiguation. Otherwise, a street number may be wrongly interpreted as a product quantity, inducing noise in the word labels.

To the best of our knowledge, Palm et al. (2019) is the only related model that directly learns from naturally produced extraction results. However, the authors only tackle the recognition of independent and non-recurring fields such as the document date and omit the extraction of structured entities. Such entities are structures composed of multiple field values. Within documents, structured information is often contained in tables. For example, a product entity is usually described in a table row with its field values, such as price and quantity, being in different columns. Our work is intended to remedy this lack by proposing end-to-end methods for processing structured information. As a first step towards full end-to-end extraction, we focus in this paper on the recognition of fields whose values always appears verbatim in the document, thus eliminating the need for normalization operations.

As illustrated in Figure 1, extracted structured information can be represented in a markup lan-

Proceedings of 4th Workshop on Structured Prediction for NLP, pages 43–52
November 20, 2020. ©2020 Association for Computational Linguistics

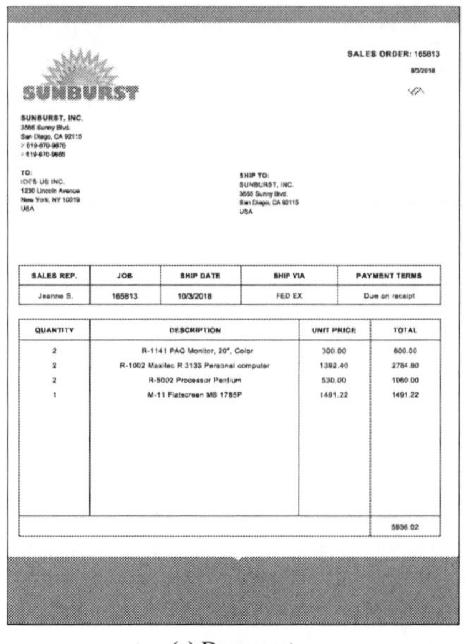 SALES ORDER: 165813

(a) Document

```
<Extraction>
    <Product>
        <IDNumber>R-1141</IDNumber>
        <Quantity>2</Quantity>
    </Product>
    <Product>
        <IDNumber>R-1002</IDNumber>
        <Quantity>2</Quantity>
    </Product>
    <Product>
        <IDNumber>R-5002</IDNumber>
        <Quantity>2</Quantity>
    </Product>
    <Product>
        <IDNumber>M-11</IDNumber>
        <Quantity>1</Quantity>
    </Product>
</Extraction>
```

(b) Extracted information

Figure 1: A purchase order (a) and the XML representation of its extracted information (b). In this example, we retrieve the ordered products which are contained in the main table of the document. Two fields are recognized for each product entity: the ID number and the quantity.

guage that describes both its content and its structure. Among many others, we choose the XML language[1] for its simplicity. We define as many XML tag pairs as the number of entity and field types to extract. A pair of opening and closing field tags delimits a list of words constituting a field instance of the corresponding type.

Following successful applications of sequence-to-sequence models in many NLP tasks (Otter et al., 2020), we employ a recurrent encoder-decoder architecture for outputting such XML representations. Conditioned on the sequence of words from the document, the decoder emits one token at each time step: either a XML tag or a word belonging to a field value. Since field values are often specific to a document or a issuer, extracted information cannot be generated from a fixed size vocabulary of words. Rather, we make use of pointing abilities of neural models (Vinyals et al., 2015) to copy words of the document that carry relevant information. Specifically, we adapt the Pointer-Generator Network (PGN) developed by See et al. (2017) for text summarization to our extraction needs. We evaluate the resulting model for extracting ordered products from purchase orders. We demonstrate that this end-to-end model performs competitively with a word classifier based model while avoiding

to create supervision at the word level.

2 Related Work

2.1 Information extraction

As mentioned before, most methods for information extraction in documents take the word labels for granted and rather focus on improving the encoding of the document.

Holt and Chisholm (2018) combine heuristic filtering for identifying word candidates and a gradient boosting decision tree for independently scoring them. The strength of their model mainly lies on the wide range of engineered features describing syntactic, semantic, positional and visual content of each word as well as its local context.

When extracting the main fields of invoices and purchase orders, Palm et al. (2017) and Sage et al. (2019) both employ recurrent connections across the document to reinforce correlations between the class predictions of words. They show empirically that Recurrent Neural Networks (RNN) surpass classifiers whose prediction dependence is only due to local context knowledge introduced in the word representations. For this purpose, they arrange the words within a document as a unidimensional sequence and pass the word representations into a bidirectional LTSM (BLSTM) network for field classification. Similar to the state-of-the-art

---

[1] https://en.wikipedia.org/wiki/XML

in Named Entity Recognition (Yadav and Bethard, 2018), Jiang et al. (2019) also add a Conditional Random Field (CRF) on top of the BLSTM to refine predictions while extracting information from Chinese contracts.

Yet, unlike plain text, word spacing and alignments in both horizontal and vertical directions convey substantial clues for extracting information of documents. By imposing a spurious unidimensional word order, these architectures significantly favor transmission of context in one direction at the expense of the other. Lately, methods that explicitly consider the two dimensional structure of documents have emerged with two different approaches.

Lohani et al. (2018), Liu et al. (2019) and Holeček et al. (2019) represent documents by graphs, with each node corresponding to a word or a group of words and edges either connecting all the nodes or only spatially near neighbors. Convolutional or recurrent mechanisms are then applied to the graph for predicting the field type of each node.

Some authors rather represent a document page as a regular two dimensional grid by downscaling the document image. Each pixel of the grid contains at most one token - either a character or a word - and its associated representation. Then, they employ fully convolutional neural networks to model the document, either with dilated convolutions (Zhao et al., 2019; Palm et al., 2019) or encoder-decoder architectures performing alternately usual and transposed convolutions (Katti et al., 2018; Denk and Reisswig, 2019; Dang and Thanh, 2019). Finally, all these works except Palm et al. (2019) output a segmentation mask representing the probabilities that each token contained in a pixel of the grid belong to the field types to extract. Katti et al. (2018) and Denk and Reisswig (2019) additionally tackle tabular data extraction by predicting the coordinates of the table rows bounding boxes to identify the invoiced products.

Instead of directly classifying each word of the document, Palm et al. (2019) output attention scores to measure the relevance of each word given the field type to extract. The relevant words are then copied and fed to learned neural parsers to generate a normalized string corresponding to the expected value of the field. The predicted string is measured by exact match with the ground truth. Evaluated on 7 fields types of invoices, their end-to-end method outperforms a logistic regression based model whose word labels are derived from end-to-end ground truth using heuristics. However, their approach cannot extract structured information such as the invoiced products.

Although there are publicly released datasets for the task of information extraction in documents (Jiang et al., 2019; Huang et al., 2019; Graliński et al., 2020), as far as we know, none of them are annotated to recognize structured data.

2.2 Structured language generation

A number of works prove that neural encoder-decoder models can produce well-formed and well-typed sequences in a structured language without supplying an explicit grammar of the language.

Extending traditional text recognition, some authors transform images of tables (Zhong et al., 2019; Deng et al., 2019) and mathematical formulas (Deng et al., 2017; Wu et al., 2018) into their LaTeX or HTML representations. After applying a convolutional encoder to the input image, they use a forward RNN based decoder to generate tokens in the target language. The decoder is enhanced with an attention mechanism over the final feature maps to help focusing on the image part that is recognized at the current time step.

Neural encoder-decoder architectures have also been used for semantic parsing which aims at converting natural language utterances to formal meaning representations (Dong and Lapata, 2016; Rabinovich et al., 2017). The representations may be an executable language such as SQL and Prolog or more abstract representations like abstract syntax trees. Text being the modality of both input and output sequences, Jia and Liang (2016), Zhong et al. (2017) and McCann et al. (2018) include attention-based copying abilities in their neural model to efficiently produce the rare or out-of-vocabulary words.

3 Approach

We assume that the text of a document is already transcribed before extracting its information. For scanned documents, we employ a commercial Optical Character Recognition (OCR) engine for retrieving the text.

The method we propose for extracting structured information from a document is depicted in Figure 2. The model is derived from the PGN of See et al. (2017) proposed for summarization of news

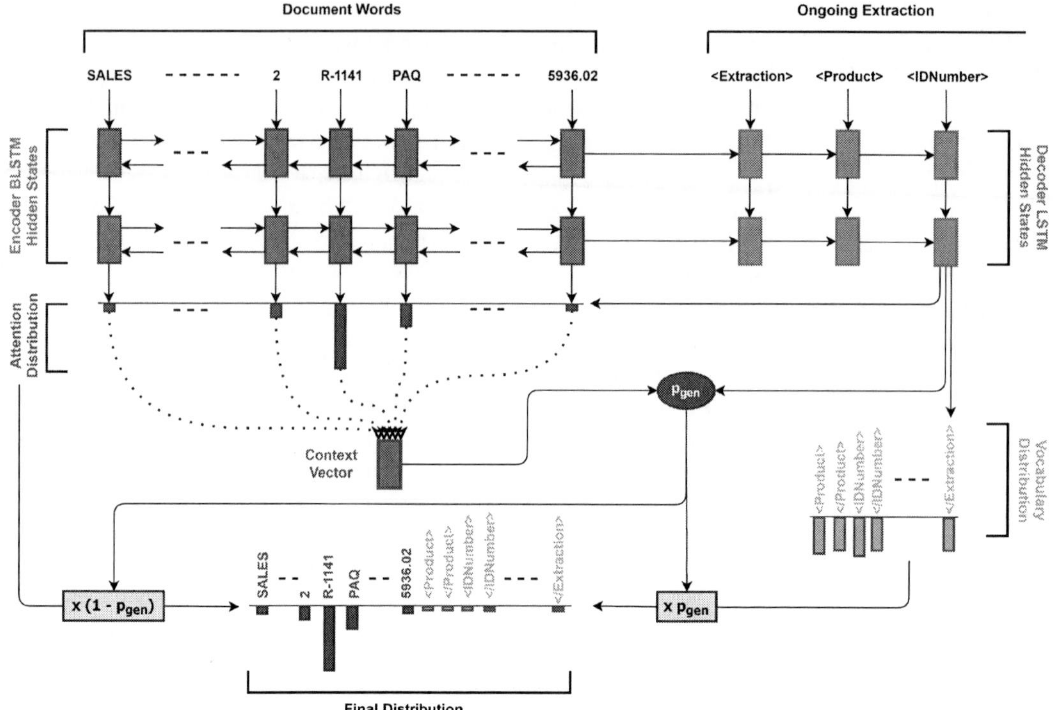

Figure 2: Illustration of the pointer-generator network for extracting structured information of the document in Figure 1. For each decoder time step, a generation probability $p_{gen} \in [0, 1]$ is calculated, which weights the probability of generating XML tags from the vocabulary versus copying words from the document carrying information. The vocabulary distribution and the attention distribution are weighted and summed to obtain the final distribution. For the illustrated time step, the model mainly points to the word R-1141, i.e. the ID number of the first product.

articles. The attention-based pointing mechanism allows to accurately reproduce factual information of articles by copying words that are not in the generator's vocabulary, e.g. rare proper nouns. Similarly, we take advantage of its pointing ability to copy the words from the document which carry relevant information while allowing the generator to produce the XML tags which structure the extracted information. In the following subsections, we describe in details our model and highlight key differences with the original PGN.

3.1 Word representation

Each word w_i of the document is represented by a vector denoted r_i. In complement to the word level embeddings used by See et al. (2017), we enrich representations with additional textual features to cope with the open vocabulary observed within the corpus of documents. First, we follow the C2W model of Ling et al. (2015) to form a textual representation q_i^c at the character level. To that end, we apply a BLSTM layer over the dense embed-

dings associated to the characters of the word and concatenate the last hidden state in both directions. We also add the number n_i of characters in the word and case features, i.e. the percentage α_i of its characters in upper case and a binary factor β_i indicating if it has a title form. We concatenate all these features to form the textual component r_i^t of the word representation:

$$r_i^t = [q_i^w, q_i^c, n_i, \alpha_i, \beta_i] \qquad (1)$$

where q_i^w is its word level embedding.

To take into account the document layout, we also compute spatial features r_i^s of the word. These encompass the coordinates of the top-left and bottom-right edges of the word bounding box, normalized by the height and width of the page. We concatenate the spatial r_i^s and textual r_i^t components to build the word representation r_i.

3.2 Encoder

The words of the document are organized as a uni-dimensional sequence of length N by reading them in a top-left to bottom-right order. The word representations $\{r_i\}_{i=1..N}$ are then fed to a two-layer BLSTM to obtain contextualized representations through the encoder hidden states $\{h_i\}_{i=1..N}$.

3.3 Decoder

Decoding is performed by a two-layer forward LSTM, producing a hidden state s_t at each time step t. An attention mechanism is added on top of the decoder to compute the attention distribution a^t over the document words and the context vector $h_t^* = \sum_{i=1}^{N} a_i^t h_i$. While See et al. (2017) use the alignment function of Bahdanau et al. (2015), we employ the *general* form of Luong et al. (2015) as this is computationally less expensive while showing similar performances:

$$e_i^t = s_t^\mathsf{T} W_a h_i \tag{2}$$
$$a^t = \text{softmax}(e^t) \tag{3}$$

where W_a is a matrix of learnable parameters.

We simplify the computing of the vocabulary distribution P_{vocab} as the generator is only in charge of producing the XML tags and thus has a vocabulary of limited size. We apply a unique dense layer instead of two and do not involve the context vector h_t^* in the expression of P_{vocab}:

$$P_{vocab} = \text{softmax}(V s_t + b) \tag{4}$$

where V and b are learnable parameters

The generation probability $p_{gen} \in [0, 1]$ for choosing between generating XML tags versus copying words from the document is computed as follows:

$$p_{gen} = \sigma(w_h^\mathsf{T} h_t^* + w_s^\mathsf{T} s_t + w_x^\mathsf{T} x_t + b_{ptr}) \tag{5}$$

where x_t is the decoder input, vectors w_h, w_s, w_x and scalar b_{ptr} are learnable parameters and σ is the sigmoid function. Then, p_{gen} weights the sum of the attention and vocabulary distributions to obtain the final distribution $P(w)$ over the extended vocabulary, i.e. the union of all XML tags and unique textual values from the document words:

$$P(w) = p_{gen} P_{vocab}(w) + (1 - p_{gen}) \sum_{i:w_i=w} a_i^t \tag{6}$$

Note that if a textual value appears multiple times in the document, the attention weights of all the corresponding words are summed for calculating its probability of being copied.

During training, the decoder input x_t is the previous token of the ground truth sequence, while in inference mode, the previous token emitted by the decoder is used. An input token is either represented by a dense embedding if the token is a XML tag or by the textual feature set r_i^t of the corresponding words $\{w_i\}$ if the token is copied from the document.

To help the model keeping track of words already copied, we concatenate the previous context vector h_{t-1}^* with the input representation x_t before applying the first decoder LSTM layer (Luong et al., 2015). We also employ the *coverage mechanism* proposed in See et al. (2017) in order to reduce repetitions in the generated sequences. The idea is to combine the attention distributions of the previous time steps in the coverage vector $c^t = \sum_{t'=1}^{t-1} a^{t'}$ to compute the current attention distribution. We adapt their mechanism to our alignment function, thus changing the equation 2 to:

$$e_i^t = s_t^\mathsf{T}(W_a h_i + c_i^t w_c) \tag{7}$$

where w_c is a vector of adjustable parameters.

The training loss is the combination of the negative log-likelihood of the target tokens $\{w_t^*\}_{t=1..T}$ and the coverage loss which penalizes the model for repeatedly paying attention to the same words:

$$loss_t = -\log P(w_t^*) + \lambda \sum_{i=1}^{N} \min(a_i^t, c_i^t) \tag{8}$$

$$loss = \frac{1}{T} \sum_{t=1}^{T} loss_t \tag{9}$$

where λ is a scalar hyperparameter.

When the decoding stage is performed, the resulting string is parsed according to the XML syntax to retrieve all the predicted entities and fields of the document.

4 Dataset

We train and evaluate our extraction model on a dataset of real world business documents which unfortunately cannot be publicly released. It consists of 219,476 purchase orders emanated by 17,664 issuers between April 2017 and May 2018. The dataset is multilingual and multicultural even if the documents mainly originate from the U.S. The number of purchase orders per issuer is at least 3 and at most 31, ensuring diversity of document layouts. Training, validation and test sets have distinct issuers to assess the ability of the model to generalize to unseen layouts. They have been constructed by randomly picking 70 %, 10 % and 20 % of the issuers, respectively. More detailed statistics of the dataset are given in the Table 1.

Table 1: Statistics of our dataset.

Training documents	154,450
Validation documents	22,261
Test documents	42,765
Words per document (Avg.)	411
Pages per document (Avg.)	1.52
Product entities per document (Avg.)	3.52
Tokens in output sequence (Avg.)	32.24
Words per ID number instance (Avg.)	1.36
Words per quantity instance (Avg.)	1.00

This dataset comes from a larger corpus of documents with their information extraction results that have been validated by end users of a commercial document automation software. Among all the types of information, we focus on the extraction of the ordered product entities which have two mandatory fields: ID number and quantity. From this corpus, we select the purchase orders whose location in the document is supplied for all its field instances. The knowledge of location comes from a layout-based incremental extraction system and ensures that we perfectly construct the labels for training a word classifier. Since a field instance can be composed of multiple words, we adopt the IOB (Inside, Outside, Beginning) tagging scheme of Ramshaw and Marcus (1999) for defining the field type of each document word.

5 Experiments

Our end-to-end model is compared on this dataset with a baseline extraction method based on a word classifier. This baseline encodes the document as the end-to-end model does, i.e. with the same operations for constructing the word representations r_i and the encoder outputs h_i. On top of the encoder, a dense layer with softmax activation is added with 5 output units. 4 of these units refer to the beginning and continuation of an instance for ID number and quantity fields. The remaining unit is dedicated to the Outside class, i.e. for the document words carrying information that we do not want to extract. The words with a predicted probability above 0.5 for one of the 4 field units are associated with the corresponding class, otherwise we attribute the Outside class. Field instances are then constructed by merging words with beginning and continuing classes of the same field type. Finally, each quantity instance is paired with an ID number instance to form the product entities. To do so, the Hungarian algorithm (Kuhn, 1955) solves a linear sum assignment problem with the vertical distance on the document as the matching cost between two field instances. For our task, this pairing strategy is flawless if the field instances are perfectly extracted by the word classifier.

The model hyperparameters are chosen according to the micro averaged gain on the validation set. The end-to-end model and baseline share the same hyperparameter values, except the number of BLSTM cells in each encoder layer that is fixed to 128 and 256 respectively, to ensure similar numbers of trainable parameters. The input character and word vocabularies are derived from the training set. We consider all observed characters while we follow the word vocabulary construction of Sage et al. (2019) designed for business documents. This results in vocabularies of respectively 5,592 and 25,677 elements. Their embedding has a size of 16 and 32 and are trained from scratch. The BLSTM layer iterating over characters of document words has 32 cells. For all BLSTM layers, each direction has $n/2$ LSTM cells and their output are concatenated to form n-dimensional vectors. The decoder layers have a size of 128 and are initialized by the last states of the encoding BLSTM layers. At inference time, we decode with a beam search of width 3 and we set the maximum length of the output sequence to the number of words in the document. This results in 1,400,908 and 1,515,733 trainable parameters for the PGN and the word classifier.

To deal with exploding gradients, we apply gradient norm clipping (Pascanu et al., 2013) with a clipping threshold of 5. The loss is minimized with the Adam optimizer, its learning rate is fixed to 0.001 the first 2 epochs and then exponentially decreases by a factor of 0.8. We stop the training when the micro gain on the validation set has not improved in the last 3 epochs. As suggested in See et al. (2017), the coverage loss is added to the minimized loss only at the end of training, for one additional epoch. We weight its contribution by setting $\lambda = 0.1$ as the original value of 1 makes the negative log-likelihood loss increase. The batch size is 8 if the model fits on GPU RAM, 4 otherwise.

The experiments are carried out on a single NVIDIA TITAN X GPU. Model training takes from 3 to 10 days for 10 to 15 epochs. Due to the computational burden, the hyperparameters values have not been optimized thoroughly. Besides, we are not able to train the models on documents with more than 1800 words, which amounts to about 4 % of the training set being put aside. Yet, we evaluate the models on all documents of the validation and test sets. The implementation is based on the seq2seq subpackage of TensorFlow Addons (Luong et al., 2017).

6 Results

6.1 Manual post-processing cost

We evaluate the models by measuring how much work is saved by using them rather than manually doing the extraction. For this purpose, we first assign the predicted products of a document to the ground truth entities, then we count the number of deletions, insertions and modifications to match the ground truth field instances from the predicted instances that have been assigned. The modification counter is incremented by one when a predicted field value and its target do not exactly match. For a given field, we estimate the manual post-processing gain with the following edit distance:

$$1 - \frac{\text{\# deletions} + \text{\# insertions} + \text{\# modifications}}{N} \tag{10}$$

where N is the number of ground truth instances in the document for this field. Micro averaged gain is calculated by summing the error counters of ID number and quantity fields and applying equation 10. We select the assignment between predicted and target entities that maximizes the micro gain of the document. To assess the post-processing gains across a set of documents, we sum the counters of each document before using equation 10.

Our evaluation methodology is closely related to Katti et al. (2018). However, they compute metrics independently for each field while we take into account the structure of entities in our evaluation.

We report in Table 2 the results of both extraction models on the test set. We retain the best epoch of each model according to the validation micro gain. All post-processing gains have positive values, meaning that it is more efficient to correct potential errors of models than manually perform the extraction from scratch (in this case, # insertions $= N$

Table 2: Post-processing gains when extracting the products from the test documents. *% Perfect* column indicates the percentage of documents perfectly processed by each model.

	ID number	Quantity	Micro avg.	% Perfect
Word classifier	0.754	0.855	0.804	67.4
PGN	0.711	0.832	0.771	68.2

and # deletions $=$ # modifications $= 0$). We note that the performances of the word classifier and PGN are quite similar. Even if its field level gains are a little behind, the PGN slightly surpasses the word classifier for recognizing whole documents. Both models significantly reduce human efforts as the end users do not have any corrections to make for more than 2 out of 3 documents. Besides, the PGN produces sequences that are well-formed according to the XML syntax for more than 99.5 % of the test documents.

6.2 Visual inspection of the attention mechanism

The comparison with the baseline confirms that the PGN has learned to produce relevant attention distributions in order to copy words carrying useful information. In particular, when the expected field value appears multiple times in the document, the PGN is able to localize the occurrence that is semantically correct, as illustrated in the document displayed in Figure 3. As shown, the PGN focuses its attention on the word 1 in the table row of the product that is currently recognized. On the contrary, the model ignores the occurrences of 1 which are contained in the rest of the product table and in the address blocks. This behaviour is noteworthy since the model is not explicitly taught to perform this disambiguation.

7 Discussion

The main difficulty faced by both models is ambiguity in the ground truth as our dataset has been annotated by users from many distinct companies. Some documents contain multiple valid values for a field of a unique product. For example, there may be the references from both recipient and issuer for the ID number. The field value which is retained as ground truth then depends on further processing of the extracted information, e.g. integration into a Enterprise Resource Planning (ERP) system.

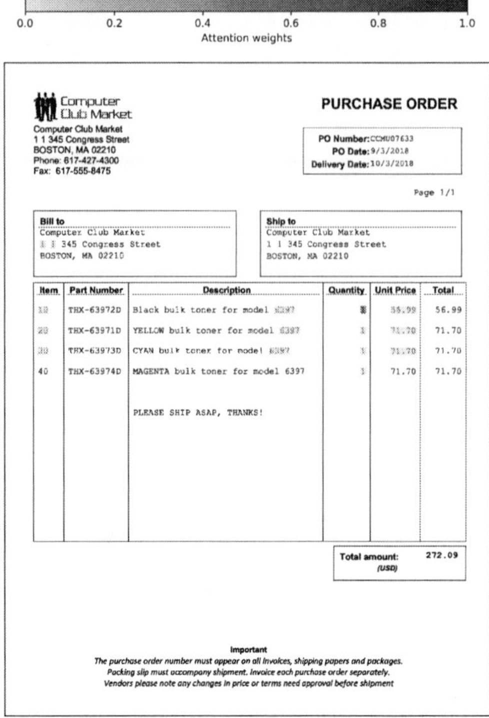

Figure 3: A sample document with filled bounding boxes around words whose colors depend on their attention weights. For sake of readability, we only highlight the top 15 words. We show attention values for the 6th time step of the pointer-generator network, after having outputted the tokens `<Product>`, `<IDNumber>`, `THX-63972D`, `</IDNumber>` and `<Quantity>`. The model rightly points to the word `1` to extract the quantity value of the first product.

This seriously prevents any extraction model from reaching the upper bound of post-processing gain metrics which is 1.

Besides, the ID number field does not always have a dedicated physical column and rather appears within the description column, without keywords clearly introducing the field instances such as in Figure 1. Also, its instances are constituted on average of more words than the quantity, making less likely the exact match between predicted and target instances. These additional complications explain the gap of model performances between the two fields.

Unlike the word classifier based approach, the PGN tends to repeat itself by duplicating some field instances and skipping others. This is especially observed for documents having a large number of products, therefore large output sequences. To mea-

sure the impact of these repetitions on metrics, we split the test set into 3 subsets according to the number of products contained in the document: no more than 3, between 4 and 14 and at least 15 entities. The last subset gathers documents with output sequences of at least 122 tokens. We recompute the metrics for each subset and report the micro averaged gains in Table 3.

Table 3: Micro averaged gains over the test set conditioned on the number N of products in the document.

	$N \leq 3$	$3 < N < 15$	$N \geq 15$
Documents	33,332	7,820	1,613
Product entities	46,893	53,771	44,094
Word classifier	0.804	0.807	0.801
PGN	0.820	0.791	0.696
Without coverage	0.799	0.817	0.671

The performances are stable for the word classifier whatever the number of entities in the document. The PGN is on par with the word classifier for the documents with a small number of products which constitute the vast majority of the dataset. However, its extraction performance greatly declines for large output sequences, indicating that the PGN is more affected by repetitions than the baseline. It is unclear why the coverage mechanism is not as successful on our task as it is for abstractive summarization (See et al., 2017). We also tried to use the temporal attention from Paulus et al. (2018) to avoid copying the same words multiple times but this was unsuccessful too.

8 Conclusion

We discussed a novel method based on pointer-generator networks for extracting structured information from documents. We showed that learning directly from the textual value of information is a viable alternative to the costly word level supervision commonly used in information extraction. In this work, we focused on purchase orders but the approach could be used to extract any structured entity as long as its information type is known at training time.

Future work should aim to: i) reduce repetitions in the output sequences, ii) add parsing abilities into our encoder-decoder in order to transform the values of copied words. This will allow to process fields that need to be normalized when being extracted.

Acknowledgment

The work presented in this paper was supported by Esker. We thank them for providing the dataset on which experiments were performed and for insightful discussions about these researches.

References

Dzmitry Bahdanau, Kyunghyun Cho, and Yoshua Bengio. 2015. Neural machine translation by jointly learning to align and translate. In *3rd International Conference on Learning Representations, ICLR 2015, San Diego, CA, USA, May 7-9, 2015, Conference Track Proceedings*.

Vincent Poulain d'Andecy, Emmanuel Hartmann, and Marçal Rusiñol. 2018. Field extraction by hybrid incremental and a-priori structural templates. In *2018 13th IAPR International Workshop on Document Analysis Systems (DAS)*, pages 251–256. IEEE.

Tuan Anh Nguyen Dang and Dat Nguyen Thanh. 2019. End-to-end information extraction by character-level embedding and multi-stage attentional u-net. In *Proceedings of the British Machine Vision Conference (BMVC)*.

Yuntian Deng, Anssi Kanervisto, Jeffrey Ling, and Alexander M Rush. 2017. Image-to-markup generation with coarse-to-fine attention. In *Proceedings of the 34th International Conference on Machine Learning-Volume 70*, pages 980–989. JMLR. org.

Yuntian Deng, David Rosenberg, and Gideon Mann. 2019. Challenges in end-to-end neural scientific table recognition. In *2019 International Conference on Document Analysis and Recognition (ICDAR)*, pages 894–901. IEEE.

Timo I. Denk and Christian Reisswig. 2019. {BERT}grid: Contextualized embedding for 2d document representation and understanding. In *Workshop on Document Intelligence at NeurIPS 2019*.

Pranjal Dhakal, Manish Munikar, and Bikram Dahal. 2019. One-shot template matching for automatic document data capture. In *2019 Artificial Intelligence for Transforming Business and Society (AITB)*, volume 1, pages 1–6. IEEE.

Li Dong and Mirella Lapata. 2016. Language to logical form with neural attention. In *Proceedings of the 54th Annual Meeting of the Association for Computational Linguistics (Volume 1: Long Papers)*, pages 33–43, Berlin, Germany. Association for Computational Linguistics.

Filip Graliński, Tomasz Stanisławek, Anna Wróblewska, Dawid Lipiński, Agnieszka Kaliska, Paulina Rosalska, Bartosz Topolski, and Przemysław Biecek. 2020. Kleister: A novel task for information extraction involving long documents with complex layout. *arXiv preprint arXiv:2003.02356*.

Martin Holeček, Antonín Hoskovec, Petr Baudiš, and Pavel Klinger. 2019. Line-items and table understanding in structured documents. *arXiv preprint arXiv:1904.12577*.

Xavier Holt and Andrew Chisholm. 2018. Extracting structured data from invoices. In *Proceedings of the Australasian Language Technology Association Workshop 2018*, pages 53–59.

Zheng Huang, Kai Chen, Jianhua He, Xiang Bai, Dimosthenis Karatzas, Shijian Lu, and CV Jawahar. 2019. Icdar2019 competition on scanned receipt ocr and information extraction. In *2019 International Conference on Document Analysis and Recognition (ICDAR)*, pages 1516–1520. IEEE.

Robin Jia and Percy Liang. 2016. Data recombination for neural semantic parsing. In *Proceedings of the 54th Annual Meeting of the Association for Computational Linguistics (Volume 1: Long Papers)*, pages 12–22, Berlin, Germany. Association for Computational Linguistics.

Zhaohui Jiang, Zheng Huang, Yunrui Lian, Jie Guo, and Weidong Qiu. 2019. Integrating coordinates with context for information extraction in document images. In *2019 International Conference on Document Analysis and Recognition (ICDAR)*, pages 363–368. IEEE.

Anoop R Katti, Christian Reisswig, Cordula Guder, Sebastian Brarda, Steffen Bickel, Johannes Höhne, and Jean Baptiste Faddoul. 2018. Chargrid: Towards understanding 2d documents. In *Proceedings of the 2018 Conference on Empirical Methods in Natural Language Processing*, pages 4459–4469.

Harold W Kuhn. 1955. The hungarian method for the assignment problem. *Naval research logistics quarterly*, 2(1-2):83–97.

Wang Ling, Chris Dyer, Alan W Black, Isabel Trancoso, Ramón Fermandez, Silvio Amir, Luís Marujo, and Tiago Luís. 2015. Finding function in form: Compositional character models for open vocabulary word representation. In *Proceedings of the 2015 Conference on Empirical Methods in Natural Language Processing*, pages 1520–1530, Lisbon, Portugal. Association for Computational Linguistics.

Xiaojing Liu, Feiyu Gao, Qiong Zhang, and Huasha Zhao. 2019. Graph convolution for multimodal information extraction from visually rich documents. In *Proceedings of the 2019 Conference of the North American Chapter of the Association for Computational Linguistics: Human Language Technologies, Volume 2 (Industry Papers)*, pages 32–39, Minneapolis, Minnesota. Association for Computational Linguistics.

Devashish Lohani, A Belaïd, and Yolande Belaïd. 2018. An invoice reading system using a graph convolutional network. In *Asian Conference on Computer Vision*, pages 144–158. Springer.

Minh-Thang Luong, Eugene Brevdo, and Rui Zhao. 2017. Neural machine translation (seq2seq) tutorial. *https://github.com/tensorflow/nmt*.

Thang Luong, Hieu Pham, and Christopher D. Manning. 2015. Effective approaches to attention-based neural machine translation. In *Proceedings of the 2015 Conference on Empirical Methods in Natural Language Processing*, pages 1412–1421, Lisbon, Portugal. Association for Computational Linguistics.

Bryan McCann, Nitish Shirish Keskar, Caiming Xiong, and Richard Socher. 2018. The natural language decathlon: Multitask learning as question answering. *arXiv preprint arXiv:1806.08730*.

Daniel W Otter, Julian R Medina, and Jugal K Kalita. 2020. A survey of the usages of deep learning for natural language processing. *IEEE Transactions on Neural Networks and Learning Systems*.

Rasmus Berg Palm, Florian Laws, and Ole Winther. 2019. Attend, copy, parse end-to-end information extraction from documents. In *2019 International Conference on Document Analysis and Recognition (ICDAR)*, pages 329–336. IEEE.

Rasmus Berg Palm, Ole Winther, and Florian Laws. 2017. Cloudscan-a configuration-free invoice analysis system using recurrent neural networks. In *2017 14th IAPR International Conference on Document Analysis and Recognition (ICDAR)*, pages 406–413. IEEE.

Razvan Pascanu, Tomas Mikolov, and Yoshua Bengio. 2013. On the difficulty of training recurrent neural networks. In *International Conference on Machine Learning*, pages 1310–1318.

Romain Paulus, Caiming Xiong, and Richard Socher. 2018. A deep reinforced model for abstractive summarization. In *International Conference on Learning Representations*.

Maxim Rabinovich, Mitchell Stern, and Dan Klein. 2017. Abstract syntax networks for code generation and semantic parsing. In *Proceedings of the 55th Annual Meeting of the Association for Computational Linguistics (Volume 1: Long Papers)*, pages 1139–1149, Vancouver, Canada. Association for Computational Linguistics.

Lance A Ramshaw and Mitchell P Marcus. 1999. Text chunking using transformation-based learning. In *Natural language processing using very large corpora*, pages 157–176. Springer.

Clément Sage, Alex Aussem, Haytham Elghazel, Véronique Eglin, and Jérémy Espinas. 2019. Recurrent Neural Network Approach for Table Field Extraction in Business Documents. In *International Conference on Document Analysis and Recognition, ICDAR 2019*, Sydney, Australia.

Abigail See, Peter J Liu, and Christopher D Manning. 2017. Get to the point: Summarization with pointer-generator networks. In *Proceedings of the 55th Annual Meeting of the Association for Computational Linguistics (Volume 1: Long Papers)*, pages 1073–1083.

Oriol Vinyals, Meire Fortunato, and Navdeep Jaitly. 2015. Pointer networks. In *Advances in neural information processing systems*, pages 2692–2700.

Jin-Wen Wu, Fei Yin, Yan-Ming Zhang, Xu-Yao Zhang, and Cheng-Lin Liu. 2018. Image-to-markup generation via paired adversarial learning. In *Joint European Conference on Machine Learning and Knowledge Discovery in Databases*, pages 18–34. Springer.

Vikas Yadav and Steven Bethard. 2018. A survey on recent advances in named entity recognition from deep learning models. In *Proceedings of the 27th International Conference on Computational Linguistics*, pages 2145–2158.

Xiaohui Zhao, Zhuo Wu, and Xiaoguang Wang. 2019. Cutie: Learning to understand documents with convolutional universal text information extractor. *arXiv preprint arXiv:1903.12363*.

Victor Zhong, Caiming Xiong, and Richard Socher. 2017. Seq2sql: Generating structured queries from natural language using reinforcement learning. *arXiv preprint arXiv:1709.00103*.

Xu Zhong, Elaheh ShafieiBavani, and Antonio Jimeno Yepes. 2019. Image-based table recognition: data, model, and evaluation. *arXiv preprint arXiv:1911.10683*.

Layer-wise Guided Training for BERT:
Learning Incrementally Refined Document Representations

Nikolaos Manginas [†]   **Ilias Chalkidis** [† ‡]   **Prodromos Malakasiotis** [† ‡]
[†] Institute of Informatics & Telecommunications, NCSR "Demokritos"
[‡] Department of Informatics, Athens University of Economics and Business
`[nmanginas,ichalkidis,pmalakasiotis]@iit.demokritos.gr`

Abstract

Although BERT is widely used by the NLP community, little is known about its inner workings. Several attempts have been made to shed light on certain aspects of BERT, often with contradicting conclusions. A much raised concern focuses on BERT's over-parameterization and under-utilization issues. To this end, we propose o novel approach to fine-tune BERT in a structured manner. Specifically, we focus on Large Scale Multilabel Text Classification (LMTC) where documents are assigned with one or more labels from a large predefined set of hierarchically organized labels. Our approach guides specific BERT layers to predict labels from specific hierarchy levels. Experimenting with two LMTC datasets we show that this structured fine-tuning approach not only yields better classification results but also leads to better parameter utilization.

1 Introduction

Despite BERT's (Devlin et al., 2019) popularity and effectiveness, little is known about its inner workings. Several attempts have been made to demystify certain aspects of BERT (Rogers et al., 2020), often leading to contradicting conclusions. For instance, Clark et al. (2019) argue that attention measures the importance of a particular word when computing the next level representation for this word. However, Kovaleva et al. (2019) showed that most attention heads contain trivial linguistic information and follow a vertical pattern (attention to `[cls]`, `[sep]`, and punctuation tokens), which could be related to under-utilization or over-parameterization issues. Other studies attempted to link specific BERT heads with linguistically interpretable functions (Htut et al., 2019; Clark et al., 2019; Kovaleva et al., 2019; Voita et al., 2019; Hoover et al., 2020; Lin et al., 2019), agreeing that no single head densely encodes enough relevant information but instead different linguistic features are learnt by different attention heads. We hypothesize that the aforementioned largely contributes to the lack of attention-based explainability of BERT. Another open topic is how the knowledge is distributed across BERT layers. Most studies agree that syntactic knowledge is gathered in the middle layers (Hewitt and Manning, 2019; Goldberg, 2019; Jawahar et al., 2019), while the final layers are more task-specific. Most importantly, it seems that any semantic knowledge is spread across the model, explaining why non-trivial tasks are better solved at the higher layers (Tenney et al., 2019).

Driven by the above discussion, we propose a novel fine-tuning approach where different parts of BERT are guided to directly solve increasingly challenging classification tasks following an underlying label hierarchy. Specifically, we focus on Large Scale Multilabel Text Classification (LMTC) where documents are assigned with one or more labels from a large predefined set. The labels are organized in a hierarchy from general to specific concepts. Our approach attempts to tie specific BERT layers with specific hierarchy levels. In effect, each of these layers is responsible for predicting the labels of the corresponding level. We experiment with two LMTC datasets (EURLEX57K, MIMIC-III) and several variations of structured BERT training. Our contributions are: (a) We propose a novel structured approach to fine-tune BERT where specific layers are tied to specific hierarchy levels; (b) We show that structured training yields better results than the baseline across all levels of the hierarchy, while also leading to better parameter utilization.

2 Datasets

EURLEX57K (Chalkidis et al., 2019) contains 57k EU legal acts from EURLEX.[1] Each act is approx.

---

[1] `http://eur-lex.europa.eu/`

Proceedings of 4th Workshop on Structured Prediction for NLP, pages 53–61
November 20, 2020. ©2020 Association for Computational Linguistics

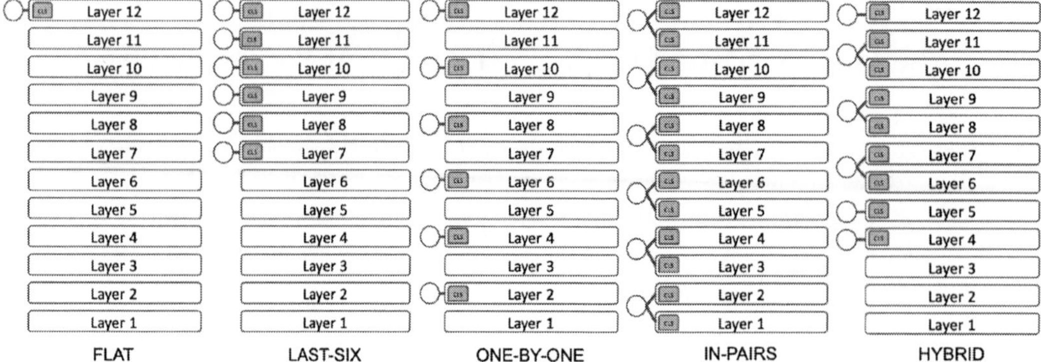

Figure 1: The five variants of BERT-based multi-label classifiers including the flat one and the four structured editions. The circles represent the classification layers attached to [cls] tokens across layers.

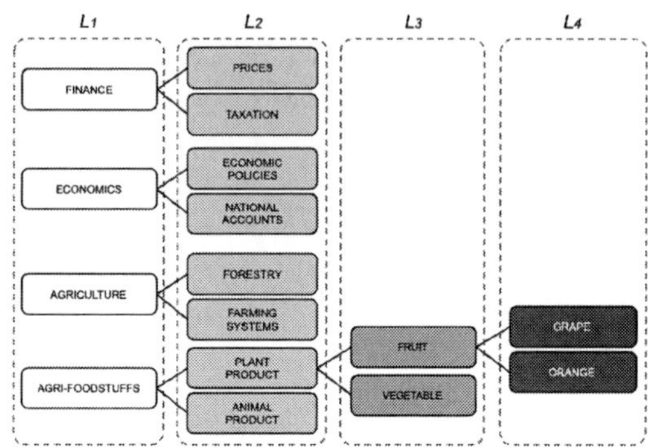

Figure 2: Examples from EUROVOC label hierarchy. Layerwise models consider all labels in the same level (L_i; dashed boxes) of the hierarchy on-par.

700 words long and is annotated with one or more concepts from EUROVOC[2] which contains 7,391 concepts organized in an 8-level hierarchy. We truncate the hierarchy to 6 levels by discarding the last 2 levels which contain 50 rarely used labels.[3]

MIMIC-III (Johnson et al., 2017) contains approx. 52k discharge summaries from US hospitals. Each summary is approx. 1.6k words long and is annotated with one or more ICD-9[4] codes. ICD-9 contains 22,395 codes organized in a 7-level hierarchy. We truncate the hierarchy to 6 levels, discarding the first level which contains only 4 general codes.[3]

Label Augmentation: In both datasets, we make the assumption that if a label l is assigned to a document then all of its ancestors should also be assigned to this document. Hence, we augment labels by annotating a document with all the ancestors of its assigned labels. For instance, in EUROVOC, if a

document is annotated with the label *grape* it will also be annotated with *grape*'s ancestors, i.e., *fruit*, *plant product*, and *agri-foodstuffs* (Figure 2). This assumption is perfectly valid, while also having the added side effect of providing a more accurate test-bed for evaluation. For example, if a classifier mistakenly annotated the document with *citrus fruit*, a sibling of *grape*, in the non-augmented case it would receive a score of zero. By contrast, in the augmented case, assuming it correctly identified all the ancestors of *citrus fruit* it would receive a much higher score of 0.75 having correctly assigned the three ancestors of *grape* but not the (more specialized) label itself. Thus, we believe the model is evaluated more fairly in the augmented case with respect to the hierarchy. This type of evaluation is also in-line with the literature on hierarchical classification (Kosmopoulos et al., 2015).

3 Structured Learning with BERT

Before we proceed with the description of our methods (Figure 1), we introduce some notation. Given a label hierarchy L of depth d, L_n denotes the set of labels in the nth level of this hierarchy ($n \leqslant d$). Also, $f_i = \sigma(W_i \cdot c_i + b_i)$ is a classification function, where W_i and b_i are trainable parameters, c_i is the [cls] token in the ith BERT layer,[5] and σ is the sigmoid activation function. Note that the sizes of W_i and b depend on the number of labels that f_i is responsible for predicting, i.e., if f_i predicts the labels of L_n, $W_i \in \mathbb{R}^{|L_n| \times 768}$ and $b_i \in \mathbb{R}^{|L_n| \times 1}$.

FLAT: This is a simple baseline which uses f_{12} to predict all labels in the hierarchy in a flat manner. In effect, $W_{12} \in \mathbb{R}^{|L| \times 768}$ and $b_i \in \mathbb{R}^{|L| \times 1}$. Note

---

[2] http://eurovoc.europa.eu/
[3] For more details on data manipulation see Appendix A.
[4] www.who.int/classifications/icd/en/

[5] We use BERT-BASE (12 layers, 768 units, 12 heads).

Labels Depth	1	2	3	4	5	6	Micro	Macro
EURLEX- BERT-BASE								
#Labels	21	127	567	3,861	2,284	481	7,341	7,341
FLAT	90.3 ± 0.2	83.9 ± 0.3	81.0 ± 0.5	74.8 ± 1.0	74.5 ± 1.2	79.9 ± 1.4	80.6 ± 0.6	80.7 ± 0.6
LAST-SIX	$\mathbf{90.7} \pm 0.1$	$\mathbf{84.6} \pm 0.0$	$\mathbf{81.9} \pm 0.2$	$\mathbf{76.8} \pm 0.2$	$\mathbf{77.2} \pm 0.5$	$\mathbf{82.2} \pm 1.1$	$\mathbf{81.7} \pm 0.1$	$\mathbf{82.2} \pm 0.1$
ONE-BY-ONE	90.0 ± 0.0	84.3 ± 0.1	81.7 ± 0.2	76.2 ± 0.2	76.7 ± 0.5	81.6 ± 0.2	81.3 ± 0.1	81.7 ± 0.0
IN-PAIRS	89.9 ± 0.2	84.3 ± 0.2	81.7 ± 0.2	76.7 ± 0.3	$\mathbf{77.2} \pm 0.6$	81.7 ± 0.4	81.4 ± 0.1	81.9 ± 0.4
HYBRID	90.5 ± 0.2	84.3 ± 0.1	81.7 ± 0.2	76.6 ± 0.4	76.6 ± 0.7	81.8 ± 0.7	81.5 ± 0.2	81.9 ± 0.0
MIMIC-III- SCIBERT								
#Labels	79	589	3,982	9,640	7,234	867	22,391	22,391
FLAT	75.5 ± 0.0	66.5 ± 0.2	57.7 ± 0.4	50.8 ± 0.4	43.2 ± 0.8	38.6 ± 3.3	60.1 ± 0.4	55.4 ± 0.9
LAST-SIX	$\mathbf{76.8} \pm 0.2$	$\mathbf{67.3} \pm 0.1$	$\mathbf{58.5} \pm 0.1$	51.2 ± 0.0	$\mathbf{43.8} \pm 0.3$	40.9 ± 0.1	$\mathbf{60.4} \pm 0.0$	$\mathbf{56.4} \pm 0.1$
ONE-BY-ONE	75.7 ± 0.0	66.7 ± 0.1	57.9 ± 0.1	50.6 ± 0.1	43.4 ± 0.3	$\mathbf{41.8} \pm 0.6$	59.8 ± 0.1	56.0 ± 0.2
IN-PAIRS	75.6 ± 0.1	66.5 ± 0.1	58.1 ± 0.1	50.9 ± 0.1	43.6 ± 0.3	40.9 ± 0.8	59.9 ± 0.1	55.9 ± 0.2
HYBRID	76.4 ± 0.1	67.0 ± 0.1	$\mathbf{58.5} \pm 0.1$	$\mathbf{51.3} \pm 0.0$	$\mathbf{43.8} \pm 0.2$	40.0 ± 0.4	60.3 ± 0.0	56.2 ± 0.1

Table 1: R-Precision $\pm$ std for all variants of BERT-BASE on EURLEX and MIMIC-III test data across hierarchy depths.

that this model achieves state-of-the-art results on EURLEX57K but not on MIMIC-III (Chalkidis et al., 2020). However, our results are not directly comparable to Chalkidis et al. (2020) because our methods operate on augmented label sets.

LAST-SIX: This method uses the classifiers f_7 through f_{12} to predict the labels in L_1 through L_6, respectively. Our intuition is that the layers 1-6 will retain and enhance their pre-trained functionality, i.e., syntactic knowledge, contextualized representations, while layers 7-12 will leverage this knowledge to better solve their individual tasks. We also expect that the model will show higher parameter utilization for the layers 7-12 since they are forced to solve gradually more refined classification tasks.

ONE-BY-ONE: This method utilizes the full depth of BERT in a *"skip one, use one"* fashion, i.e., it uses classifiers f_i, $i \in \{2, 4, \dots, 12\}$. In effect, the odd layers $(1, 3, \dots, 11)$ are updated only indirectly, through the classification tasks of the even layers. We expect that the odd layers will learn rich latent representations to facilitate the classifiers of the even layers. Spreading the classification tasks across the whole depth of the model will potentially lead to better parameter utilization. On the other hand, it could harm the model's pre-trained functionality and hence its performance.

IN-PAIRS: This method also exploits the full depth of BERT, but now the layers are grouped in 6 pairs, $p_n \in \{(1, 2), (3, 4), \dots, (11, 12)\}$. The classifier responsible for the labels of L_n operates on the concatenated [cls] tokens of the corresponding pair, e.g., $f_1 = \sigma(W_1 \cdot [c_1; c_2] + b_1)$ is trained on the labels of L_1. We expect IN-PAIRS to have better pa-

rameter utilization than ONE-BY-ONE, although the risk of hindering performance is now even higher.

HYBRID: Similarly to LAST-SIX, this method skips some of the lower BERT layers (3 instead of 6). Also, it ties L_1, L_2, and L_6, which are the hierarchy levels with the fewest labels to layers 4, 5, and 12, respectively. Finally, similarly to IN-PAIRS the remaining BERT layers are grouped in pairs and are tied to the rest of the hierarchy levels. We expect the first three layers to retain and enhance their pre-trained functionality, while the hierarchy levels with a large number of labels will benefit from the additional parameters at their disposal.

4 Experiments

We report R-Precision (Manning et al., 2009) at each hierarchy level as well as micro (flat) and macro averages across all levels.[6] Table 1 shows the results in both datasets. In EURLEX57K our structured methods always outperform the baseline mostly by a large margin. LAST-SIX achieves the best overall results and is superior than the other structured methods in all hierarchy levels indicating that allowing the lower layers to retain and enhance their pre-trained functionality is crucial. Similar observations can be made for MIMIC-III, but in this case the importance of not damaging BERT's pre-trained functionality is even higher, as evident by the only minor improvements ONE-BY-ONE and IN-PAIRS have compared to FLAT.[7]

---

[6] See Appendices B and C for a detailed description on experimental setup and a discussion on LMTC evaluation.

[7] This is probably due to the additional difficulties of the clinical domain. See Appendix D for a discussion.

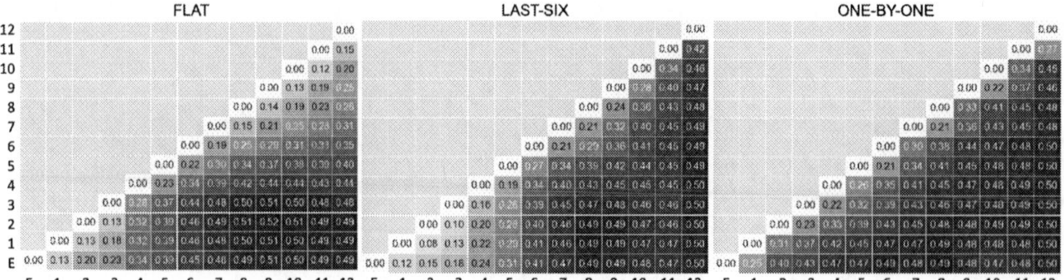

Figure 3: Angular distance between `[cls]` representations across layers.

Figure 4: KL-Divergence between attention distributions across layers.

Layer	1		2		3		4		5		6		7		8		9		10		11		12	
FLAT	4.7	1.3	3.9	0.7	2.5	0.9	3.6	1.7	3.3	2.6	3.2	3.2	3.4	3.1	2.7	2.6	2.1	2.1	2.6	1.8	2.2	1.2	2.4	0.6
LAST-SIX	4.6	1.5	4.2	0.6	4.1	0.8	3.9	1.1	2.7	2.7	2.9	3.6	2.9	3.0	2.6	2.9	3.0	4.2	4.5	3.9	4.3	2.3	5.2	0.6
ONE-BY-ONE	4.5	1.9	4.1	2.4	4.0	4.7	4.0	3.8	3.7	4.2	2.8	2.9	4.6	2.7	4.0	3.0	3.9	1.7	3.9	1.8	4.4	1.4	4.5	0.2
IN-PAIRS	4.4	1.9	3.9	3.0	3.9	4.6	4.1	4.2	3.2	3.6	3.5	3.5	4.1	2.5	3.5	2.8	3.7	2.0	3.7	1.4	4.2	1.1	5.1	0.2
HYBRID	4.6	2.0	4.5	0.9	4.2	1.7	4.2	2.1	3.8	3.4	3.1	3.7	4.1	3.8	3.8	3.6	4.1	2.8	4.3	2.5	4.1	1.1	4.7	0.3

Table 2: Entropy (left column) and KL-Divergence (right column) of attention distributions per layer.

5 Discussion on model utilization

Comparing `[cls]` representations: Figure 3 shows the average angular distances between the `[cls]` representations of each layer on development data of EURLEX57K.[8] The angular distance is calculated on unit (L_2 normalized) vectors, takes values in $[0, 1]$, and a distance of 0.5 indicates an angle of 90°. We observe that ONE-BY-ONE leads to larger angles between the representations than LAST-SIX which in turn yields larger angles than FLAT. In effect, ONE-BY-ONE and to a lesser extent LAST-SIX lead to a better parameter utilization than FLAT. To better support this claim we provide a geometric interpretation. We first L_2 normalize all `[cls]` representations. Each normalized representation can be interpreted as a vector having its initial point at the origin and its terminal point at the surface of a 768-dimensional hyper-sphere (centered at the origin). The larger the angle between two `[cls]` vectors the further apart they are on the hyper-sphere's surface. Effectively, `[cls]` vectors with large angles between them cover a larger sub-area of the hyper-sphere's surface indicating that the vector space is utilized to a higher extent which directly implies better parameter utilization.

Comparing attention distributions: Figure 4 shows the KL-Divergence of the average (across heads) attention for all layers on the development data of EURLEX57K.[8] A high KL-Divergence indicates that two layers attend to different sub-word units. Moreover, Table 2 reports the entropy (left column per layer) of the average (across heads) attention distribution per layer. A high entropy indicates that a layer attends to more sub-word units. Table 2 also reports the average KL-Divergence (right column per layer) between the attention distributions of each possible pair of heads in a layer. A high KL-Divergence indicates that each head attends to different sub-word units. A first observation is that FLAT attends to almost the same sub-word units across layers (small entropy differences and KL-Divergence across layers). Interestingly,

[8]For brevity, we only show the heatmaps of three methods. We include the missing ones in Appendix E.

the different attention heads focus on different sub-word units only in the middle layers (5-8). On the other hand, all the structured methods show better utilization of the attention mechanism, having higher entropy and KL-Divergence both across heads (Table 2) and across layers (Figure 4).

6 Related Work

Our approach is similar to Wehrmann et al. (2018) but they experiment with fully connected networks, which are not well suited for text classification, contrary to stacked transformers (Vaswani et al., 2017; Devlin et al., 2019). Similarly, Yan et al. (2015) used Convolutional Neural Networks, albeit with shallow hierarchies (2 levels). Although our approach leverages the label hierarchy it should not be confused with hierarchical classification methods (Silla and Freitas, 2011), which typically employ one classifier per node and cannot scale-up to large hierarchies when considering neural classifiers. A notable exception is the work of You et al. (2019) who employed one bidirectional LSTM with label-wise attention (You et al., 2018) per hierarchy node. However, for their method to scale-up, they use probabilistic label trees (Khandagale et al., 2019) to organize the labels in their own shallow hierarchy which does not follow the abstraction level of the original hierarchy. To the best of our knowledge we are the first to apply this approach to pre-trained language models.

7 Conclusions and Further Work

We proposed a novel guided approach to fine-tune BERT, where specific layers are tied to specific hierarchy levels. Experimenting with two LMTC datasets, we showed that structured training not only yields better results than a flat baseline, but also leads to better parameter utilization. In the future we will try to further increase the parameter utilization by guiding BERT's attention heads to explicitly focus on specific hierarchy parts. We also plan to improve the explainability of our methods with respect to the utilization of their parameters.

References

Iz Beltagy, Kyle Lo, and Arman Cohan. 2019. SciB-ERT: A pretrained language model for scientific text. In *Proceedings of the 2019 Conference on Empirical Methods in Natural Language Processing and the 9th International Joint Conference on Natural Language Processing (EMNLP-IJCNLP)*, pages 3606–3611, Hong Kong, China.

Ilias Chalkidis, Emmanouil Fergadiotis, Prodromos Malakasiotis, and Ion Androutsopoulos. 2019. Large-Scale Multi-Label Text Classification on EU Legislation. In *Proceedings of the 57th Annual Meeting of the Association for Computational Linguistics*, pages 6314–6322, Florence, Italy.

Ilias Chalkidis, Manos Fergadiotis, Sotiris Kotitsas, Prodromos Malakasiotis, Nikolaos Aletras, and Ion Androutsopoulos. 2020. An empirical study on large-scale multi-label text classification including few and zero-shot labels.

Kevin Clark, Urvashi Khandelwal, Omer Levy, and Christopher D. Manning. 2019. What does BERT look at? an analysis of BERT's attention. In *Proceedings of the 2019 ACL Workshop BlackboxNLP: Analyzing and Interpreting Neural Networks for NLP*, pages 276–286, Florence, Italy. Association for Computational Linguistics.

Jacob Devlin, Ming-Wei Chang, Kenton Lee, and Kristina Toutanova. 2019. BERT: Pre-training of Deep Bidirectional Transformers for Language Understanding. *Proceedings of the Annual Conference of the North American Chapter of the Association for Computational Linguistics: Human Language Technologies*, abs/1810.04805.

Yoav Goldberg. 2019. Assessing bert's syntactic abilities.

John Hewitt and Christopher D. Manning. 2019. A structural probe for finding syntax in word representations. In *Proceedings of the 2019 Conference of the North American Chapter of the Association for Computational Linguistics: Human Language Technologies, Volume 1 (Long and Short Papers)*, pages 4129–4138, Minneapolis, Minnesota. Association for Computational Linguistics.

Benjamin Hoover, Hendrik Strobelt, and Sebastian Gehrmann. 2020. exBERT: A Visual Analysis Tool to Explore Learned Representations in Transformer Models. In *Proceedings of the 58th Annual Meeting of the Association for Computational Linguistics: System Demonstrations*, pages 187–196, Online. Association for Computational Linguistics.

Phu Mon Htut, Jason Phang, Shikha Bordia, and Samuel R. Bowman. 2019. Do attention heads in bert track syntactic dependencies?

Ganesh Jawahar, Benoît Sagot, and Djamé Seddah. 2019. What does BERT learn about the structure of language? In *Proceedings of the 57th Annual Meeting of the Association for Computational Linguistics*, pages 3651–3657, Florence, Italy. Association for Computational Linguistics.

Alistair EW Johnson, David J. Stone, Leo A. Celi, and Tom J. Pollard. 2017. MIMIC-III, a freely accessible critical care database. *Nature*.

Sujay Khandagale, Han Xiao, and Rohit Babbar. 2019. Bonsai - Diverse and Shallow Trees for Extreme Multi-label Classification. *CoRR*, abs/1904.08249.

Diederik P. Kingma and Jim Ba. 2015. Adam: A method for stochastic optimization. In *Proceedings of the 5th International Conference on Learning Representations*.

Aris Kosmopoulos, Ioannis Partalas, Eric Gaussier, Georgios Paliouras, and Ion Androutsopoulos. 2015. Evaluation measures for hierarchical classification: a unified view and novel approaches. *Data Mining and Knowledge Discovery*, 29(3):820–865.

Olga Kovaleva, Alexey Romanov, Anna Rogers, and Anna Rumshisky. 2019. Revealing the dark secrets of BERT. In *Proceedings of the 2019 Conference on Empirical Methods in Natural Language Processing and the 9th International Joint Conference on Natural Language Processing (EMNLP-IJCNLP)*, pages 4365–4374, Hong Kong, China. Association for Computational Linguistics.

Yongjie Lin, Yi Chern Tan, and Robert Frank. 2019. Open sesame: Getting inside BERT's linguistic knowledge. In *Proceedings of the 2019 ACL Workshop BlackboxNLP: Analyzing and Interpreting Neural Networks for NLP*, pages 241–253, Florence, Italy. Association for Computational Linguistics.

Christopher D. Manning, Prabhakar Raghavan, and Hinrich Schütze. 2009. *Introduction to Information Retrieval*. Cambridge University Press.

Anthony Rios and Ramakanth Kavuluru. 2018. Few-Shot and Zero-Shot Multi-Label Learning for Structured Label Spaces. In *Proceedings of the 2018 Conference on Empirical Methods in Natural Language Processing*, pages 3132–3142. Association for Computational Linguistics.

Anna Rogers, Olga Kovaleva, and Anna Rumshisky. 2020. A primer in bertology: What we know about how bert works. *arXiv preprint arXiv:2002.12327*.

Carlos N Silla and Alex A Freitas. 2011. A survey of hierarchical classification across different application domains. *Data Mining and Knowledge Discovery*, 22(1-2):31–72.

Ian Tenney, Dipanjan Das, and Ellie Pavlick. 2019. BERT rediscovers the classical NLP pipeline. In *Proceedings of the 57th Annual Meeting of the Association for Computational Linguistics*, pages 4593–4601, Florence, Italy. Association for Computational Linguistics.

Ashish Vaswani, Noam Shazeer, Niki Parmar, Jakob Uszkoreit, Llion Jones, Aidan N. Gomez, Lukasz Kaiser, and Illia Polosukhin. 2017. Attention Is All You Need. In *31th Annual Conference on Neural Information Processing Systems*, Long Beach, CA, USA.

Elena Voita, David Talbot, Fedor Moiseev, Rico Sennrich, and Ivan Titov. 2019. Analyzing multi-head self-attention: Specialized heads do the heavy lifting, the rest can be pruned. In *Proceedings of the 57th Annual Meeting of the Association for Computational Linguistics*, pages 5797–5808, Florence, Italy. Association for Computational Linguistics.

Jonatas Wehrmann, Ricardo Cerri, and Rodrigo Barros. 2018. Hierarchical multi-label classification networks. In *Proceedings of the 35th International Conference on Machine Learning*, volume 80 of *Proceedings of Machine Learning Research*, pages 5075–5084, Stockholmsmässan, Stockholm Sweden. PMLR.

Zhicheng Yan, Hao Zhang, Robinson Piramuthu, Vignesh Jagadeesh, Dennis DeCoste, Wei Di, and Yizhou Yu. 2015. Hd-cnn: Hierarchical deep convolutional neural networks for large scale visual recognition. In *2015 IEEE International Conference on Computer Vision (ICCV)*, pages 2740–2748.

Ronghui You, Suyang Dai, Zihan Zhang, Hiroshi Mamitsuka, and Shanfeng Zhu. 2018. Attentionxml: Extreme multi-label text classification with multi-label attention based recurrent neural networks. *arXiv preprint arXiv:1811.01727*.

Ronghui You, Zihan Zhang, Ziye Wang, Suyang Dai, Hiroshi Mamitsuka, and Shanfeng Zhu. 2019. Attentionxml: Label tree-based attention-aware deep model for high-performance extreme multi-label text classification. In *Advances in Neural Information Processing Systems 32*, pages 5812–5822. Curran Associates, Inc.

A Data manipulation

Hierarchy truncation: In order to directly apply all our methods, we truncate both hierarchies and reduce their depth to six. We believe this truncation is justified since in EUROVOC the last two layers contain a very small number of labels, which are rarely, if at all, assigned and in ICD-9 the first layer also contains a very small number of labels which are very general and can be trivially classified (Table 3). In both cases it seems that only minimal information is lost which would have small practical use in the classification tasks.

Document Truncation: Documents in both datasets are often above the 512 token limit of BERT. To reduce document size, we perform a number of pre-processing normalizations, including removal of numeric tokens, punctuation and stop-words.[9] In EURLEX documents have been tokenized using SpaCy's default tokenizer,[10] while in

---

[9] Similar procedures are very common in classification, thus we believe they do not harm text semantics.

[10] https://spacy.io

Depth	EUROVOC	ICD-9
1	21	4*
2	127	79
3	568	589
4	4,545	3,982
5	2,335	9,640
6	497	7,234
7	79*	867
8	6*	-
Overall	8,178 / 8,093	22,395 / 22,391

Table 3: Label distribution across EUROVOC and ICD-9 hierarchy levels. Concepts (labels) are arranged from more abstract (level 1-2) to more specialized ones (levels 6-8). Labels with an asterisk are truncated in our experiments.

MIMIC-III, we use regular expressions tailored for the biomedical domain. While document length is severely reduced post normalization, if a document still has a larger number of tokens, i.e. more than 512, we use the first 512 tokens and ignore the rest.

B Experimental Setup

All our methods build on BERT-BASE and are implemented in Tensorflow 2. For EURLEX we use the original BERT-BASE (Devlin et al., 2019), while for MIMIC-III we use SCIBERT (Beltagy et al., 2019), which has the same architecture (12 layers, 768 hidden units, 12 attention heads), and better suits biomedical documents.[11] Our models are tuned by grid searching three learning rates $(2e\text{-}5, 3e\text{-}5, 5e\text{-}5)$ and two drop-out rates $(0, 0.1)$. We use the Adam optimizer (Kingma and Ba, 2015) with early stopping on validation loss. In preliminary experiments, we found that weighting individual losses with respect to the number of labels in each level is crucial. We therefore weigh each loss by the percentage of labels at the corresponding level, i.e., $w_n = \frac{|L_n|}{|L|}$, where $|L_n|$ is the number of labels in the nth level of the hierarchy and $|L|$ is the total number of labels across all levels, e.g., in EURLEX57K, $w_1 = \frac{21}{8093} \approx 0.0026$.

C Evaluation in LMTC

The literature of LMTC (Rios and Kavuluru, 2018; Chalkidis et al., 2019) mostly uses information retrieval evaluation measures. We support the premise that when the number of labels is that large the problem mimics retrieval with each document acting as a query and the model having to score relevant labels higher than the rest. However in our study, it would be really confusing

---

to report the standard retrieval metrics Recall@R, Precision@K, nDCG@K since we evaluate our classifiers at each hierarchy depth and reasonable values for K have large fluctuations between levels, as the number of labels per level vastly varies (see Table 3). Instead, we prefer R-Precision (Manning et al., 2009), which is the Precision@R where R is the number of gold labels associated with each document. It follows that R-Precision can neither under-estimate (penalize) nor over-estimate the performance of the models (Chalkidis et al., 2019).

D Peculiarities of MIMIC-III dataset

In our experiments we observe a hindered performance in MIMIC-III, which can be attributed to a number of characteristics of the dataset. Firstly, documents contain a lot of non-trivial biomedical terminology which naturally makes the classification task more difficult. Further, discharge summaries describe a patient's condition during their hospitalization and therefore proper label annotations change throughout the document as the patient's diagnosis changes or as they exhibit new symptoms, e.g., *"the patient was admitted to the hospital with <u>no heart issues</u>, [. . .] the patient had a heart failure and died."*. Both the in-domain language and the constant change of events make the dataset more challenging than EURLEX57K, where documents are more organized and well-written also with simpler language.

It therefore seems reasonable that in MIMIC-III allowing lower BERT layers to retain and enhance the preliminary functionality, without explicitly guiding them, is of utmost importance. We would like to highlight that even though we use SCIBERT (Beltagy et al., 2019), which is based on a new scientific vocabulary, we observe that specialized biomedical terms are often over-fragmented in multiple sub-word units, e.g. 'atelectasis' splits into ['ate', '##lect', '##asis']. Thus, the initial layers need to decipher these over-fragmented sub-word units and reconstruct the original word semantics. On the contrary, in EURLEX57K, classifying general concepts in the initial layers, even considering only the sub-word unit embeddings is plausible.

E Discussion on model utilization

We present additional results for the rest of the methods (IN-PAIRS, HYBRID). Figure 5 shows the average angular distances between the [cls] representations of each layer (Figure 5) for all con-

---

[11] We use the Transformers library of Huggingface (`https://github.com/huggingface/transformers`).

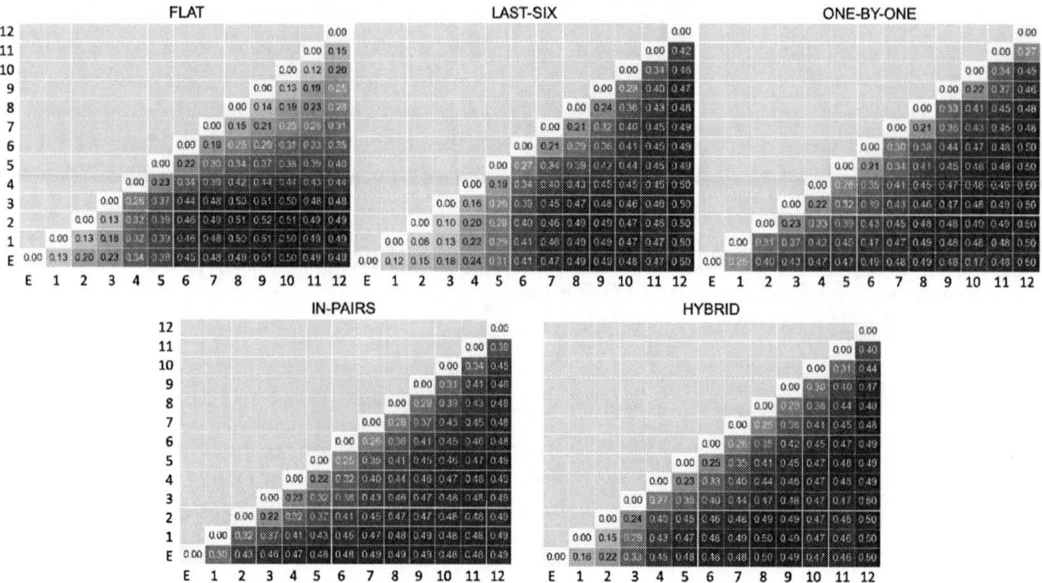

Figure 5: Angular distance between `[cls]` representations across layers in the development dataset of EURLEX57K.

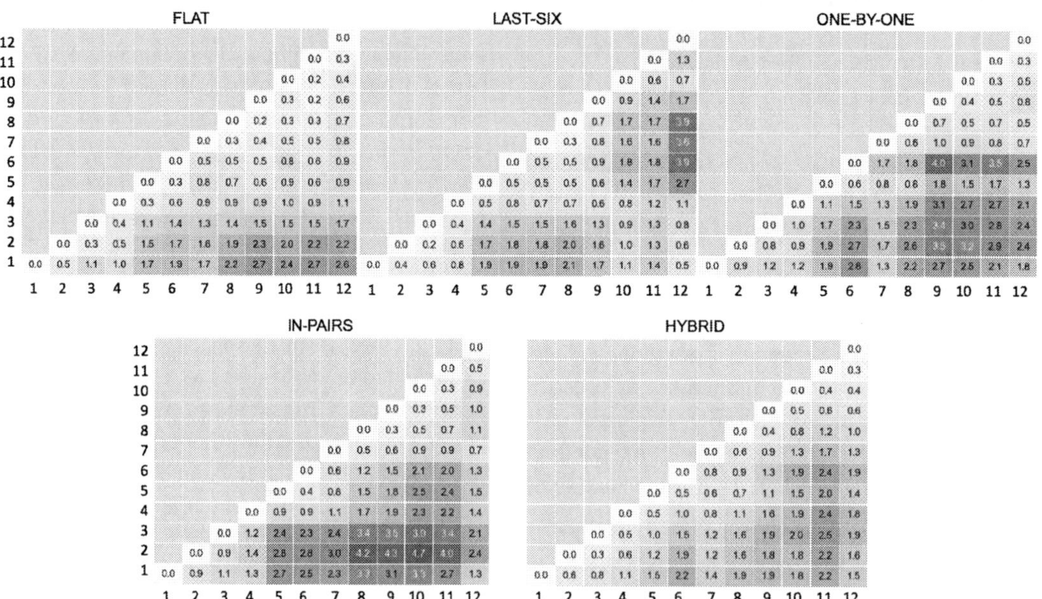

Figure 6: KL-Divergence between attention distributions across layers in the development dataset of EURLEX57K.

sidered methods. We observe that the distances of IN-PAIRS between consecutive `[cls]` representations follow a similar pattern with those of ONE-BY-ONE, with the exception of 0.25+ distances which are more dense in the upper layers for IN-PAIRS. This is reasonable, since in IN-PAIRS all layers directly contribute to the classification tasks. The pattern of HYBRID is very similar to ONE-BY-ONE and IN-PAIRS, except for the first three non-guided

layers in which distances bear close resemblance to those of the corresponding layers in LAST-SIX. Similar observations hold for MIMIC-III (Figure 7). Finally, Figure 6 shows the KL-Divergence of the average (across heads) attention for all layers on the development data. All structured methods show better utilization of the attention mechanism than FLAT, having higher KL-Divergence across layers. Contrary, in MIMIC-III, all structured methods fol-

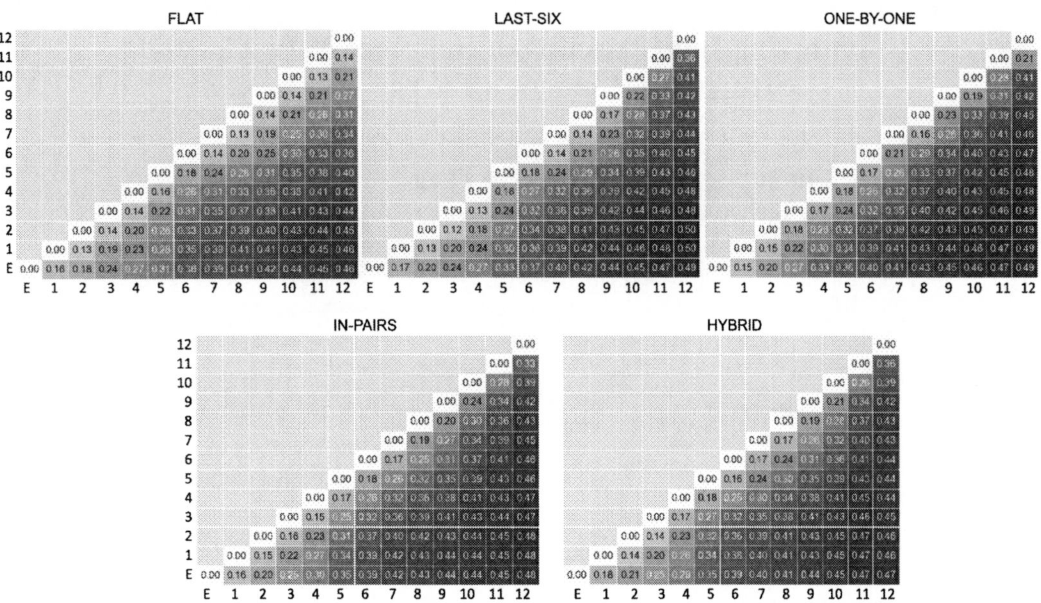

Figure 7: Angular distance between `[cls]` representations across layers in the development dataset of MIMIC-III.

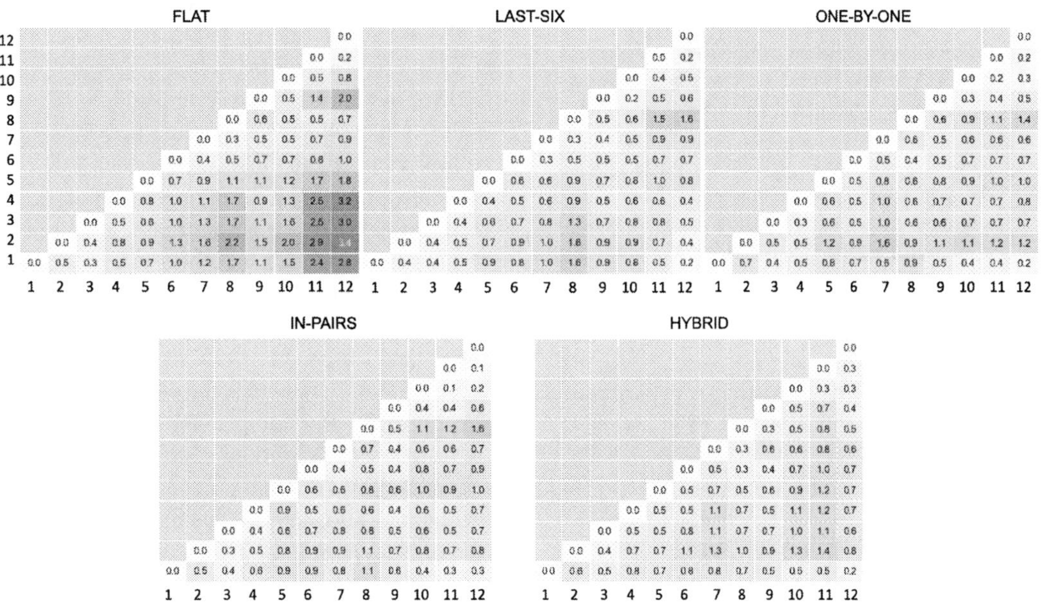

Figure 8: KL-Divergence between attention distributions across layers in the development dataset of MIMIC-III.

low a similar pattern of low KL-Divergence across layers (Figure 8), even lower than the upper layers of FLAT, i.e., the models attend to similar sub-word positions across layers. We aim to further study and explain this behaviour in future work.

Improving Joint Training of Inference Networks and Structured Prediction Energy Networks

Lifu Tu[1]   **Richard Yuanzhe Pang**[2]*   **Kevin Gimpel**[1]
[1]Toyota Technological Institute at Chicago, Chicago, IL 60637, USA
[2]New York University, New York, NY 10011, USA
`lifu@ttic.edu, yzpang@nyu.edu, kgimpel@ttic.edu`

Abstract

Deep energy-based models are powerful, but pose challenges for learning and inference (Belanger and McCallum, 2016). Tu and Gimpel (2018) developed an efficient framework for energy-based models by training "inference networks" to approximate structured inference instead of using gradient descent. However, their alternating optimization approach suffers from instabilities during training, requiring additional loss terms and careful hyperparameter tuning. In this paper, we contribute several strategies to stabilize and improve this joint training of energy functions and inference networks for structured prediction. We design a compound objective to jointly train both cost-augmented and test-time inference networks along with the energy function. We propose joint parameterizations for the inference networks that encourage them to capture complementary functionality during learning. We empirically validate our strategies on two sequence labeling tasks, showing easier paths to strong performance than prior work, as well as further improvements with global energy terms.

1 Introduction

Energy-based modeling (LeCun et al., 2006) associates a scalar compatibility measure to each configuration of input and output variables. Belanger and McCallum (2016) formulated deep energy-based models for structured prediction, which they called structured prediction energy networks (SPENs). SPENs use arbitrary neural networks to define the scoring function over input/output pairs. However, this flexibility leads to challenges for learning and inference. The original work on SPENs used gradient descent for structured inference (Belanger and McCallum, 2016; Belanger et al., 2017). Tu

and Gimpel (2018, 2019) found improvements in both speed and accuracy by replacing the use of gradient descent with a method that trains a neural network (called an "inference network") to do inference directly. Their formulation, which jointly trains the inference network and energy function, is similar to training in generative adversarial networks (Goodfellow et al., 2014), which is known to suffer from practical difficulties in training due to the use of alternating optimization (Salimans et al., 2016). To stabilize training, Tu and Gimpel (2018) experimented with several additional terms in the training objectives, finding performance to be dependent on their inclusion.

Moreover, when using the approach of Tu and Gimpel (2018), there is a mismatch between the training and test-time uses of the trained inference network. During training with hinge loss, the inference network is actually trained to do "cost-augmented" inference. However, at test time, the goal is to simply minimize the energy without any cost term. Tu and Gimpel (2018) fine-tuned the cost-augmented network to match the test-time criterion, but found only minimal change from this fine-tuning. This suggests that the cost-augmented network was mostly acting as a test-time inference network by convergence, which may be hindering the potential contributions of cost-augmented inference in max-margin structured learning (Tsochantaridis et al., 2004; Taskar et al., 2004).

In this paper, we contribute a new training objective for SPENs that addresses the above concern and also contribute several techniques for stabilizing and improving learning. We empirically validate our strategies on two sequence labeling tasks from natural language processing (NLP), namely part-of-speech tagging and named entity recognition. We show easier paths to strong performance than prior work, as well as further improvements with global energy terms. We summarize our list

---

* Work done at the University of Chicago and Toyota Technological Institute at Chicago.

Proceedings of 4th Workshop on Structured Prediction for NLP, pages 62–73
November 20, 2020. ©2020 Association for Computational Linguistics">

of contributions as follows.

- We design a compound objective under the SPEN framework to jointly train the "training-time" cost-augmented inference network and test-time inference network (Section 3).

- We propose shared parameterizations for the two inference networks so as to encourage them to capture complementary functionality while reducing the total number of trained parameters (Section 3.1). Quantitative and qualitative analysis shows clear differences in the characteristics of the two networks (Table 3).

- We present three methods to streamline and stabilize training that help with both the old and new objectives (Section 4).

- We propose global energy terms to capture long-distance dependencies and obtain further improvements (Section 5).

While SPENs have been used for multiple NLP tasks, including multi-label classification (Belanger and McCallum, 2016), part-of-speech tagging (Tu and Gimpel, 2018), and semantic role labeling (Belanger et al., 2017), they are not widely used in NLP. Structured prediction is extremely common in NLP, but is typically approached using methods that are more limited than SPENs (such as conditional random fields) or models that suffer from a train/test mismatch (such as most auto-regressive models). SPENs offer a maximally expressive framework for structured prediction while avoiding the train/test mismatch and therefore offer great potential for NLP. However, the training and inference have deterred NLP researchers. While we have found benefit from training inference networks for machine translation in recent work (Tu et al., 2020b), that work assumed a fixed, pretrained energy function. Our hope is that the methods in this paper will enable SPENs to be applied to a larger set of applications, including generation tasks in the future.

2 Background

We denote the input space by $\mathcal{X}$. For an input $x \in \mathcal{X}$, we denote the structured output space by $\mathcal{Y}(x)$. The entire space of structured outputs is denoted $\mathcal{Y} = \cup_{x \in \mathcal{X}} \mathcal{Y}(x)$. A SPEN (Belanger and McCallum, 2016) defines an **energy function** $E_\Theta : \mathcal{X} \times \mathcal{Y} \to \mathbb{R}$ parameterized by Θ that computes a scalar energy for an input/output pair. At test time,

for a given input x, prediction is done by choosing the output with lowest energy:

$$\hat{y} = \arg\min_{y \in \mathcal{Y}(x)} E_\Theta(x, y) \tag{1}$$

However, solving equation (1) requires combinatorial algorithms because $\mathcal{Y}$ is a structured, discrete space. This becomes intractable when E_Θ does not decompose into a sum over small "parts" of y. Belanger and McCallum (2016) relaxed this problem by allowing the **discrete vector** y to be continuous; $\mathcal{Y}_R$ denotes the **relaxed output space**. They solved the relaxed problem by using gradient descent to iteratively minimize the energy with respect to y. The energy function parameters Θ are trained using a structured hinge loss which requires repeated cost-augmented inference during training. Using gradient descent for the repeated cost-augmented inference steps is time-consuming and makes learning unstable (Belanger et al., 2017).

Tu and Gimpel (2018) replaced gradient descent with a neural network trained to do efficient inference. This "inference network" $\mathbf{A}_\Psi : \mathcal{X} \to \mathcal{Y}_R$ is parameterized by Ψ and trained with the goal that

$$\mathbf{A}_\Psi(x) \approx \arg\min_{y \in \mathcal{Y}_R(x)} E_\Theta(x, y) \tag{2}$$

When training the energy function parameters Θ, Tu and Gimpel (2018) replaced the cost-augmented inference step in the structured hinge loss from Belanger and McCallum (2016) with a cost-augmented inference network $\mathbf{F}_\Phi$:

$$\mathbf{F}_\Phi(x) \approx \arg\min_{y \in \mathcal{Y}_R(x)} \left(E_\Theta(x, y) - \triangle(y, y^*) \right) \tag{3}$$

where $\triangle$ is a structured cost function that computes the distance between its two arguments. We use L1 distance for $\triangle$. This inference problem involves finding an output with low energy but high cost relative to the gold standard. Thus, it is not well-aligned with the test-time inference problem.

Here is the specific objective to jointly train Θ (parameters of the energy function) and Φ (parameters of the cost-augmented inference network):

$$\min_\Theta \max_\Phi \sum_{\langle x_i, y_i \rangle \in \mathcal{D}} [\triangle(\mathbf{F}_\Phi(x_i), y_i)$$
$$- E_\Theta(x_i, \mathbf{F}_\Phi(x_i)) + E_\Theta(x_i, y_i)]_+ \tag{4}$$

where $\mathcal{D}$ is the set of training pairs, $[h]_+ = \max(0, h)$, and $\triangle$ is a structured cost function that computes the distance between its two arguments.

Tu and Gimpel (2018) alternatively optimized Θ and Φ, which is similar to training in generative adversarial networks (Goodfellow et al., 2014). The inference network is analogous to the generator and the energy function is analogous to the discriminator. As alternating optimization can be difficult in practice (Salimans et al., 2016), Tu & Gimpel experimented with including several additional terms in the above objective to stabilize training.

After the training of the energy function, an inference network $\mathbf{A}_\Psi$ for test-time prediction is fine-tuned with the goal shown in Eq. (2). More specifically, for the fine-tuning step, we first initialize Ψ with Φ; next, we do gradient descent according to the following objective to learn Ψ:

$$\Psi \leftarrow \arg\min_{\Psi'} \sum_{x \in \mathcal{X}} E_\Theta(x, A_{\Psi'}(x))$$

where $\mathcal{X}$ is a set of training or validation inputs. It could also be the test inputs in a transductive setting.

3   An Objective for Joint Learning of Inference Networks

One challenge with the above optimization problem is that it requires training a separate inference network $\mathbf{A}_\Psi$ for test-time prediction after the energy function is trained. In this paper, we propose an alternative that trains the energy function and both inference networks jointly. In particular, we use a "compound" objective that combines two widely-used losses in structured prediction. We first present it without inference networks:

$$\min_{\Theta} \sum_{\langle x_i, y_i \rangle \in \mathcal{D}}$$

$$\underbrace{\left[\max_{y} (\triangle(y, y_i) - E_\Theta(x_i, y) + E_\Theta(x_i, y_i)) \right]_+}_{\text{margin-rescaled hinge loss}}$$

$$+ \lambda \underbrace{\left[\max_{y} (-E_\Theta(x_i, y) + E_\Theta(x_i, y_i)) \right]_+}_{\text{perceptron loss}} \quad (5)$$

As indicated, this loss can be viewed as the sum of the margin-rescaled hinge and perceptron losses for SPENs. Two different inference problems are represented. The margin-rescaled hinge loss contains cost-augmented inference, shown as part of Eq. (3). The perceptron loss contains the test-time inference problem, which is shown in Eq. (1). Tu

and Gimpel (2018) used a single inference network for solving both problems, so it was trained as a cost-augmented inference network during training and then fine-tuned as a test-time inference network afterward. We avoid this issue by training two inference networks, $\mathbf{A}_\Psi$ for test-time inference and $\mathbf{F}_\Phi$ for cost-augmented inference:

$$\min_{\Theta} \max_{\Phi, \Psi} \sum_{\langle x_i, y_i \rangle \in \mathcal{D}}$$

$$[\triangle(\mathbf{F}_\Phi(x_i), y_i) - E_\Theta(x_i, \mathbf{F}_\Phi(x_i)) + E_\Theta(x_i, y_i)]_+$$

$$+ \lambda \left[-E_\Theta(x_i, \mathbf{A}_\Psi(x_i)) + E_\Theta(x_i, y_i) \right]_+ \quad (6)$$

We treat this optimization problem as a minimax game and find a saddle point for the game similar to Tu and Gimpel (2018) and Goodfellow et al. (2014). We use minibatch stochastic gradient descent and alternately optimize Θ, Φ, and Ψ. The objective for the energy parameters Θ in minibatch $\mathcal{M}$ is:

$$\hat{\Theta} \leftarrow \arg\min_{\Theta} \sum_{\langle x_i, y_i \rangle \in \mathcal{M}}$$

$$\left[\triangle(\mathbf{F}_\Phi(x_i), y_i) - E_\Theta(x_i, \mathbf{F}_\Phi(x_i)) + E_\Theta(x_i, y_i) \right]_+$$

$$+ \lambda \left[-E_\Theta(x_i, \mathbf{A}_\Psi(x_i)) + E_\Theta(x_i, y_i) \right]_+$$

When we remove 0-truncation (see Sec. 4.1 for the motivation), the objective for the inference network parameters in minibatch $\mathcal{M}$ is:

$$\hat{\Psi}, \hat{\Phi} \leftarrow \arg\max_{\Psi, \Phi} \sum_{\langle x_i, y_i \rangle \in \mathcal{M}} \triangle(\mathbf{F}_\Phi(x_i), y_i) -$$

$$E_\Theta(x_i, \mathbf{F}_\Phi(x_i)) - \lambda E_\Theta(x_i, \mathbf{A}_\Psi(x_i))$$

3.1   Joint Parameterizations

If we were to train independent inference networks $\mathbf{A}_\Psi$ and $\mathbf{F}_\Phi$, this new objective could be much slower than the approach of Tu and Gimpel (2018). However, the compound objective offers several natural options for defining joint parameterizations of the two inference networks. We consider three options which are visualized in Figure 1 and described below:

- **separated**: $\mathbf{F}_\Phi$ and $\mathbf{A}_\Psi$ are two independent networks with their own architectures and parameters as shown in Figure 1(a).
- **shared**: $\mathbf{F}_\Phi$ and $\mathbf{A}_\Psi$ share a "feature" network as shown in Figure 1(b). We consider this option because both $\mathbf{F}_\Phi$ and $\mathbf{A}_\Psi$ are trained to produce output labels with low energy. However $\mathbf{F}_\Phi$ also needs to produce output labels with high cost $\triangle$ (i.e., far from the gold standard).

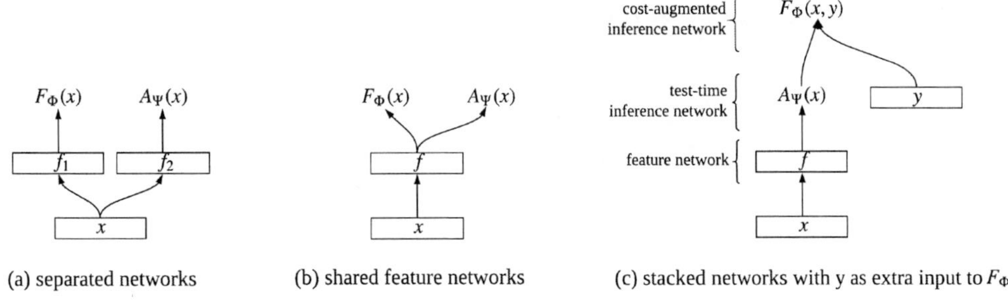

Figure 1: Joint parameterizations for cost-augmented inference network $\mathbf{F}_\Phi$ and test-time inference network $\mathbf{A}_\Psi$.

- **stacked**: the cost-augmented network $\mathbf{F}_\Phi$ is a function of the output of the test-time network $\mathbf{A}_\Psi$ *and* the gold standard output $\boldsymbol{y}$. That is, $\mathbf{F}_\Phi(\boldsymbol{x}, \boldsymbol{y}) = q(\mathbf{A}_\Psi(\boldsymbol{x}), \boldsymbol{y})$ where q is a parameterized function. This is depicted in Figure 1(c). We block the gradient at $\mathbf{A}_\Psi$ when updating Φ.

For the q function in the stacked option, we use an affine transformation on the concatenation of the inference network label distribution and the gold standard one-hot vector. That is, denoting the vector at position t of the cost-augmented network output by $\mathbf{F}_\Phi(\boldsymbol{x}, \boldsymbol{y})_t$, we have:

$$\mathbf{F}_\Phi(\boldsymbol{x}, \boldsymbol{y})_t = \mathrm{softmax}(W_q[\mathbf{A}_\Psi(\boldsymbol{x})_t; \boldsymbol{y}(t)] + b_q)$$

where semicolon (;) is vertical concatenation, $\boldsymbol{y}(t)$ (position t of $\boldsymbol{y}$) is an L-dimensional one-hot vector, $\mathbf{A}_\Psi(\boldsymbol{x})_t$ is the vector at position t of $\mathbf{A}_\Psi(\boldsymbol{x})$, W_q is an $L \times 2L$ matrix, and b_q is a bias.

One motivation for these parameterizations is to reduce the total number of parameters in the procedure. Generally, the number of parameters is expected to decrease when moving from separated to shared to stacked. We will compare the three options empirically in our experiments, in terms of both accuracy and number of parameters.

Another motivation, specifically for the third option, is to distinguish the two inference networks in terms of their learned functionality. With all three parameterizations, the cost-augmented network will be trained to produce an output that differs from the gold standard, due to the presence of the $\triangle(\cdot)$ term in the combined objective. However, Tu and Gimpel (2018) found that the trained cost-augmented network was barely affected by fine-tuning for the test-time inference objective. This suggests that the cost-augmented network was mostly acting as a test-time inference network by the time of convergence. With the stacked parameterization, however, we explicitly provide the gold standard $\boldsymbol{y}$ to the cost-augmented network, permitting it to learn to change the predictions of the test-time network in appropriate ways to improve the energy function.

4   Training Stability and Effectiveness

We now discuss several methods that simplify and stabilize training SPENs with inference networks. When describing them, we will illustrate their impact by showing training trajectories for the Twitter part-of-speech tagging task.

4.1   Removing Zero Truncation

Tu and Gimpel (2018) used the following objective for the cost-augmented inference network (maximizing it with respect to Φ): $l_0 =$

$$[\triangle(\mathbf{F}_\Phi(\boldsymbol{x}), \boldsymbol{y}) - E_\Theta(\boldsymbol{x}, \mathbf{F}_\Phi(\boldsymbol{x})) + E_\Theta(\boldsymbol{x}, \boldsymbol{y})]_+$$

where $[h]_+ = \max(0, h)$. However, there are two potential reasons why l_0 will equal zero and trigger no gradient update. First, E_Θ (the energy function, corresponding to the discriminator in a GAN) may already be well-trained, and it can easily separate the gold standard output from the cost-augmented inference network output. Second, the cost-augmented inference network (corresponding to the generator in a GAN) could be so poorly trained that the energy of its output is very large, leading the margin constraints to be satisfied and l_0 to be zero.

In standard margin-rescaled max-margin learning in structured prediction (Taskar et al., 2004; Tsochantaridis et al., 2004), the cost-augmented inference step is performed exactly (or approximately

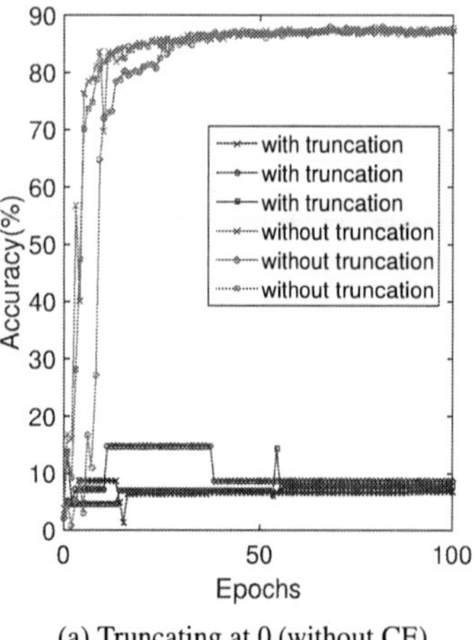

(a) Truncating at 0 (without CE).

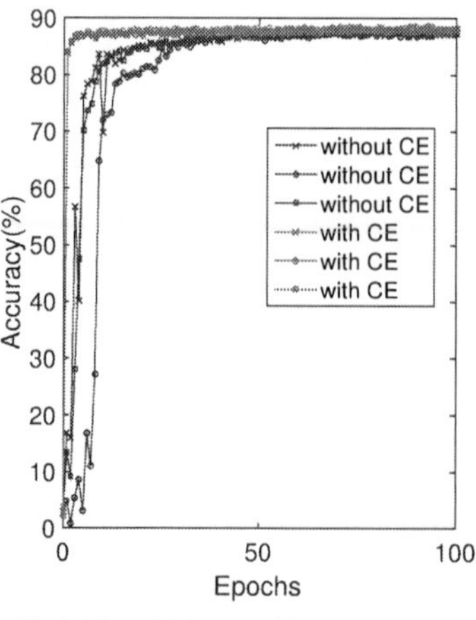

(b) Adding CE loss (without truncation).

Figure 2: Part-of-speech tagging training trajectories. The three curves in each setting correspond to different random seeds. (a) Without the local CE loss, training fails when using zero truncation. (b) The CE loss reduces the number of epochs for training. Tu and Gimpel (2018) used zero truncation and CE during training.

with reasonable guarantee of effectiveness), ensuring that when l_0 is zero, the energy parameters are well trained. However, in our case, l_0 may be zero simply because the cost-augmented inference network is undertrained, which will be the case early in training. Then, when using zero truncation, the gradient of the inference network parameters will be 0. This is likely why Tu and Gimpel (2018) found it important to add several stabilization terms to the l_0 objective. We find that by instead removing the truncation, learning stabilizes and becomes less dependent on these additional terms. Note that we retain the truncation at zero when updating the energy parameters Θ.

As shown in Figure 2(a), without any stabilization terms and with truncation, the inference network will barely move from its starting point and learning fails overall. However, without truncation, the inference network can work well even without any stabilization terms.

4.2 Local Cross Entropy (CE) Loss

Tu and Gimpel (2018) proposed adding a local cross entropy (CE) loss, which is the sum of the label cross entropy losses over all positions in the sequence, to stabilize inference network training. We similarly find this term to help speed up convergence and improve accuracy. Figure 2(b) shows faster convergence to high accuracy when adding the local CE term. See Section 7 for more details.

4.3 Multiple Inference Network Update Steps

When training SPENs with inference networks, the inference network parameters are nested within the energy function. We found that the gradient components of the inference network parameters consequently have smaller absolute values than those of the energy function parameters. So, we alternate between $k \geq 1$ steps of optimizing the inference network parameters ("I steps") and one step of optimizing the energy function parameters ("E steps"). We find this strategy especially helpful when using complex inference network architectures.

To analyze, we compute the cost-augmented loss $l_1 = \triangle(\mathbf{F}_\Phi(\boldsymbol{x}), \boldsymbol{y}) - E_\Theta(\boldsymbol{x}, \mathbf{F}_\Phi(\boldsymbol{x}))$ and the margin-rescaled hinge loss $l_0 = [\triangle(\mathbf{F}_\Phi(\boldsymbol{x}), \boldsymbol{y}) - E_\Theta(\boldsymbol{x}, \mathbf{F}_\Phi(\boldsymbol{x})) + E_\Theta(\boldsymbol{x}, \boldsymbol{y})]_+$ averaged over all training pairs $(\boldsymbol{x}, \boldsymbol{y})$ after each set of I steps. The I steps update Ψ and Φ to maximize these losses. Meanwhile the E steps update Θ to minimize these losses. Figs. 3(a) and (b) show l_1 and l_0 during training for different numbers (k) of I steps for every one E step. Fig. 3(c) shows the norm of the energy parameters after the E steps, and Fig. 3(d) shows the norm of $\frac{\partial E_\Theta(\boldsymbol{x}, \mathbf{A}_\Psi)}{\partial \Psi}$ after the I steps.

With $k = 1$, the setting used by Tu and Gimpel (2018), the inference network lags behind the energy, making the energy parameter updates very small, as shown by the small norms in Fig. 3(c). The inference network gradient norm (Fig. 3(d)) remains high, indicating underfitting. However, increasing k too much also harms learning, as evi-

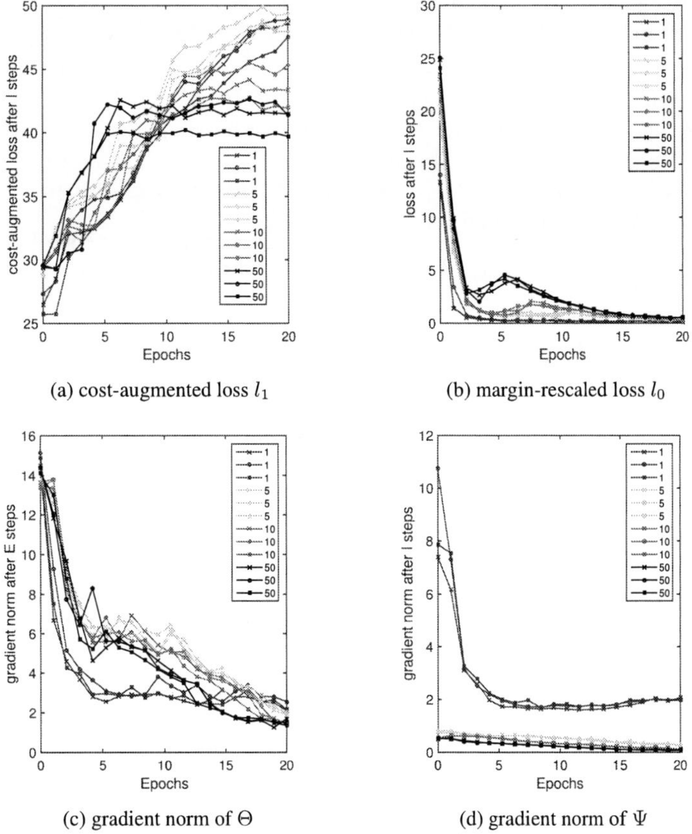

(a) cost-augmented loss l_1

(b) margin-rescaled loss l_0

(c) gradient norm of Θ

(d) gradient norm of Ψ

Figure 3: POS training trajectories with different numbers of I steps. The three curves in each setting correspond to different random seeds. (a) cost-augmented loss after I steps; (b) margin-rescaled hinge loss after I steps; (c) gradient norm of energy function parameters after E steps; (d) gradient norm of test-time inference network parameters after I steps.

denced by the "plateau" effect in the l_1 curves for $k = 50$; this indicates that the energy function is lagging behind the inference network. Using $k = 5$ leads to more of a balance between l_1 and l_0 and gradient norms that are mostly decreasing during training. We treat k as a hyperparameter that is tuned in our experiments.

There is a potential connection between our use of multiple I steps and a similar procedure used in GANs (Goodfellow et al., 2014). In the GAN objective, the discriminator D is updated in the inner loop, and they alternate between multiple update steps for D and one update step for G. In this section, we similarly found benefit from multiple steps of inner loop optimization for every step of the outer loop. However, the analogy is limited, since GAN training involves sampling noise vectors and using them to generate data, while there are no noise vectors or explicitly-generated samples in our framework.

5 Energies for Sequence Labeling

For our sequence labeling experiments in this paper, the input x is a length-T sequence of tokens, and the output y is a sequence of labels of length T. We use y_t to denote the output label at position t, where y_t is a vector of length L (the number of labels in the label set) and where $y_{t,j}$ is the jth entry of the vector y_t. In the original output space $\mathcal{Y}(x)$, $y_{t,j}$ is 1 for a single j and 0 for all others. In the relaxed output space $\mathcal{Y}_R(x)$, $y_{t,j}$ can be interpreted as the probability of the tth position being labeled with label j. We then use the following energy for sequence labeling (Tu and Gimpel, 2018):

$$
\begin{aligned}
E_\Theta(x, y) = -\Bigg(& \sum_{t=1}^{T} \sum_{j=1}^{L} y_{t,j} \left(U_j^\top b(x, t) \right) \\
& + \sum_{t=1}^{T} y_{t-1}^\top W y_t \Bigg)
\end{aligned}
\tag{7}
$$

where $U_j \in \mathbb{R}^d$ is a parameter vector for label j and the parameter matrix $W \in \mathbb{R}^{L \times L}$ contains label-pair parameters. Also, $b(x, t) \in \mathbb{R}^d$ denotes the "input feature vector" for position t. We define b to be the d-dimensional BiLSTM (Hochreiter and Schmidhuber, 1997) hidden vector at t. The full set of energy parameters Θ includes the U_j vectors, W, and the parameters of the BiLSTM.

Global Energies for Sequence Labeling. In addition to new training strategies, we also experiment with several global energy terms for sequence labeling. Eq. (7) shows the base energy, and to capture long-distance dependencies, we include global energy (GE) terms in the form of Eq. (8).

We use h to denote an LSTM tag language model (TLM) that takes a sequence of labels as input and returns a distribution over next labels. We define $\overline{y}_t = h(y_0, \ldots, y_{t-1})$ to be the distribution given the preceding label vectors (under a LSTM language model). Then, the energy term is:

$$E^{\mathrm{TLM}}(y) = - \sum_{t=1}^{T+1} \log\left(y_t^\top \overline{y}_t\right) \quad (8)$$

where y_0 is the start-of-sequence symbol and y_{T+1} is the end-of-sequence symbol. This energy returns the negative log-likelihood under the TLM of the candidate output y. Tu and Gimpel (2018) pretrained their h on a large, automatically-tagged corpus and fixed its parameters when optimizing Θ. Our approach has one critical difference. We instead *do not* pretrain h, and its parameters are learned when optimizing Θ. We show that even without pretraining, our global energy terms are still able to capture useful additional information.

We also propose new global energy terms. Define $\overline{y}_t = h(y_0, \ldots, y_{t-1})$ where h is an LSTM TLM that takes a sequence of labels as input and returns a distribution over next labels. First, we add a TLM in the backward direction (denoted $\overline{y}_t'$ analogously to the forward TLM). Second, we include words as additional inputs to forward and backward TLMs. We define $\widetilde{y}_t = g(x_0, \ldots, x_{t-1}, y_0, \ldots, y_{t-1})$ where g is a forward LSTM TLM. We define the backward version similarly (denoted $\widetilde{y}_t'$). The global energy is therefore

$$E^{\mathrm{GE}}(y) = - \sum_{t=1}^{T+1} \log(y_t^\top \overline{y}_t) + \log(y_t^\top \overline{y}_t')$$
$$+ \gamma\big(\log(y_t^\top \widetilde{y}_t) + \log(y_t^\top \widetilde{y}_t')\big) \quad (9)$$

Here γ is a hyperparameter that is tuned. We experiment with three settings for the global energy: GE(a): forward TLM as in Tu and Gimpel (2018); GE(b): forward and backward TLMs ($\gamma = 0$); GE(c): all four TLMs in Eq. (9).

6　Experimental Setup

We consider two sequence labeling tasks: Twitter part-of-speech (POS) tagging (Gimpel et al., 2011) and named entity recognition (NER; Tjong Kim Sang and De Meulder, 2003).

Twitter Part-of-Speech (POS) Tagging. We use the Twitter POS data from Gimpel et al. (2011) and Owoputi et al. (2013) which contain 25 tags. We use 100-dimensional skip-gram (Mikolov et al., 2013) embeddings from Tu et al. (2017). Like Tu and Gimpel (2018), we use a BiLSTM to compute the input feature vector for each position, using hidden size 100. We also use BiLSTMs for the inference networks. The output of the inference network is a softmax function, so the inference network will produce a distribution over labels at each position. The Δ is L1 distance. We train the inference network using stochastic gradient descent (SGD) with momentum and train the energy parameters using Adam (Kingma and Ba, 2014). We also explore training the inference network using Adam when not using the local CE loss.[1] In experiments with the local CE term, its weight is set to 1.

Named Entity Recognition (NER). We use the CoNLL 2003 English dataset (Tjong Kim Sang and De Meulder, 2003). We use the BIOES tagging scheme, following previous work (Ratinov and Roth, 2009), resulting in 17 NER labels. We use 100-dimensional pretrained GloVe embeddings (Pennington et al., 2014). The task is evaluated using F1 score computed with the `conlleval` script. The architectures for the feature networks in the energy function and inference networks are all BiLSTMs. The architectures for tag language models are LSTMs. We use a dropout `keep-prob` of 0.7 for all LSTM cells. The hidden size for all LSTMs is 128. We use Adam (Kingma and Ba, 2014) and do early stopping on the development set. We use a learning rate of $5 \cdot 10^{-4}$. Similar to above, the weight for the CE term is set to 1.

We consider three NER modeling configurations. **NER** uses only words as input and pretrained, fixed

---

[1] We find that Adam works better than SGD when training the inference network without the local cross entropy term.

loss	zero trunc.	CE	POS acc (%)	NER F1 (%)	NER+ F1 (%)
margin-rescaled	yes	no	13.9	3.91	3.91
	no	no	87.9	85.1	88.6
	yes	yes	89.4*	85.2*	89.5*
	no	yes	89.4	85.2	89.5
perceptron	no	no	88.2	84.0	88.1
	no	yes	88.6	84.7	89.0

Table 1: Test results for POS and NER for several SPEN configurations. Results with * correspond to the setting of Tu and Gimpel (2018). The inference network architecture is a one-layer BiLSTM.

GloVe embeddings. **NER+** uses words, the case of the first letter, POS tags, and chunk labels, as well as pretrained GloVe embeddings with fine-tuning. **NER++** includes everything in **NER+** as well as character-based word representations obtained using a convolutional network over the character sequence in each word. Unless otherwise indicated, our SPENs use the energy in Eq. (7).

7 Results and Analysis

Effect of Zero Truncation and Local CE Loss. Table 1 shows results for zero truncation and the local CE term. Training fails for both tasks when using zero truncation without CE. Removing truncation makes learning succeed and leads to effective models even without using CE. However, when using the local CE term, truncation has little effect on performance. The importance of CE in prior work (Tu and Gimpel, 2018) is likely due to the fact that truncation was being used.

The local CE term is useful for both tasks, though it appears more helpful for tagging.[2] This may be because POS tagging is a more local task. Regardless, for both tasks, as shown in Section 4.2, the inclusion of the CE term speeds convergence and improves training stability. For example, on NER, using the CE term reduces the number of epochs chosen by early stopping from $\sim$100 to $\sim$25. For POS, using the CE term reduces the number of epochs from $\sim$150 to $\sim$60.

Effect of Compound Objective and Joint Parameterizations. The compound objective is the sum of the margin-rescaled and perceptron losses, and outperforms them both (see Table 2). Across all tasks, the shared and stacked parameterizations are more accurate than the previous objectives. For the separated parameterization, the performance

drops slightly for NER, likely due to the larger number of parameters. The shared and stacked options have fewer parameters to train than the separated option, and the stacked version processes examples at the fastest rate during training.

The top part of Table 3 shows how the performance of the test-time inference network $\mathbf{A}_\Psi$ and the cost-augmented inference network $\mathbf{F}_\Phi$ vary when using the new compound objective. The differences between $\mathbf{F}_\Phi$ and $\mathbf{A}_\Psi$ are larger than in the baseline configuration, showing that the two are learning complementary functionality. With the stacked parameterization, the cost-augmented network $\mathbf{F}_\Phi$ receives as an additional input the gold standard label sequence, which leads to the largest differences as the cost-augmented network can explicitly favor incorrect labels.[3]

The bottom part of Table 3 shows qualitative differences between the two inference networks. On the POS development set, we count the differences between the predictions of $\mathbf{A}_\Psi$ and $\mathbf{F}_\Phi$ when $\mathbf{A}_\Psi$ makes the correct prediction.[4] $\mathbf{F}_\Phi$ tends to output tags that are highly confusable with those output by $\mathbf{A}_\Psi$. For example, it often outputs proper noun when the gold standard is common noun or vice versa. It also captures the ambiguities among adverbs, adjectives, and prepositions.

Global Energies. The results are shown in Table 4. Adding the backward (b) and word-augmented TLMs (c) improves over using only the forward TLM from Tu and Gimpel (2018). With the global energies, our performance is comparable to several strong results (90.94 of Lample et al., 2016 and 91.37 of Ma and Hovy, 2016). However, it is still lower than the state of the art (Akbik et al., 2018; Devlin et al., 2019), likely due to the lack of contextualized embeddings. In other work, we proposed and evaluated several other high-order energy terms for sequence labeling using our framework (Tu et al., 2020a).

8 Related Work

There are several efforts aimed at stabilizing and improving learning in generative adversarial networks (GANs) (Goodfellow et al., 2014; Salimans et al., 2016; Zhao et al., 2017; Arjovsky et al., 2017). Progress in training GANs has come largely

---

[2] We found the local CE term to be useful for both the cost-augmented and test-time inference networks during training.

[3] We also tried a BiLSTM in the final layer of the stacked parameterization but results were similar to the simpler affine architecture, so we only report results for the latter.

[4] We used the stacked parameterization.

	POS				NER				NER+
	acc. (%)	$|T|$	$|I|$	speed	F1 (%)	$|T|$	$|I|$	speed	F1 (%)
BiLSTM	88.8	166K	166K	–	84.9	239K	239K	–	89.3

SPENs with inference networks (Tu and Gimpel, 2018):

	POS				NER				NER+
margin-rescaled	89.4	333K	166K	–	85.2	479K	239K	–	89.5
perceptron	88.6	333K	166K	–	84.4	479K	239K	–	89.0

SPENs with inference networks, compound objective, CE, no zero truncation (this paper):

	POS				NER				NER+
separated	89.7	500K	166K	66	85.0	719K	239K	32	89.8
shared	89.8	339K	166K	78	85.6	485K	239K	38	90.1
stacked	**89.8**	**335K**	**166K**	**92**	**85.6**	**481K**	**239K**	**46**	**90.1**

Table 2: Test results for POS and NER. $|T|$ is the number of trained parameters; $|I|$ is the number of parameters needed during inference. Training speeds (examples/second) are shown for joint parameterizations to compare them in terms of efficiency. Best setting (best performance with fewest parameters and fastest training) is in bold.

		POS	NER
		$\mathbf{A}_\Psi - \mathbf{F}_\Phi$	$\mathbf{A}_\Psi - \mathbf{F}_\Phi$
margin-rescaled		0.2	0
compound	separated	2.2	0.4
	shared	1.9	0.5
	stacked	**2.6**	**1.7**

test-time ($\mathbf{A}_\Psi$)	cost-augmented ($\mathbf{F}_\Phi$)
common noun	proper noun
proper noun	common noun
common noun	adjective
proper noun	proper noun + possessive
adverb	adjective
preposition	adverb
adverb	preposition
verb	common noun
adjective	verb

Table 3: Top: differences in accuracy/F1 between test-time inference networks $\mathbf{A}_\Psi$ and cost-augmented networks $\mathbf{F}_\Phi$ (on development sets). The "margin-rescaled" row uses a SPEN with the local CE term and without zero truncation, where $\mathbf{A}_\Psi$ is obtained by fine-tuning $\mathbf{F}_\Phi$ as done by Tu and Gimpel (2018). Bottom: most frequent output differences between $\mathbf{A}_\Psi$ and $\mathbf{F}_\Phi$ on the development set.

	NER	NER+	NER++
margin-rescaled	85.2	89.5	90.2
compound, stacked, CE, no truncation	85.6	90.1	90.8
+ global energy GE(a)	85.8	90.2	90.7
+ global energy GE(b)	85.9	90.2	90.8
+ global energy GE(c)	**86.3**	**90.4**	**91.0**

Table 4: NER test F1 scores with global energy terms.

from overcoming learning difficulties by modifying loss functions and optimization, and GANs have become more successful and popular as a result. Notably, Wasserstein GANs (Arjovsky et al., 2017) provided the first convergence measure in GAN training using Wasserstein distance. To compute Wasserstein distance, the discriminator uses weight clipping, which limits network capacity. Weight clipping was subsequently replaced with a gradient norm constraint (Gulrajani et al., 2017). Miyato et al. (2018) proposed a novel weight normalization technique called spectral normalization. These methods may be applicable to the similar optimization problems solved in learning SPENs. Another direction may be to explore alternative training objectives for SPENs, such as those that use weaker supervision than complete structures (Rooshenas et al., 2018, 2019; Naskar et al., 2020).

9 Conclusions and Future Work

We contributed several strategies to stabilize and improve joint training of SPENs and inference networks. Our use of joint parameterizations mitigates the need for inference network fine-tuning, leads to complementarity in the learned inference networks, and yields improved performance overall. These developments offer promise for SPENs to be more easily applied to a broad range of NLP tasks.

Future work will explore other structured prediction tasks, such as parsing and generation. We have taken initial steps in this direction, considering constituency parsing with the sequence-to-sequence model of Tran et al. (2018). Preliminary experiments are positive,[5] but significant challenges remain, specifically in defining appropriate inference network architectures to enable efficient learning.

Acknowledgments

We would like to thank the reviewers for insightful comments. This research was supported in part by an Amazon Research Award to K. Gimpel.

---

[5]On NXT Switchboard (Calhoun et al., 2010), the baseline achieves 82.80 F1 on the development set and the SPEN (stacked parameterization) achieves 83.22. More details are in the appendix.

References

Alan Akbik, Duncan Blythe, and Roland Vollgraf. 2018. Contextual string embeddings for sequence labeling. In *Proceedings of the 27th International Conference on Computational Linguistics*, pages 1638–1649, Santa Fe, New Mexico, USA. Association for Computational Linguistics.

Martín Arjovsky, Soumith Chintala, and Léon Bottou. 2017. Wasserstein generative adversarial networks. In *Proceedings of the 34th International Conference on Machine Learning*.

David Belanger and Andrew McCallum. 2016. Structured prediction energy networks. In *Proceedings of the 33rd International Conference on Machine Learning*.

David Belanger, Bishan Yang, and Andrew McCallum. 2017. End-to-end learning for structured prediction energy networks. In *Proceedings of the 34th International Conference on Machine Learning*.

Sasha Calhoun, Jean Carletta, Jason M Brenier, Neil Mayo, Dan Jurafsky, Mark Steedman, and David Beaver. 2010. The NXT-format Switchboard Corpus: a rich resource for investigating the syntax, semantics, pragmatics and prosody of dialogue. *Language resources and evaluation*, 44(4):387–419.

Jacob Devlin, Ming-Wei Chang, Kenton Lee, and Kristina Toutanova. 2019. BERT: Pre-training of deep bidirectional transformers for language understanding. In *Proceedings of the 2019 Conference of the North American Chapter of the Association for Computational Linguistics: Human Language Technologies, Volume 1 (Long and Short Papers)*, pages 4171–4186, Minneapolis, Minnesota. Association for Computational Linguistics.

Kevin Gimpel, Nathan Schneider, Brendan O'Connor, Dipanjan Das, Daniel Mills, Jacob Eisenstein, Michael Heilman, Dani Yogatama, Jeffrey Flanigan, and Noah A. Smith. 2011. Part-of-speech tagging for twitter: Annotation, features, and experiments. In *Proceedings of the 49th Annual Meeting of the Association for Computational Linguistics: Human Language Technologies*, pages 42–47, Portland, Oregon, USA. Association for Computational Linguistics.

Ian Goodfellow, Jean Pouget-Abadie, Mehdi Mirza, Bing Xu, David Warde-Farley, Sherjil Ozair, Aaron Courville, and Yoshua Bengio. 2014. Generative adversarial nets. In *Advances in Neural Information Processing Systems*, pages 2672–2680.

Ishaan Gulrajani, Faruk Ahmed, Martin Arjovsky, Vincent Dumoulin, and Aaron C Courville. 2017. Improved training of Wasserstein GANs. In I. Guyon, U. V. Luxburg, S. Bengio, H. Wallach, R. Fergus, S. Vishwanathan, and R. Garnett, editors, *Advances in Neural Information Processing Systems 30*, pages 5767–5777.

Sepp Hochreiter and Jürgen Schmidhuber. 1997. Long short-term memory. *Neural Computation*.

Diederik P. Kingma and Jimmy Ba. 2014. Adam: A method for stochastic optimization. *arXiv preprint arXiv:1412.6980*.

Guillaume Lample, Miguel Ballesteros, Sandeep Subramanian, Kazuya Kawakami, and Chris Dyer. 2016. Neural architectures for named entity recognition. In *Proceedings of the 2016 Conference of the North American Chapter of the Association for Computational Linguistics: Human Language Technologies*, pages 260–270, San Diego, California. Association for Computational Linguistics.

Yann LeCun, Sumit Chopra, Raia Hadsell, Marc'Aurelio Ranzato, and Fu-Jie Huang. 2006. A tutorial on energy-based learning. In *Predicting Structured Data*. MIT Press.

Xuezhe Ma and Eduard Hovy. 2016. End-to-end sequence labeling via bi-directional LSTM-CNNs-CRF. In *Proceedings of the 54th Annual Meeting of the Association for Computational Linguistics (Volume 1: Long Papers)*, pages 1064–1074, Berlin, Germany. Association for Computational Linguistics.

Tomas Mikolov, Ilya Sutskever, Kai Chen, Greg S Corrado, and Jeff Dean. 2013. Distributed representations of words and phrases and their compositionality. In *Advances in Neural Information Processing Systems*, pages 3111–3119.

Takeru Miyato, Toshiki Kataoka, Masanori Koyama, and Yuichi Yoshida. 2018. Spectral normalization for generative adversarial networks. In *Proceedings of International Conference on Learning Representations (ICLR)*.

Subhajit Naskar, Amirmohammad Rooshenas, Simeng Sun, Mohit Iyyer, and Andrew McCallum. 2020. Energy-based reranking: Improving neural machine translation using energy-based models. *arXiv preprint arXiv:2009.13267*.

Olutobi Owoputi, Brendan O'Connor, Chris Dyer, Kevin Gimpel, Nathan Schneider, and Noah A. Smith. 2013. Improved part-of-speech tagging for online conversational text with word clusters. In *Proceedings of the 2013 Conference of the North American Chapter of the Association for Computational Linguistics: Human Language Technologies*, pages 380–390, Atlanta, Georgia. Association for Computational Linguistics.

Jeffrey Pennington, Richard Socher, and Christopher Manning. 2014. Glove: Global vectors for word representation. In *Proceedings of the 2014 Conference on Empirical Methods in Natural Language Processing (EMNLP)*, pages 1532–1543, Doha, Qatar. Association for Computational Linguistics.

Lev Ratinov and Dan Roth. 2009. Design challenges and misconceptions in named entity recognition. In *Proceedings of the Thirteenth Conference on Computational Natural Language Learning (CoNLL-2009)*, pages 147–155.

Amirmohammad Rooshenas, Aishwarya Kamath, and Andrew McCallum. 2018. Training structured prediction energy networks with indirect supervision. In *Proceedings of the 2018 Conference of the North American Chapter of the Association for Computational Linguistics: Human Language Technologies, Volume 2 (Short Papers)*, pages 130–135.

Amirmohammad Rooshenas, Dongxu Zhang, Gopal Sharma, and Andrew McCallum. 2019. Search-guided, lightly-supervised training of structured prediction energy networks. In H. Wallach, H. Larochelle, A. Beygelzimer, F. d'Alché-Buc, E. Fox, and R. Garnett, editors, *Advances in Neural Information Processing Systems 32*, pages 13522–13532.

Tim Salimans, Ian Goodfellow, Wojciech Zaremba, Vicki Cheung, Alec Radford, and Xi Chen. 2016. Improved techniques for training GANs. In *Advances in Neural Information Processing Systems*, pages 2234–2242.

Ben Taskar, Carlos Guestrin, and Daphne Koller. 2004. Max-margin Markov networks. In *Advances in Neural Information Processing Systems*, pages 25–32.

Erik F. Tjong Kim Sang and Fien De Meulder. 2003. Introduction to the CoNLL-2003 shared task: Language-independent named entity recognition. In *Proceedings of the Seventh Conference on Natural Language Learning at HLT-NAACL 2003*, pages 142–147.

Trang Tran, Shubham Toshniwal, Mohit Bansal, Kevin Gimpel, Karen Livescu, and Mari Ostendorf. 2018. Parsing speech: a neural approach to integrating lexical and acoustic-prosodic information. In *Proceedings of the 2018 Conference of the North American Chapter of the Association for Computational Linguistics: Human Language Technologies, Volume 1 (Long Papers)*, pages 69–81, New Orleans, Louisiana. Association for Computational Linguistics.

Ioannis Tsochantaridis, Thomas Hofmann, Thorsten Joachims, and Yasemin Altun. 2004. Support vector machine learning for interdependent and structured output spaces. In *Proceedings of the Twenty-first International Conference on Machine Learning*.

Lifu Tu and Kevin Gimpel. 2018. Learning approximate inference networks for structured prediction. In *Proceedings of International Conference on Learning Representations (ICLR)*.

Lifu Tu and Kevin Gimpel. 2019. Benchmarking approximate inference methods for neural structured prediction. In *Proceedings of the 2019 Conference of the North American Chapter of the Association for Computational Linguistics: Human Language Technologies, Volume 1 (Long and Short Papers)*, pages 3313–3324, Minneapolis, Minnesota. Association for Computational Linguistics.

Lifu Tu, Kevin Gimpel, and Karen Livescu. 2017. Learning to embed words in context for syntactic tasks. In *Proceedings of the 2nd Workshop on Representation Learning for NLP*, pages 265–275.

Lifu Tu, Tianyu Liu, and Kevin Gimpel. 2020a. An exploration of arbitrary-order sequence labeling via energy-based inference networks. In *Proceedings of the 2020 Conference on Empirical Methods in Natural Language Processing*.

Lifu Tu, Richard Yuanzhe Pang, Sam Wiseman, and Kevin Gimpel. 2020b. ENGINE: Energy-based inference networks for non-autoregressive machine translation. In *Proceedings of the 58th Annual Meeting of the Association for Computational Linguistics*, pages 2819–2826, Online. Association for Computational Linguistics.

Junbo Jake Zhao, Michaël Mathieu, and Yann Le-Cun. 2017. Energy-based generative adversarial network. In *Proceedings of International Conference on Learning Representations (ICLR)*.

A Appendices

A.1 Constituency Parsing Experiments

We linearize the constituency parsing outputs, similar to Tran et al. (2018). We use the following equation plus global energy in the form of Eq. (8) as the energy function:

$$
E_\Theta(\boldsymbol{x}, \boldsymbol{y}) = -\left(\sum_{t=1}^{T} \sum_{j=1}^{L} y_{t,j} \left(U_j^\top b(\boldsymbol{x}, t) \right) \right. \\
\left. + \sum_{t=1}^{T} \boldsymbol{y}_{t-1}^\top W \boldsymbol{y}_t \right)
$$

Here, b has a seq2seq-with-attention architecture identical to Tran et al. (2018). In particular, here is the list of implementation decisions.

- We can write $b = g \circ f$ where f (which we call the "feature network") takes in an input sentence, passes it through the encoder, and passes the encoder output to the decoder feature layer to obtain hidden states; g takes in the hidden states and passes them into the rest of the layers in the decoder. In our experiments, the cost-augmented inference network $\mathbf{F}_\Phi$, test-time inference network $\mathbf{A}_\Psi$, and b of the energy function above share the same feature network (defined as f above).

- The feature network (f) component of b is pretrained using the feed-forward local cross-entropy objective. The cost-augmented inference network $\mathbf{F}_\Phi$ and the test-time inference network $\mathbf{A}_\Psi$ are both pretrained using the feed-forward local cross-entropy objective.

The seq2seq baseline achieves 82.80 F1 on the development set in our replication of Tran et al. (2018). Using a SPEN with our stacked parameterization, we obtain 83.22 F1.

Reading the Manual: Event Extraction as Definition Comprehension

Yunmo Chen[1]   Tongfei Chen[1]   Seth Ebner[1]
Aaron Steven White[2]   Benjamin Van Durme[1]
[1]Johns Hopkins University   [2]University of Rochester
{yunmo,tongfei,seth,vandurme}@jhu.edu
aaron.white@rochester.edu

Abstract

We ask whether text understanding has progressed to where we may extract event information through incremental refinement of *bleached statements* derived from annotation manuals. Such a capability would allow for the trivial construction and extension of an extraction framework by intended end-users through declarations such as, *Some person was born in some location at some time*. We introduce an example of a model that employs such statements, with experiments illustrating we can extract events under closed ontologies and generalize to unseen event types simply by reading new definitions.

1 Introduction

This work is aimed at the disconnect between how human annotators and machines carry out information extraction: humans read annotation manuals consisting of guidelines and illustrative examples then label data, whereas machines label data (by making predictions) based purely on previously seen examples (Figure 1). We explore the feasibility of building a model that has access to information derived from annotation manuals. Specifically we focus on the task of event extraction and convert annotation guidelines describing event types into natural language *bleached statements*. An example bleached statement for the ACE 2005 (Walker et al., 2006) LIFE:BE-BORN event type is:

some person was born in some location at some time
_______PERSON_______________PLACE__________TIME

The bleached statement describes a general occurrence of an event of a given type. The event's arguments are initialized with bleached placeholders (e.g. *some person*) to be replaced with extracted spans from the text, eventually resulting in, e.g.:

Barack Obama was born in Hawaii at some time
___PERSON_______________PLACE______TIME

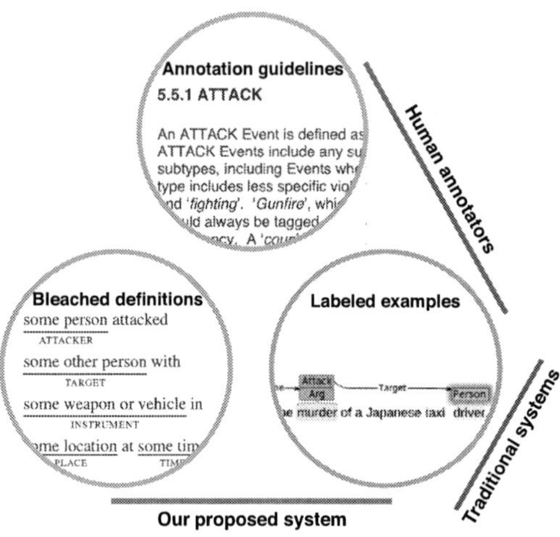

Figure 1: Comparison of data sources for human annotators, traditional information extraction systems, and our proposed approach. Human annotators use annotation guidelines and limited illustrative examples, traditional systems use large amounts of labeled examples, and our system uses bleached statements (derived from annotation guidelines) and labeled examples.

We are motivated to consider these statements owing to the rapid progress in sentence-level representation learning and machine reading comprehension: can a contemporary encoder *understand* event statements well enough that their derived representation may be directly employed in extraction?

Bleached statements are straightforward to write and accommodate various levels of expressiveness in both the choice of arguments present and in the lexicalization of the trigger.[1] These features allow for easy adaptation as an ontology changes: simply introduce new or modified statements. In the case where the amount of labeled examples is small or non-existent, a bleached statement serves as a sort

---

[1] For example, for a CONFLICT:ATTACK event, we could use the simple trigger "attacked" or the more descriptive phrase "violently caused physical harm or damage to."

Proceedings of 4th Workshop on Structured Prediction for NLP, pages 74–83
November 20, 2020. ©2020 Association for Computational Linguistics

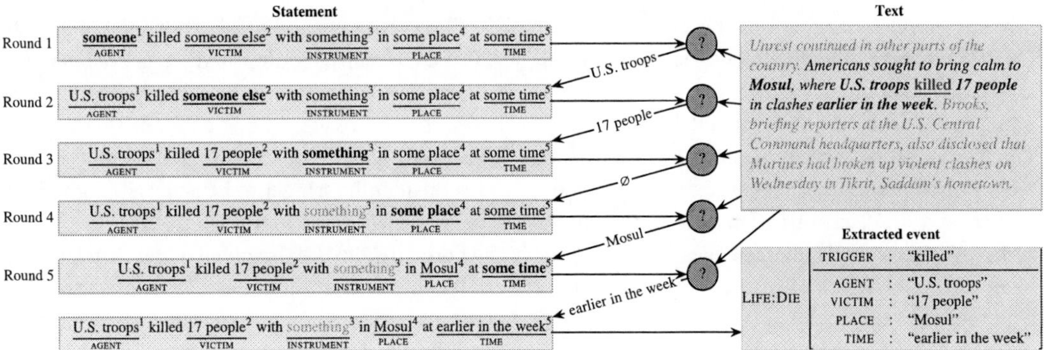

Figure 2: An example of our approach on a sentence from the ACE 2005 dataset for the LIFE:DIE event. The bleached statement is incrementally populated with values from the text (in the order denoted by the superscripts), and not all event arguments are supported by the text. The grayed out text in the paragraph is given for context to the reader, but our model operates on single-sentence contexts.

of canonical example provided ahead of further annotation. We would like a solution where one simply declared the intended information, where any traditional labeled examples were used for disambiguation and fine-tuning, rather than being a critical component in building a model.

As an example of such a solution, we propose a model which incrementally populates bleached statements by querying partially filled statements against text. This strategy is similar to the tasks of machine reading comprehension (MRC) and question answering (QA), in which an answer span is predicted in response to a question about a document. Conceptually this may also be considered a form of incremental recognizing textual entailment (RTE) (Dagan et al., 2006) where we iteratively refine a hypothesis that is supported by the document context. Experimental results demonstrate that zero- and few-shot event extraction are feasible with this approach. While our intent here is exploratory, we manage to achieve state-of-the-art performance on trigger identification and trigger classification on the ACE 2005 dataset. The contributions of this work are: **(i)** A novel approach to event extraction that takes into account annotation guidelines through bleached statements; **(ii)** A multiple-span selection model that demonstrates the feasibility of the approach for event extraction as well as for zero- and few-shot settings.

2   Background

Event extraction is traditionally viewed as three subtasks: (1) event trigger detection, where triggers of events (words that most clearly express the occurrences of events) are detected; (2) entity men-

tion detection, where all potential arguments (entity mentions) to events are detected; and (3) argument role prediction, where relations between detected arguments and trigger words are recognized with respect to each event type's defined set of roles.

Much prior work adopts a pipelined approach to these 3 subtasks or focuses on a subset of the subtasks based on gold entity mention spans. These include feature-based approaches (Ji and Grishman, 2008; Liao and Grishman, 2010; McClosky et al., 2011; Huang and Riloff, 2012; Li et al., 2013, *inter alia*) and neural approaches (Nguyen and Grishman, 2015; Chen et al., 2015, 2017; Nguyen and Grishman, 2018; Sha et al., 2018, *inter alia*).

Because pipelined approaches suffer from error propagation in which the error from earlier subtasks (e.g. entity mention detection) is inherited by later subtasks, joint modeling of the 3 subtasks has been attempted. Yang and Mitchell (2016) attempts to jointly model the three components with hand-crafted features, but still need to detect entity mentions and event triggers separately. Nguyen and Nguyen (2019) jointly models the three tasks using neural networks with shared underlying representations. The models proposed in these two works are the baselines used in this paper.

Huang et al. (2018) approach zero-shot event extraction by stipulating a graph structure for each event type and finding the event type graph structure whose learned representation most closely matches the learned representation of the parsed AMR (Banarescu et al., 2013) structure of a text. In contrast, our approach forgoes explicit graph-structured semantic representations such as AMR.

Researchers have introduced large question answering (QA) / machine reading comprehension (MRC) datasets in a cloze style (Hermann et al., 2015; Onishi et al., 2016), where a query sentence contains a placeholder and the model fills the blank. Our work can be viewed as an extension to such work, where multiple placeholders are extracted.

Li et al. (2019) casts relation extraction as multi-turn QA with natural language questions, where in each turn one argument of the relation is found.. The method requires writing a question for each entity type and each relation type. In (Levy et al., 2017), sets of crowdsourced paraphrastic questions are written for each relation type in the ontology. In contrast, for each event type we use a single declarative bleached statement derived from the annotation guidelines. Soares et al. (2019) proposes a model for relation extraction by filling in two blanks given a contextual relation statement.

These three methods focus on binary relation extraction, and do not readily generalize to n-ary events or relations. Our approach naturally supports variable arity events and relations.

3 Problem Formulation

A *bleached statement* consists of: the statement tokens $S = (s_1, s_2, \cdots, s_n)$; a placeholder dictionary $R = \{(r_k : I_k)\}_{k=1,\cdots,K}$, where r_k is the predefined *role* of that argument (e.g. AGENT, PATIENT); and an index set $I_k \subseteq \{1, \cdots, n\}$, a set containing indices of tokens in the statement S (i.e. if $I = \{i_1, \cdots, i_l\}$, then $(s_{i_1}, \cdots, s_{i_l})$ is a placeholder).[2] An example bleached statement in the ACE 2005 dataset for the event type LIFE:DIE (also used in our Figure 2 for illustration purposes) is:

$$\underbrace{\text{someone}}_{\text{AGENT}} \text{ killed } \underbrace{\text{someone else}}_{\text{VICTIM}} \text{ with } \underbrace{\text{something}}_{\text{INSTRUMENT}}$$
$$\text{in } \underbrace{\text{some place}}_{\text{PLACE}} \text{ at } \underbrace{\text{some time}}_{\text{TIME}}$$

This statement is accompanied by the following placeholder dictionary, in which each role is mapped to an index set that highlights the placeholder in the bleached statement[3]:

$$R = \begin{bmatrix} \text{AGENT} & : & \{1\} \\ \text{VICTIM} & : & \{3, 4\} \\ \text{INSTRUMENT} & : & \{6\} \\ \text{PLACE} & : & \{8, 9\} \\ \text{TIME} & : & \{11, 12\} \end{bmatrix}$$

---

[2] Our bleached statements are inspired in part by linguistic resource creation efforts by White and Rawlins (2018).

[3] The model itself does not see the role names. They are used only for human readability and evaluation.

The event extraction task as defined in the ACE 2005 dataset also requires finding an *event trigger*— a span in the text that most clearly expresses the event's occurrence. In this example, the trigger is the word *"killed"*. For a consistent implementation, we consider the trigger to be a special argument of the event, with role name TRIGGER.

Formally, the task is: given a bleached statement S, its placeholder dictionary R, and text tokens T, return a dictionary $\hat{R}$ that contains the event trigger and the the extracted arguments. Such a result is shown in the bottom right of Figure 2. Note that the INSTRUMENT role is not filled in the example because the model does not find a span to fill it.

4 Approach

Given a bleached statement with multiple placeholders, we do not fill the placeholders in parallel—instead, we fill them incrementally in an enforced order.[4] In each step, the model attempts to fill a single focused placeholder, which is replaced by the extracted span(s) thereby creating a refined statement (see Figure 2). In this work we fill the placeholders in the statement *from left to right* and leave other orders as future work.

Formally, in each round, our model returns multiple arguments (see "Multiple Argument Selector" section below) for each placeholder:

$$A \leftarrow \text{GETARGS}(S, I, T),$$

where S is the (partially refined) statement, I is the index set that covers the focused placeholder (which corresponds to a role), and T is the text to extract from. The returned argument set A contains a number of text spans (potentially zero) in T that replace the placeholder in S picked out by I.

If A is the empty set, then the model did not find an appropriate text span to replace the placeholder. If the answer set A is not empty, we replace the placeholder with the extracted span. Note that in some cases, there can be more than one argument that fits a role. Consider the following bleached statement (for the ACE 2005 event LIFE:MARRY), focused on the first placeholder *"some people"*:

$$\underbrace{\text{some people}^1}_{\text{PERSON}} \text{ married in } \underbrace{\text{some location}^2}_{\text{PLACE}} \text{ at } \underbrace{\text{some time}^3}_{\text{TIME}}$$

We expect multiple arguments for the same role PERSON in this event. If our model returns

---

[4] The enforced order is denoted in our examples by indices on the placeholders and the values that fill them.

Algorithm 1 Argument extraction

Input: statement S, placeholder dictionary R, text T
Output: extracted argument structure E

> **function** EXTRACTARGS(S, R, T)
>> $i \leftarrow 1$ ▷ i-th round
>> $S^{(1)} \leftarrow S$ ▷ the initial statement
>> $E \leftarrow \varnothing$ ▷ extracted event
>> **for** $(r, I) \in R$ **do**
>>> $A \leftarrow$ GETARGS($S^{(i)}, I, T$)
>>> **if** $A \neq \varnothing$ **then**
>>>> $S^{(i+1)} \leftarrow$ replace the I tokens in $S^{(i)}$ with A ▷ refine the statement
>>>> $E \leftarrow E \cup (r : A)$
>>> **else** $S^{(i+1)} \leftarrow S^{(i)}$ ▷ skip to the next role
>>> **end if**
>>> $i \leftarrow i + 1$
>> **end for**
>> **return** E
> **end function**

Algorithm 2 Event extraction

Input: ontology $\mathcal{O}$, text T
Output: extracted event structures $\mathcal{E}$

> **function** EXTRACTEVENTS($\mathcal{O}, T$)
>> $\mathcal{E} \leftarrow \varnothing$
>> **for** $(\tau, S, R) \in \mathcal{O}$ **do**
>>> $triggers \leftarrow$ TRIGGERID(S, R, T)
>>> **for** $t \in triggers$ **do**
>>>> $S' \leftarrow$ ANCHORTRIGGER(S, t)
>>>> $E \leftarrow$ EXTRACTARGS(S', R, T)
>>>> $\hat{R} \leftarrow E \cup ($TRIGGER $: t)$
>>>> $\mathcal{E} \leftarrow \mathcal{E} \cup \hat{R}$
>>> **end for**
>> **end for**
>> **return** $\mathcal{E}$ ▷ all events extracted from T
> **end function**

$A = \{$"Kim", "Pat"$\}$, i.e. a set containing multiple extracted arguments, we replace the placeholder with all arguments, concatenated with the "*and*" token, and shift the focus to the next placeholder, creating the refined statement:

Kim and Pat[1] married in **some location**[2] at some time[3]
    PERSON   PLACE   TIME

If our model returns nothing, i.e. $A = \varnothing$, we simply skip the placeholder and move the focus to the next placeholder. For example, if the model finds no argument for the PLACE role, the refined statement of the next iteration would be

Kim and Pat[1] married in some location[2] at **some time**[3]
    PERSON   PLACE   TIME

We run this iterative process until all roles of an event are visited. An advantage of this method is that during the incremental refinement process, the statement always remains a natural language sentence. The incremental process for extracting event arguments is formalized in Algorithm 1, given the initial bleached statement S, the role dictionary R, and the text T to extract from.

Annotation manuals of interest usually define multiple event types. For each event type τ described in the manual, we require a bleached statement S and a role dictionary R. These together form our ontology $\mathcal{O} = \{(\tau_k, S_k, R_k)\}$. To perform full event extraction (Algorithm 2), we first run a trigger detection model for *all event types* (see "Trigger Identification" section below) specified in the ontology. For those event types whose trigger is found, we proceed with argument extraction (Algorithm 1).

4.1 Model

Architecture for MRC In light of recent advancements in NLP from large-scale pre-training, we use BERT (Devlin et al., 2019) as our sequence encoder. We first review the answer selector architecture for machine reading comprehension (MRC) used in BERT, then extend it for our approach.

Under the formulation of MRC, each training data point is of the form (S, T) where S is a natural language question with tokens $S = (s_1, \cdots, s_n)$ and T is the text to extract answers from, with tokens $T = (t_1, \cdots, t_m)$. The model returns a span in T or predicts that the question is not answerable, in which case an empty span is returned.

To perform MRC, Devlin et al. (2019) proposed the following architecture. First the question S and the text T are concatenated with special delimiters and passed through the BERT contextualizer:

$$\text{BERT}\left([\text{CLS}, s_1, \cdots, s_n, \text{SEP}, t_1, \cdots, t_m, \text{SEP}]\right),$$

where CLS is a special sentinel token whose embedding encompasses the whole string, and SEP is a sentence separator. We denote the output encoding of each question token s_i ($1 \leq i \leq n$) as $\mathbf{s}_i \in \mathbb{R}^d$, and the encoding of each text token t_j ($1 \leq j \leq m$) as $\mathbf{t}_j \in \mathbb{R}^d$. Additionally, two vectors, $\mathbf{b}_{\text{left}}$ and $\mathbf{b}_{\text{right}}$, for the left and right boundaries of the answer span are learned. The probability of each token t_j $(1 \leq j \leq m)$ being the left or right boundary of the answer span is computed as

$$P_{\text{left}}(t_j) \propto \exp(\mathbf{b}_{\text{left}} \cdot \mathbf{t}_j); \; P_{\text{right}}(t_j) \propto \exp(\mathbf{b}_{\text{right}} \cdot \mathbf{t}_j)$$

The two vectors $\mathbf{b}_{\text{left}}$ and $\mathbf{b}_{\text{right}}$ act as attention *query vectors* to the text, resulting in a soft pointer over the text tokens.

Multiple Argument Selector   Our scenario is fundamentally different from MRC in two ways: (1) Our query is not formulated as a natural language question; instead, it is a cloze-style problem with a natural language statement and a highlighted blank to fill; (2) For some cases, there can be more than one answer for a given blank. Previous MRC models support extracting only at most one answer.

To accommodate these requirements, we propose a new architecture for this scenario that describes the GETARGS function in Algorithm 1. Given a bleached statement $S = (s_1, \cdots, s_n)$ with a highlighted placeholder span with indices $I = \{i_1, \cdots, i_l\} \subseteq \{1, \cdots, n\}$, instead of two attention query vectors $\mathbf{b}_{\text{left}}$ and $\mathbf{b}_{\text{right}}$ to get the left and right boundary for the answer span, we consider the problem of answer span selection as a *tagging* problem, first proposed in Yao et al. (2013), where answer spans are tagged using a linear chain CRF (Lafferty et al., 2001). By considering answer span selection as tagging, our model selects potentially multiple spans for a query.

We enforce the constraint that all extracted spans come from the same sentence in the text, but in general this constraint need not be enforced. Additionally, our model operates on single-sentence contexts, so information available in other sentences is not considered.

We use the BIO tagging scheme (Ramshaw and Marcus, 1995), where each token in the text is tagged with B (beginning), I (inside), or O (outside). In a linear-chain CRF, the probability of an output tag sequence $y_1, \cdots, y_j$ (for each j, $y_j \in \{B, I, O\}$) given the text $T = (t_1, \cdots, t_j)$ is

$$P(y_1, \cdots, y_j | t_1, \cdots, t_j) \propto \prod_{j=1}^{m} \psi(y_{j-1}, y_j, j), \quad (1)$$

where we define the potential function $\psi(y_{j-1}, y_j, j)$ as the output of a neural function described below. Our model is trained to maximize P.

We first compute an attentive representation for a placeholder with respect to each text token t_j, using the attention mechanism proposed by Luong et al. (2015), since the placeholder is of variable length but we desire a fixed-size vector representation:

$$a_{ij} = \frac{\exp\left(\mathbf{s}_i \cdot \mathbf{t}_j\right)}{\sum_{i' \in I} \exp\left(\mathbf{s}_{i'} \cdot \mathbf{t}_j\right)} \quad (2)$$

$$\tilde{\mathbf{s}}_j = \sum_{i \in I} a_{ij} \mathbf{s}_i \quad (3)$$

Then the attentive placeholder representation $\tilde{\mathbf{s}}_j$, together with its corresponding text token representation $\mathbf{t}_j$, are joined using various matching methods proposed in Mou et al. (2016):[5]

$$\mathbf{x}_j = \left[\tilde{\mathbf{s}}_j \; ; \; \mathbf{t}_j \; ; \; |\tilde{\mathbf{s}}_j - \mathbf{t}_j| \; ; \; \tilde{\mathbf{s}}_j \odot \mathbf{t}_j \right] \quad (4)$$

yielding the joined feature vector $\mathbf{x}_j \in \mathbb{R}^{4d}$.

Finally the joined feature vector $\mathbf{x}_j$ is passed through a multi-layer feed-forward neural network to get the final potential function for each token and each predicted tag type $y_j \in \{B, I, O\}$:

$$\psi(y_{j-1}, y_j, j) = \text{FFNN}_{y_j}(\mathbf{x}_j) \quad (5)$$

In our experiments, we pass $\mathbf{x}_j$ through 4 layers, with output dimensions $2d, d, d$, and 1, respectively, and tanh as the nonlinearity function between layers.

Trigger Identification   Triggers of events can be thought as a special argument, which usually is the main verb (or a nominalized verb) that expresses the occurrence of an event. We reuse the argument selection model for trigger identification: the highlighted token set for the trigger is all tokens in the statement that are not part of any standard argument:

$$I_{\text{trigger}} = \{1, \cdots, n\} \setminus \bigcup_{(r, I) \in R} I \quad (6)$$

For example, the highlighted token set for the trigger of the statement in Figure 2 consists of the tokens underlined below:

> someone <u>killed</u> someone else <u>with</u> something <u>in</u> some place <u>at</u> some time

4.2   Training Data Generation

We generate data examples in the form of (S, I, T) triples to train the argument extractor, where S is a bleached statement, I is the index set of the focused

---

[5] $|\cdot|$ is elementwise absolute value, $\odot$ is elementwise product, and $[;]$ is vector concatenation.

placeholder, and T is the text. Algorithm 1 generates a sequence of bleached statements, where each successive statement is a refinement of its predecessor. During training, instead of replacing placeholders with their predicted arguments $A \leftarrow \text{GETARGS}(S, I, T)$, we replace them with the gold argument(s) from the event extraction dataset.

Negative Sampling For trigger identification, we augment each example with negative samples from the set of event types not found in the example's text. For each event, $\alpha\%$ of the non-occurring event types are taken as negative samples. We tune $\alpha \in \{10, 20, 30, 40, 50\}$.

4.3 Recasting MRC Data for Pre-training

SQuAD (Rajpurkar et al., 2016) is a reading comprehension dataset consisting of questions on a set of Wikipedia articles, where the answer to each question is a span of text extracted from the corresponding reading passage. Its version 2.0 (Rajpurkar et al., 2018) contains additional data that poses unanswerable questions to reading comprehension systems. To do well, a system should learn to abstain from answering when no answer is supported by the text.

We employ recast versions of the training and development splits of SQuAD 2.0 as pre-training data for our event extraction system. We cast each SQuAD natural language question to a format similar to our bleached statements, where the *wh-* question phrases of the questions are tagged as the placeholders to be filled. For example, given the following SQuAD question,

> *What form of oxygen is composed of 3 oxygen atoms?*

the extracted *wh-* phrase is "*What form of oxygen*", which is chosen as the single placeholder in this statement. This is answered as

> <u>ozone</u> is composed of 3 oxygen atoms?
> ANSWER

This methodology is linguistically motivated, as both questions (as in SQuAD) and bleached statements (this work) reduce to logical forms with the same predicate. The denotations can be written (using a generic operator Q) as

$$Qx. [\![\text{form of oxygen}]\!] (x)$$
$$\wedge [\![\text{composed of three oxygen atoms}]\!] (x)$$

where Q is λ for the question and is $\exists$ for the bleached statement. Hence the *wh-* phrase is semantically similar to an existentially quantified phrase (e.g. *some form of oxygen*, where *some* introduces existential quantification), despite their pragmatic difference in illocutionary force (inquiring vs. stating). Additionally, *wh-* phrases presuppose the existence of their answer referent; to use a *wh-* phrase when no referent exists would be infelicitous. Hence *wh-* question phrases serve the same function as the existentially quantified placeholder phrases in our bleached statements, and so the recast SQuAD questions are appropriate data for pre-training.

We extract *wh-* phrases through syntactic analysis of the questions. We define the *wh-* phrase of a question to be the maximum span in its constituency parse that bears any of the question tags in the Penn Treebank (Marcus et al., 1993) parsing annotation guideline.[6]

We employ the neural span-based constituency parser (Stern et al., 2017) in the AllenNLP (Gardner et al., 2018) toolkit to parse the SQuAD questions for extracting the *wh-* phrases.

5 Experiments and Discussions

5.1 Event Extraction on ACE 2005

We evaluate our approach on the ACE 2005 dataset and use the same data splits as previous work, in which 40 newswire documents are used as the test set, another 30 documents of different genres are selected as the development set, and the remaining 529 documents constitute the training set (Li et al., 2013; Yang and Mitchell, 2016; Nguyen and Nguyen, 2019). Following previous work, we use four evaluation metrics: (1) *Trigger Identification*: a trigger is correctly identified if its span offsets exactly match a reference trigger; (2) *Trigger Classification*: a trigger is correctly classified if its span offsets and event subtype exactly match a reference trigger; (3) *Argument Identification*: an argument is correctly identified if its span offsets and corresponding event subtype exactly match a reference argument; and (4) *Argument Classification*: an argument is correctly classified if its span offsets, corresponding event subtype, and argument role exactly match a reference argument. The overall

---

[6]These include the following tags (followed by examples): WHADJP (how many), WHADVP (why), WHNP (which book), textttWHPP (by whose authority), WDT (which), WP (who), WP$ (whose), WRB (where).

Model	Trigger						Argument					
	Identification			Classification			Identification			Classification		
	P	R	F_1	P	R	F_1	P	R	F_1	P	R	F_1
JOINTFEATURE	**77.6**	65.4	71.0	**75.1**	63.3	68.7	**73.7**	38.5	50.6	**70.6**	36.9	48.4
JOINT3EE	70.5	74.5	72.5	68.0	71.8	69.8	59.9	**59.8**	**59.9**	52.1	**52.1**	**52.1**
Ours w/ partial data	64.5	62.3	63.4	60.9	58.7	59.8	43.1	42.8	43.0	35.2	34.9	35.0
Ours w/o pre-training	50.0	**85.7**	63.2	48.1	**82.4**	60.7	29.3	55.0	38.2	24.7	46.4	32.2
Ours w/ full data	68.9	77.3	**72.9**	66.7	74.7	**70.5**	44.9	41.2	43.0	44.3	40.7	42.4

Table 1: P(recision), R(ecall), and F_1 obtained by models on the ACE 2005 dataset. Best results are **bolded**. Using the full training set improves F_1 performance over using the partial training set on all metrics except argument identification (equal). Pre-training on the recast SQuAD 2.0 dataset improves F_1 performance over no pre-training on all metrics.

performance is evaluated using *precision* (P), *recall* (R), and *F-measure* (F_1) for each metric.

We use BERT for sequence encoding.[7] For pre-training on the recast SQuAD 2.0 dataset, we follow the previously mentioned pre-processing strategy. We pre-train on the training set of SQuAD 2.0 and perform early stopping using the development partition. Examples that do not have exactly 1 *wh*-phrase are discarded.[8] The maximum sequence length is 512 word pieces, the maximum query length is 128 word pieces, the learning rate is 3×10^{-5} with an Adam optimizer, the maximum gradient norm for gradient clipping is set to 1.0, and the number of training epochs is 3.

After pre-training on SQuAD 2.0, we fine-tune the model on ACE 2005. While keeping other hyperparameters unchanged, we set the learning rate to 1×10^{-5} and the number of training epochs to 8. During fine-tuning, we employ negative sampling and set the negative sampling rate to 30%.

In addition to fine-tuning on the full training set of ACE 2005, we consider a single-genre "partial" training setting in which the model is trained only on the 58 documents that appear in the newswire portion of the full training set.

Experimental Results & Discussion We train our model using full and partial training data and compare with two joint event extraction model baselines. The JOINTFEATURE model (Yang and Mitchell, 2016) is a feature-based model that ex-

ploits document-level information; the JOINT3EE model (Nguyen and Nguyen, 2019) is a neural model that achieves state-of-the-art performance on ACE 2005. These two models represent the state-of-the-art performance for feature-based and neural models, respectively.

Table 1 reports the performance of the systems on the four evaluation metrics. Training on the full training set improves F_1 performance over training on the partial training set, giving the largest improvement on trigger identification and classification. Additionally, pre-training on the recast SQuAD 2.0 dataset provides large F_1 improvements (4.8%–10.2% absolute F_1 increase) on all four evaluation metrics. Our model also tends to have higher recall than precision, especially on trigger identification and classification, and suffers from low precision compared to prior work. Our model achieves state-of-the-art performance on trigger identification and trigger classification.

Because our model does not explicitly incorporate entity mention detection, we hypothesize that our MRC-inspired approach predicts answer spans that are semantically correct but do not exactly match the gold answers, hurting performance on argument-related subtasks. We compare predicted arguments with gold references and find the following sources of errors:

- *Relative clauses*: Our model predicts *Mosul* whereas the gold answer is *Mosul, where U.S. troops killed 17 people in clashes earlier in the week.*

- *Counts*: The gold annotation is *300 billion yen* but our model predicts *300 billion*.

- *Durations*: The gold annotation is *lasted two*

---

[7] We use the BERT-BASE-CASED model, which has 12 layers, 768-dimensional hidden embeddings, 12 attention heads, and 110 million parameters.

[8] Our effective training set contains 128,649 examples after 1,670 were discarded, and the effective development set contains 11,772 examples after 100 were discarded.

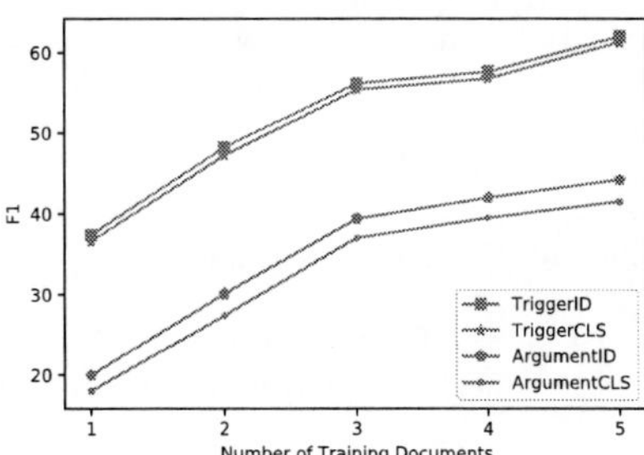

Figure 3: Few-shot experimental results on FrameNet.

Frame	Trigger		Argument	
	Id.	Cls.	Id.	Cls.
ARRIVING	9.1	9.1	6.1	6.1
ATTACK	66.4	66.4	42.1	42.1
GETTING	17.6	17.6	14.3	13.8
INTENTIONALLY_CREATE	12.5	12.5	7.1	7.1
KILLING	22.4	22.4	13.1	7.0
MANUFACTURING	37.4	37.4	27.6	26.7
SCRUTINY	16.6	16.6	11.7	11.0
STATEMENT	0.6	0.6	0.7	0.5
SUPPLY	3.1	3.1	1.7	1.5
USING	10.4	10.4	10.0	8.8
Macro-averaged F_1	19.6	19.6	13.4	12.46

Table 2: Zero-shot results on FrameNet frames. Trigger classification performance is equivalent to trigger identification performance because we evaluate on only one frame in each zero-shot learning experiment.

hours but our model predicts *two hours*.

5.2 Few-shot Learning on FrameNet

In order to evaluate our approach under a lower-resource setting than the partial training setting, we consider few- and zero-shot learning on annotated documents from FrameNet.[9] 7 documents are excluded from FrameNet's 107 annotated documents because they do not have frame annotations. The arguments in our bleached statements consist of only the frame's core *frame elements*. We use the same four evaluation metrics as used for ACE 2005.

We split the remaining 100 documents into 5 training documents and 95 test documents and experiment with training on between 1 and 5 documents.[10] We pick the top-10 most frequent frames that represent events and write bleached statements based on their frame definitions.

Following the same pre-training setup, we then train the model using the same hyperparameters as the model fine-tuned on ACE 2005.

Experimental Results & Discussion The results in Figure 3 show that F_1 performance on all evaluation metrics increases as more documents are added to the training set. The marginal utility of adding training documents almost monotonically decreases as the training set increases, so that performance from training on 3 documents roughly matches performance from training on 5 documents.

5.3 Zero-shot Learning on FrameNet

We additionally investigate the model's ability to generalize to unseen event types using the same dataset as the few-shot setting. We employ a leave-one-out strategy to the frames in Table 2, training on 9 frames and testing on the other 1.

Experimental Results & Discussion The results in Table 2 reveal a large variation in performance on the frames. The best performance is achieved on the ATTACK frame, but frames such as STATEMENT achieve poor performance.

We report the *macro-averaged* F_1 over all frames to reveal overall performance instead of *micro-average*, since we care how the approach generalizes to different frames. Overall, the macro-averaged F_1 shows that the model can feasibly extract information about events of unseen types, but performance varies greatly across frames.

Possible reasons why the STATEMENT frame has low performance include: (1) the event type being too general, (2) the bleached statement being poorly constructed, (3) the span for the "message" role being long and difficult to tag exactly correctly using the `BIO` scheme.

6 Conclusion & Future Work

We present an approach to event extraction that uses bleached statements to give a model access to information contained in annotation manuals. Our model incrementally refines the statements with values extracted from text. We also demonstrate the feasibility of making predictions on event types seen rarely or not at all. Future work can apply our approach to *n*-ary relation extraction.

---

[9] We use the Full Text Annotation portion of FrameNet.
[10] Because we do not perform a hyperparameter sweep in this setting, we do not use a development set.

Acknowledgments

This research was supported by the JHU HLTCOE, DARPA AIDA, DARPA KAIROS, IARPA BETTER, and NSF-BCS (1748969/1749025). The U.S. Government is authorized to reproduce and distribute reprints for Governmental purposes. The views and conclusions contained in this publication are those of the authors and should not be interpreted as representing official policies or endorsements of DARPA or the U.S. Government.

References

Laura Banarescu, Claire Bonial, Shu Cai, Madalina Georgescu, Kira Griffitt, Ulf Hermjakob, Kevin Knight, Philipp Koehn, Martha Palmer, and Nathan Schneider. 2013. Abstract meaning representation for sembanking. In *Proceedings of the 7th Linguistic Annotation Workshop and Interoperability with Discourse*, pages 178–186.

Yubo Chen, Shulin Liu, Xiang Zhang, Kang Liu, and Jun Zhao. 2017. Automatically labeled data generation for large scale event extraction. In *Proc. ACL*, pages 409–419.

Yubo Chen, Liheng Xu, Kang Liu, Daojian Zeng, and Jun Zhao. 2015. Event extraction via dynamic multipooling convolutional neural networks. In *Proc. ACL*, pages 167–176.

Ido Dagan, Oren Glickman, and Bernardo Magnini. 2006. The pascal recognising textual entailment challenge. In *Machine Learning Challenges. Evaluating Predictive Uncertainty, Visual Object Classification, and Recognising Tectual Entailment*, pages 177–190, Berlin, Heidelberg. Springer Berlin Heidelberg.

Jacob Devlin, Ming-Wei Chang, Kenton Lee, and Kristina Toutanova. 2019. BERT: Pre-training of deep bidirectional transformers for language understanding. In *Proceedings of the 2019 Conference of the North American Chapter of the Association for Computational Linguistics: Human Language Technologies, Volume 1 (Long and Short Papers)*, pages 4171–4186, Minneapolis, Minnesota. Association for Computational Linguistics.

Matt Gardner, Joel Grus, Mark Neumann, Oyvind Tafjord, Pradeep Dasigi, Nelson F. Liu, Matthew E. Peters, Michael Schmitz, and Luke Zettlemoyer. 2018. AllenNLP: A deep semantic natural language processing platform. *CoRR*, abs/1803.07640.

Karl Moritz Hermann, Tomás Kociský, Edward Grefenstette, Lasse Espeholt, Will Kay, Mustafa Suleyman, and Phil Blunsom. 2015. Teaching machines to read and comprehend. In *Proc. NeurIPS*, pages 1693–1701.

Lifu Huang, Heng Ji, Kyunghyun Cho, Ido Dagan, Sebastian Riedel, and Clare Voss. 2018. Zero-shot transfer learning for event extraction. In *Proceedings of the 56th Annual Meeting of the Association for Computational Linguistics (Volume 1: Long Papers)*, pages 2160–2170, Melbourne, Australia. Association for Computational Linguistics.

Ruihong Huang and Ellen Riloff. 2012. Modeling textual cohesion for event extraction. In *Proc. AAAI*.

Heng Ji and Ralph Grishman. 2008. Refining event extraction through cross-document inference. In *Proceedings of ACL-08: HLT*, pages 254–262, Columbus, Ohio. Association for Computational Linguistics.

John D. Lafferty, Andrew McCallum, and Fernando C. N. Pereira. 2001. Conditional random fields: Probabilistic models for segmenting and labeling sequence data. In *Proc. ICML*, pages 282–289.

Omer Levy, Minjoon Seo, Eunsol Choi, and Luke Zettlemoyer. 2017. Zero-shot relation extraction via reading comprehension. In *Proceedings of the 21st Conference on Computational Natural Language Learning (CoNLL 2017)*, pages 333–342, Vancouver, Canada. Association for Computational Linguistics.

Qi Li, Heng Ji, and Liang Huang. 2013. Joint event extraction via structured prediction with global features. In *Proceedings of the 51st Annual Meeting of the Association for Computational Linguistics (Volume 1: Long Papers)*, pages 73–82, Sofia, Bulgaria. Association for Computational Linguistics.

Xiaoya Li, Fan Yin, Zijun Sun, Xiayu Li, Arianna Yuan, Duo Chai, Mingxin Zhou, and Jiwei Li. 2019. Entity-relation extraction as multi-turn question answering. In *Proceedings of the 57th Annual Meeting of the Association for Computational Linguistics*, pages 1340–1350, Florence, Italy. Association for Computational Linguistics.

Shasha Liao and Ralph Grishman. 2010. Using document level cross-event inference to improve event extraction. In *Proceedings of the 48th Annual Meeting of the Association for Computational Linguistics*, pages 789–797, Uppsala, Sweden. Association for Computational Linguistics.

Thang Luong, Hieu Pham, and Christopher D. Manning. 2015. Effective approaches to attention-based neural machine translation. In *Proceedings of the 2015 Conference on Empirical Methods in Natural Language Processing*, pages 1412–1421, Lisbon, Portugal. Association for Computational Linguistics.

Mitchell P. Marcus, Beatrice Santorini, and Mary Ann Marcinkiewicz. 1993. Building a large annotated corpus of english: The penn treebank. *Computational Linguistics*, 19(2):313–330.

David McClosky, Mihai Surdeanu, and Christopher D. Manning. 2011. Event extraction as dependency parsing. In *Proc. ACL*, pages 1626–1635.

Lili Mou, Rui Men, Ge Li, Yan Xu, Lu Zhang, Rui Yan, and Zhi Jin. 2016. Natural language inference by tree-based convolution and heuristic matching. In *Proceedings of the 54th Annual Meeting of the Association for Computational Linguistics (Volume 2: Short Papers)*, pages 130–136, Berlin, Germany. Association for Computational Linguistics.

Thien Huu Nguyen and Ralph Grishman. 2015. Event detection and domain adaptation with convolutional neural networks. In *Proc. ACL*, pages 365–371.

Thien Huu Nguyen and Ralph Grishman. 2018. Graph convolutional networks with argument-aware pooling for event detection. In *Proc. AAAI*, pages 5900–5907.

Trung Minh Nguyen and Thien Huu Nguyen. 2019. One for all: Neural joint modeling of entities and events. In *Proc. AAAI*, pages 6851–6858.

Takeshi Onishi, Hai Wang, Mohit Bansal, Kevin Gimpel, and David A. McAllester. 2016. Who did what: A large-scale person-centered cloze dataset. In *Proc. EMNLP*, pages 2230–2235.

Pranav Rajpurkar, Robin Jia, and Percy Liang. 2018. Know what you don't know: Unanswerable questions for SQuAD. In *Proceedings of the 56th Annual Meeting of the Association for Computational Linguistics (Volume 2: Short Papers)*, pages 784–789, Melbourne, Australia. Association for Computational Linguistics.

Pranav Rajpurkar, Jian Zhang, Konstantin Lopyrev, and Percy Liang. 2016. SQuAD: 100,000+ questions for machine comprehension of text. In *Proceedings of the 2016 Conference on Empirical Methods in Natural Language Processing*, pages 2383–2392, Austin, Texas. Association for Computational Linguistics.

Lance Ramshaw and Mitch Marcus. 1995. Text chunking using transformation-based learning. In *Third Workshop on Very Large Corpora*.

Lei Sha, Feng Qian, Baobao Chang, and Zhifang Sui. 2018. Jointly extracting event triggers and arguments by dependency-bridge RNN and tensor-based argument interaction. In *Proc. AAAI*, pages 5916–5923.

Livio Baldini Soares, Nicholas FitzGerald, Jeffrey Ling, and Tom Kwiatkowski. 2019. Matching the blanks: Distributional similarity for relation learning. In *Proc. ACL*, pages 2895–2905.

Mitchell Stern, Jacob Andreas, and Dan Klein. 2017. A minimal span-based neural constituency parser. In *Proceedings of the 55th Annual Meeting of the Association for Computational Linguistics (Volume 1: Long Papers)*, pages 818–827, Vancouver, Canada. Association for Computational Linguistics.

Christopher Walker, Stephanie Strassel, Julie Medero, and Kazuaki Maeda. 2006. ACE 2005 multilingual training corpus (LDC2006T06). *Philadelphia: Linguistic Data Consortium*.

Aaron Steven White and Kyle Rawlins. 2018. The role of veridicality and factivity in clause selection. In *Proceedings of the 48th Meeting of the North East Linguistic Society*.

Bishan Yang and Tom M. Mitchell. 2016. Joint extraction of events and entities within a document context. In *Proceedings of the 2016 Conference of the North American Chapter of the Association for Computational Linguistics: Human Language Technologies*, pages 289–299, San Diego, California. Association for Computational Linguistics.

Xuchen Yao, Benjamin Van Durme, Chris Callison-Burch, and Peter Clark. 2013. Answer extraction as sequence tagging with tree edit distance. In *Proceedings of the 2013 Conference of the North American Chapter of the Association for Computational Linguistics: Human Language Technologies*, pages 858–867, Atlanta, Georgia. Association for Computational Linguistics.

On the Discrepancy between Density Estimation and Sequence Generation

Jason Lee
New York University
jason@cs.nyu.edu

Dustin Tran
Google AI
trandustin@google.com

Orhan Firat
Google AI
orhanf@google.com

Kyunghyun Cho
New York University
kyunghyun.cho@nyu.edu

Abstract

Many sequence-to-sequence generation tasks, including machine translation and text-to-speech, can be posed as estimating the density of the output y given the input x: $p(y|x)$. Given this interpretation, it is natural to evaluate sequence-to-sequence models using conditional log-likelihood on a test set. However, the goal of sequence-to-sequence generation (or structured prediction) is to find the best output $\hat{y}$ given an input x, and each task has its own downstream metric R that scores a model output by comparing against a set of references y^*: $R(\hat{y}, y^*|x)$. While we hope that a model that excels in density estimation also performs well on the downstream metric, the exact correlation has not been studied for sequence generation tasks. In this paper, by comparing several density estimators on five machine translation tasks, we find that the correlation between rankings of models based on log-likelihood and BLEU varies significantly depending on the range of the model families being compared. First, log-likelihood is highly correlated with BLEU when we consider models within the same family (e.g. autoregressive models, or latent variable models with the same parameterization of the prior). However, we observe no correlation between rankings of models across different families: (1) among non-autoregressive latent variable models, a flexible prior distribution is better at density estimation but gives worse generation quality than a simple prior, and (2) autoregressive models offer the best translation performance overall, while latent variable models with a normalizing flow prior give the highest held-out log-likelihood across all datasets.

1 Introduction

Sequence-to-sequence generation tasks can be cast as conditional density estimation $p(y|x)$ where x and y are input and output sequences. In this framework, density estimators are trained to maximize the conditional log-likelihood, and also evaluated using log-likelihood on a test set. However, many sequence generation tasks require finding the best output $\hat{y}$ given an input x at test time, and the output is evaluated against a set of references y^* on a task-specific metric: $R(\hat{y}, y^*|x)$. For example, machine translation systems are evaluated using BLEU scores (Papineni et al., 2002), image captioning systems use METEOR (Banerjee and Lavie, 2005) and text-to-speech systems use MOS (mean opinion scores). As density estimators are optimized on log-likelihood, we want models with higher held-out log-likelihoods to give better generation quality, but the correlation has not been well studied for sequence generation tasks. In this work, we investigate the correlation between rankings of density estimators based on (1) test log-likelihood and (2) the downstream metric for machine translation.

On five language pairs from three machine translation datasets (WMT'14 En↔De, WMT'16 En↔Ro, IWSLT'16 De→En), we compare the held-out log-likelihood and BLEU scores of several density estimators: (1) autoregressive models (Vaswani et al., 2017), (2) latent variable models with a non-autoregressive decoder and a simple (diagonal Gaussian) prior (Shu et al., 2019), and (3) latent variable models with a non-autoregressive decoder and a flexible (normalizing flow) prior (Ma et al., 2019).

We present two key observations. First, among models within the same family, we find that log-likelihood is strongly correlated with BLEU. The correlation is almost perfect for autoregressive models and high for latent variable models with the same prior. Between models of different families, however, log-likelihood and BLEU are not correlated. Latent variable models with a flow prior are in fact the best density estimators (even better than autoregressive models), but they give the

Proceedings of 4th Workshop on Structured Prediction for NLP, pages 84–94
November 20, 2020. ©2020 Association for Computational Linguistics

worst generation quality. Gaussian prior models offer comparable or better BLEU scores, while autoregressive models give the best BLEU scores overall. From these findings, we conclude that the correlation between log-likelihood and BLEU scores varies significantly depending on the range of model families considered.

Second, we find that knowledge distillation drastically hurts density estimation performance across different models and datasets, but consistently improves translation quality of non-autoregressive models. For autoregressive models, distillation slightly hurts translation quality. Among latent-variable models, iterative inference with a delta posterior (Shu et al., 2019) significantly improves the translation quality of latent variable models with a Gaussian prior, whereas the improvement is relatively small for the flow prior. Overall, for fast generation, we recommend a latent variable non-autoregressive model using a simple prior (rather than a flexible one), knowledge distillation, and iterative inference. This is 5–7x faster than the autoregressive model at the expense of 2 BLEU scores on average, and it improves upon latent variable models with a flexible prior across generation speed, BLEU, and parameter count.

2 Background

Sequence-to-sequence generation is a supervised learning problem of generating an output sequence given an input sequence. For many such tasks, conditional density estimators have been very successful (Sutskever et al., 2014; Bahdanau et al., 2015; Vinyals et al., 2015; Vinyals and Le, 2015).

To learn the distribution of an output sequence, it is crucial to give enough capacity to the model to be able to capture the dependencies among the output variables. We explore two ways to achieve this: (1) directly modeling the dependencies with an autoregressive factorization of the variables, and (2) letting latent variables capture the dependencies, so the distribution of the output sequence can be factorized given the latent variables and therefore more quickly be generated. We discuss both classes of density estimators in depth below. We denote the training set as a set of tuples $\{(\mathbf{x}_n, \mathbf{y}_n)\}_{n=1}^N$ and each input and output example as sequences of random variables $\mathbf{x} = \{x_1, \ldots, x_{T'}\}$ and $\mathbf{y} = \{y_1, \ldots, y_T\}$ (where we drop the subscript n for notational simplicity). We use θ to denote the model parameters.

2.1 Autoregressive Models

Learning Autoregressive models factorize the joint distribution of the sequence of output variables $\mathbf{y} = \{y_1, \ldots, y_T\}$ as a product of conditional distributions:

$$\log p_{\text{AR}}(\mathbf{y}|\mathbf{x}) = \sum_{t=1}^T \log p_\theta(y_t|y_{<t}, \mathbf{x}).$$

They are trained to maximize the log-likelihood of the training data: $L_{\text{AR}}(\theta) = \frac{1}{N}\sum_{n=1}^N \log p_{\text{AR}}(\mathbf{y}_n|\mathbf{x}_n)$.

Parameterization Recurrent neural networks and their gated variants are natural parameterizations of autoregressive models (Elman, 1990; Hochreiter and Schmidhuber, 1997; Chung et al., 2014). By ensuring that no future information $y_{\geq t}$ is used in predicting the current timestep y_t, non-recurrent architectures can also parameterize autoregressive models, such as convolutions (van den Oord et al., 2016; Gehring et al., 2017) and Transformers (Vaswani et al., 2017), which are feedforward networks with self-attention.

Inference Finding the most likely output sequence given an input sequence under an autoregressive model amounts to solving a search problem: $\text{argmax}_{y_{1:T}} \sum_{t=1}^T \log p_\theta(y_t|y_{<t}, \mathbf{x})$. As the size of the search space grows exponentially with the length of the output sequence T, solving this exactly is intractable. Therefore, approximate search algorithms are often used such as greedy search or beam search.

2.2 Latent Variable Models

Learning Latent variable models posit a joint distribution of observed variables ($\mathbf{y}$) and unobserved variables ($\mathbf{z}$). They are trained to maximize the marginal log-likelihood of the training data:

$$\log p_{\text{LVM}}(\mathbf{y}|\mathbf{x}) = \log \int_{\mathbf{z}} p_\theta(\mathbf{y}|\mathbf{z}, \mathbf{x})\, p_\theta(\mathbf{z}|\mathbf{x}) d\mathbf{z}. \tag{1}$$

As the marginalization over $\mathbf{z}$ makes computing the marginal log-likelihood and posterior inference intractable, variational inference proposes to use a parameterized family of distributions $q_\phi(\mathbf{z}|\mathbf{y}, \mathbf{x})$ to approximate the true posterior $p(\mathbf{z}|\mathbf{y}, \mathbf{x})$. Then, we have the evidence lowerbound (ELBO) (Wainwright and Jordan, 2008; Kingma and Welling,

2014):

$$\log p_{\text{LVM}}(\mathbf{y}|\mathbf{x}) \geq \text{ELBO}(\mathbf{y}, \mathbf{x}; \theta, \phi) \qquad (2)$$
$$= \mathop{\mathbb{E}}_{\mathbf{z} \sim q_\phi} \big[\log p_\theta(\mathbf{y}, \mathbf{z}|\mathbf{x}) - \log q_\phi(\mathbf{z}|\mathbf{y}, \mathbf{x})\big],$$

where $p_\theta(\mathbf{y}|\mathbf{z}, \mathbf{x})$ is the decoder, $q_\phi(\mathbf{z}|\mathbf{y}, \mathbf{x})$ is the variational posterior and $p_\theta(\mathbf{z}|\mathbf{x})$ is the prior. Both the model and variational parameters θ, ϕ are estimated to maximize ELBO over the training set: $L_{\text{LVM}}(\theta, \phi) = \frac{1}{N} \sum_{n=1}^{N} \text{ELBO}(\mathbf{y}_n, \mathbf{x}_n; \theta, \phi)$.

Parameterization As latent variables can capture the dependencies between the output variables, the decoding distribution can be factorized: $p_\theta(\mathbf{y}|\mathbf{z}, \mathbf{x}) = \prod_{t=1}^{T} p_\theta(y_t|\mathbf{z}, \mathbf{x})$. The approximate posterior distribution is also often factorized, which can be parameterized by any neural network that outputs mean and standard deviation for each output position: $q_\phi(z_{1:T}|\mathbf{y}, \mathbf{x}) = \prod_{t=1}^{T} \mathcal{N}\big(z_t\big|\mu_{\phi,t}(\mathbf{y}, \mathbf{x}), \sigma_{\phi,t}(\mathbf{y}, \mathbf{x})\big)$. We discuss prior distributions in §2.3.

Inference Generating the most likely output given an input with a latent variable model requires optimizing ELBO with respect to the output: $\text{argmax}_{\mathbf{y}} \text{ELBO}(\mathbf{y}, \mathbf{x}; \theta, \phi)$. As computing the expectation in Eq. 2 is intractable, we instead optimize a proxy lowerbound using a delta posterior (Shu et al., 2019):

$$\delta(\mathbf{z}|\boldsymbol{\mu}) = \begin{cases} 1, & \text{if } \mathbf{z} = \boldsymbol{\mu} \\ 0, & \text{otherwise} \end{cases}$$

Then, the ELBO reduces to:

$$\mathop{\mathbb{E}}_{\mathbf{z} \sim \delta(\mathbf{z}|\boldsymbol{\mu})} \big[p_\theta(\mathbf{y}|\mathbf{z}, \mathbf{x}) + p_\theta(\mathbf{z}|\mathbf{x})\big] + \overbrace{\mathcal{H}(\delta)}^{=0},$$
$$= \log p_\theta(\mathbf{y}|\boldsymbol{\mu}, \mathbf{x}) + \log p_\theta(\boldsymbol{\mu}|\mathbf{x}). \qquad (3)$$

We maximize Eq. 3 with iterative refinement: the EM algorithm alternates between (1) matching the proxy to the original lowerbound by setting $\boldsymbol{\mu} = \mathbb{E}_{q_\phi}[\mathbf{z}]$, and (2) maximizing the proxy lowerbound with respect to $\mathbf{y}$ by: $\hat{\mathbf{y}} = \text{argmax}_{\mathbf{y}}(\log p_\theta(\mathbf{y}|\boldsymbol{\mu}, \mathbf{x}))$. The delta posterior is initialized using the prior (e.g. $\boldsymbol{\mu} = \mathbb{E}_{\mathbf{z} \sim p_\theta(\mathbf{z}|\mathbf{x})}[\mathbf{z}]$ in case of a Gaussian prior) so that the inference algorithm is fully deterministic, a desirable property for sequence generation tasks. We study the effect of iterative refinement on BLEU score in detail.

2.3 Prior for Latent Variable Models

Several work have discovered that the prior distribution plays a critical role in balancing the variational posterior and the decoder, and a standard normal distribution may be too rigid for the aggregate posterior to match (Hoffman and Johnson, 2016; Rosca et al., 2018). Indeed, follow-up work found that more flexible prior distributions outperform simple priors on several density estimation tasks (Tomczak and Welling, 2018; Bauer and Mnih, 2019). Therefore, we explore two choices for the prior distribution: a factorized Gaussian and a normalizing flow.

Diagonal Gaussian A simple model of the conditional prior is a factorized Gaussian distribution:

$$\log p_\theta(z_{1:T}|\mathbf{x}) = \sum_{t=1}^{T} \log \mathcal{N}\big(z_t\big|\mu_{\theta,t}(\mathbf{x}), \sigma_{\theta,t}(\mathbf{x})\big),$$

where each latent variable z_t is modeled as a diagonal Gaussian with mean and standard deviation computed from a learned function.

Normalizing Flow Normalizing flows (Tabak and Turner, 2013; Rezende and Mohamed, 2015; Papamakarios et al., 2019) offer a general method to construct complex probability distributions over continuous random variables. It consists of (1) a base distribution $p_b(\epsilon)$ (often chosen as a standard Gaussian distribution) and an invertible transformation f and its inverse f^{-1}, such that $f(\mathbf{z}) = \epsilon$, $f^{-1}(\epsilon) = \mathbf{z}$. As our prior is conditioned on $\mathbf{x}$, so are the transformations: $f(\mathbf{z}; \mathbf{x}) = \epsilon$, $f^{-1}(\epsilon; \mathbf{x}) = \mathbf{z}$. Then, by change-of-variables, we can evaluate the exact density of the latent variable $\mathbf{z}$ under the flow prior:

$$\log p_\theta(\mathbf{z}|\mathbf{x}) = \log p_b\big(f(\mathbf{z}; \mathbf{x})\big) + \log \left|\det \frac{\partial f(\mathbf{z}; \mathbf{x})}{\partial \mathbf{z}}\right|.$$

Affine coupling flows (Dinh et al., 2017) enable efficient generation and computation of the Jacobian determinant by constructing each transformation such that only a subset of the random variables undergoes affine transformation, using parameters computed from the remaining variables:

$$\mathbf{z}_{\text{id}}, \mathbf{z}_{\text{tr}} = \text{split}(\mathbf{z})$$
$$\mathbf{s}, \mathbf{b} = g_{\text{param}}(\mathbf{z}_{\text{id}}) \qquad (4)$$
$$f(\mathbf{z}) = \text{concat}(\mathbf{z}_{\text{id}}; \ \mathbf{s} \cdot \mathbf{z}_{\text{tr}} + \mathbf{b}),$$

where g_{param} can be arbitrarily complex as it needs not be invertible. As invertibility is closed under function composition and the Jacobian determinant is multiplicative, increasingly flexible coupling flows can be constructed by stacking multiple flow layers and reordering such that all the variables are transformed.

2.4 Knowledge Distillation

While most density estimators for sequence generation tasks are trained to maximize the log-likelihood of the training data, recent work have shown that it is possible to improve the performance of non-autoregressive models significantly by training them on the predictions of a pre-trained autoregressive model (Gu et al., 2018; van den Oord et al., 2018). While Zhou et al. (2019) recently found that distillation reduces complexity of the training data, its effect on density estimation performance has not been studied.

3 Problem Definition

On a sequence generation task, a conditional density estimator $F \in \mathcal{H}$ (where $\mathcal{H}$ is a hypothesis set of density estimators in §2) is trained to maximize the log-likelihood (or its approximation) of the training set $\{(x_n, y_n)\}_{n=1}^{N}$:

$$L(F) = \frac{1}{N} \sum_{n=1}^{N} \log p_F(y_n | x_n).$$

Once training converges, the model F is evaluated on the test set $\{(x_m, y_m)\}_{m=1}^{M}$ using a downstream metric R:

$$R(F) = R\big(\{(x_m, y_m, \hat{y}_m)\}_{m=1}^{M}\big),$$

where $\hat{y}_m = \operatorname{argmax}_y \log p_F(y | x_m)$.

To perform model selection, we can rank a set of density estimators $\{F_1, \ldots, F_K\}$ based on either the held-out log-likelihood or the downstream metric. We measure the correlation between the rankings given by the log-likelihood $L(F)$ and the downstream metric $R(F)$.

4 Experimental Setup

On machine translation, we train several autoregressive models and latent variable models and analyze the correlation between their rankings based on log-likelihood and BLEU.

4.1 Datasets and Preprocessing

We use five language pairs from three translation datasets: IWSLT'16 De→En[1] (containing 197K

training, 2K development and 2K test sentence pairs), WMT'16 En↔Ro[2] (612K, 2K, 2K pairs) and WMT'14 En↔De[3] (4.5M, 3K, 3K pairs). For WMT'14 En↔De and WMT'16 En↔Ro, both directions are used.

We use the preprocessing scripts with default hyperparameters from the `tensor2tensor` framework.[4] Namely, we use wordpiece tokenization (Schuster and Nakajima, 2012) with 32K wordpieces on all datasets. For WMT'16 En↔Ro, we follow Sennrich et al. (2016) and normalize Romanian and remove diacritics before applying wordpiece tokenization. For training, we discard sentence pairs if either the source or the target length exceeds 64 tokens. As splitting along the time dimension (Ma et al., 2019) in the coupling flow layer requires that the length of the output sequence is a multiple of 2 at each level, `<EOS>` tokens are appended to the target sentence until its length is a multiple of 4.

4.2 Autoregressive Models

We use three Transformer (Vaswani et al., 2017) models of different sizes: Transformer-big (Tr-L), Transformer-base (Tr-B) and Transformer-small (Tr-S). The first two models have the same hyperparameters as in Vaswani et al. (2017). Transformer-small has 2 attention heads, 5 encoder and decoder layers, $d_{\text{model}} = 256$ and $d_{\text{filter}} = 1024$.

4.3 Latent Variable Models

The latent variable models in our experiments are composed of the source sentence encoder, length predictor, prior, decoder and posterior. The source sentence encoder is implemented with a standard Transformer encoder. Given the hidden states of the source sentence, the length predictor (a 2-layer MLP) predicts the length difference between the source and target sentences as a categorical distribution in $[-30, 30]$. We implement the decoder $p_\theta(\mathbf{y}|\mathbf{z}, \mathbf{x})$ with a standard Transformer decoder that outputs the logits of all target tokens in parallel. The approximate posterior $q_\phi(\mathbf{z}|\mathbf{y}, \mathbf{x})$ is implemented as a Transformer decoder with a final Linear layer with weight normalization (Salimans

------

[2] `www.statmt.org/wmt16/translation-task.html`
[3] `www.statmt.org/wmt14/translation-task.html`
[4] `https://github.com/tensorflow/tensor2tensor/blob/master/tensor2tensor/bin/t2t-datagen`

------

[1] `https://wit3.fbk.eu/`

and Kingma, 2016) to output the mean and standard deviation (having dimensionality d_{latent}). Both the decoder and the approximate posterior attend to the source hidden states.

Diagonal Gaussian Prior The diagonal Gaussian prior is implemented with a Transformer decoder which receives a sequence of positional encodings of length T as input, and outputs the mean and standard deviation of each target token (of dimensionality d_{latent}). We train two models of different sizes: Gauss-base (Ga-B) and Gauss-large (Ga-L). Gauss-base has 4 attention heads, 3 posterior layers, 3 decoder layers and 6 encoder layers, whereas Gauss-large has 8 attention heads, 4 posterior layers, 6 decoder layers, 6 encoder layers. $(d_{\text{model}}, d_{\text{latent}}, d_{\text{filter}})$ is (512, 512, 2048) for WMT experiments and (256, 256, 1024) for IWSLT experiments.

Normalizing Flow Prior The flow prior is implemented with Glow (Kingma and Dhariwal, 2018). We use a single Transformer decoder layer with a final Linear layer with weight normalization to parameterize g_{param} in Eq. 4. This produces the shift and scale parameters for the affine transformation. Our flow prior has the multi-scale architecture with three levels (Dinh et al., 2017): at the end of each level, half of the latent variables are modeled with a standard Gaussian distribution. We use three split patterns and multi-headed 1x1 convolution from Ma et al. (2019). We experiment with the following hyperparameter settings: Flow-small (Fl-S) with 12/12/8 flow layers in each level and Flow-base (Fl-B) with 12/24/16 flow layers in each level. The first level corresponds to the latent distribution and the last level corresponds to the base distribution. $(d_{\text{model}}, d_{\text{latent}}, d_{\text{filter}})$ is (320, 320, 640) for all experiments. For the Transformer decoder in g_{param}, we use 4 attention heads for Flow-small and 8 attention heads for Flow-base.

4.4 Training and Optimization

We use the Adam optimizer (Kingma and Ba, 2015) with the learning rate schedule used by Vaswani et al. (2017). The norm of the gradients is clipped at 1.0. We perform early stopping and choose the learning rate warmup steps and dropout rate based on the BLEU score on the development set. To train non-autoregressive models, the loss from the length predictor is minimized jointly with negative ELBO loss.

Knowledge Distillation Following previous work (Kim and Rush, 2016; Gu et al., 2018; Lee et al., 2018), we construct a distilled dataset by decoding the training set using Transformer-base with beam width 4. For IWSLT'16 De→En, we use Transformer-small.

Latent Variable Models To ease optimization of latent variable models (Bowman et al., 2016; Higgins et al., 2017), we set the weight of the KL term to 0 for the first 5,000 SGD steps and linearly increase it to 1 over the next 20,000 steps. Similarly with Mansimov et al. (2019), we find it helpful to add a small regularization term to the training objective that matches the approximate posterior with a standard Gaussian distribution: $\alpha \cdot \text{KL}\big[q_\phi(\mathbf{z}|\mathbf{y}, \mathbf{x}) \,\|\, \mathcal{N}(0, \mathbf{I})\big]$, as the original KL term $\text{KL}\big[q_\phi(\mathbf{z}|\mathbf{y}, \mathbf{x}) \,\|\, p_\theta(\mathbf{z}|\mathbf{x})\big]$ does not have a local point minimum but a valley of minima. We find $\alpha = 10^{-4}$ to work best.

Flow Prior Models We perform data-dependent initialization of actnorm parameters for the flow prior (Kingma and Dhariwal, 2018) at the 5,000-th step, which is at the beginning of KL scheduling.

4.5 Evaluation Metrics

Log-likelihood is the main metric for measuring density estimation (data modeling) performance. We compute exact log-likelihood for autoregressive models. For latent variable models, we estimate the marginal log-likelihood by importance sampling with 1K samples from the approximate posterior and using the ground truth target length.

BLEU measures the similarity (in terms of n-gram overlap) between a generated output and a set of references, regardless of the model. It is a standard metric for generation quality of machine translation systems.

Generation Speed In addition to the quality-driven metrics, we measure the generation speed of each model in the number of sentences generated per second on a single V100 GPU.

5 Results

5.1 Correlation between rankings of models

Table 1 presents the comparison of three model families (Transformer, Gauss, Flow) on five language pairs in terms of generation quality (BLEU) and log-likelihood (LL). We present two sets of results: one from models trained on raw data (Raw),

		BLEU (↑)		LL (↑)	
		RAW	DIST.	RAW	DIST.
WMT'14 EN→DE	TR-S	24.54	24.94	-1.77	-2.36
	TR-B	28.18	27.86	-1.44	-2.19
	TR-L	<u>29.39</u>	28.29	-1.35	-2.23
	GA-B	15.74	24.54	-1.51	-2.44
	GA-L	17.33	**25.53**	-1.47	-2.24
	FL-S	18.17	21.98	-1.41	-2.13
	FL-B	18.57	21.82	**-1.23**	-2.05
	FL-B$^{(*)}$	18.55	21.45		
	FL-L$^{(*)}$	20.85	23.72		
WMT'14 DE→EN	TR-S	29.15	28.40	-1.66	-2.24
	TR-B	32.21	32.24	-1.42	-2.12
	TR-L	<u>33.16</u>	32.24	-1.35	-2.05
	GA-B	21.64	29.29	-1.41	-2.17
	GA-L	23.03	**30.30**	-1.31	-2.04
	FL-S	23.17	27.14	-1.28	-1.73
	FL-B	23.12	26.72	**-1.20**	-1.71
	FL-B$^{(*)}$	23.36	26.16		
	FL-L$^{(*)}$	25.40	28.39		
WMT'16 EN→RO	TR-S	30.12	29.57	-1.72	-1.95
	TR-B	<u>33.46</u>	33.28	-1.63	-2.52
	GA-B	28.03	29.71	-2.38	-3.48
	GA-L	28.16	**30.91**	-2.44	-3.54
	FL-S	26.85	28.63	-1.53	-2.42
	FL-B	27.49	29.09	**-1.50**	-2.31
	FL-B$^{(*)}$	29.26	29.34		
	FL-L$^{(*)}$	29.86	29.73		
WMT'16 RO→EN	TR-S	29.33	28.87	-1.84	-1.93
	TR-B	<u>32.19</u>	31.15	-1.79	-2.28
	GA-B	26.48	27.81	-2.41	-2.92
	GA-L	27.35	**28.02**	-2.32	-3.01
	FL-S	26.03	26.12	-1.65	-2.05
	FL-B	27.14	27.33	**-1.64**	-2.01
	FL-B$^{(*)}$	30.16	30.44		
	FL-L$^{(*)}$	30.69	30.72		
IWSLT	TR-S	31.54	<u>31.72</u>	-1.84	-2.56
	GA-B	24.36	26.80	-1.98	-2.70
	FL-S	23.64	26.69	-1.66	-2.28
	FL-B	24.89	**27.00**	**-1.57**	-2.46
	FL-B$^{(*)}$	24.75	27.75		

Table 1: Test BLEU score and log-likelihood of each model. Raw: models trained on raw data. Dist.: models trained on distilled data. Tr-S: Transformer-small. Tr-B: Transformer-base. Tr-L: Transformer-big. Ga-B: Gauss-base. Ga-L: Gauss-large. Fl-S: Flow-small. Fl-B: Flow-base. Fl-L: Flow-large. We use beam search with width 4 for inference with autoregressive models, and one step of iterative inference (Shu et al., 2019) for latent variable models. On most datasets, our Flow-base model gives comparable results to those from Ma et al. (2019), which are denoted with (∗). We boldface the best log-likelihood overall and the best BLEU score among the latent variable models. We underscore best BLEU score among the autoregressive models.

	TR-B	GA-B	FL-B
RAW	0.926	0.831	0.678
DIST.	-0.758	-0.897	-0.873

Table 2: Pearson's correlation between log-likelihood and BLEU across the training checkpoints of Transformer-base, Gauss-base and Flow-base on WMT'14 En→De.

and another from models trained on distilled data (Dist.) (which we mostly discuss in §5.2). We use the original test set in computing the log-likelihood and BLEU scores of the distilled models, so the results are comparable with the undistilled models. We make two main observations:

1. Log-likelihood is highly correlated with BLEU when considering models within the same family.

(a) Among autoregressive models (Tr-S, Tr-B and Tr-L), there is a perfect correlation between log-likelihood and BLEU. On all five language pairs (undistilled), the rankings of autoregressive models based on log-likelihood and BLEU are identical.

(b) Among non-autoregressive latent variable models with the same prior distribution, there is a strong but not perfect correlation. Between Gauss-large and Gauss-base, the model with higher held-out log-likelihood also gives higher BLEU on four out of five datasets. Similarly, Flow-base gives higher log-likelihood and BLEU score than Flow-small on all datasets except WMT'14 De→En.

2. Log-likelihood is not correlated with BLEU when comparing models from different families.

(a) Between latent variable models with different prior distributions, we observe no correlation between log-likelihood and BLEU. On four out of five language pairs (undistilled), Flow-base gives much higher log-likelihood but similar or worse BLEU score than Gauss-base. With distillation, Gauss-large considerably outperforms Flow-base in BLEU on all datasets, while Flow-base gives better log-likelihood.

(b) Overall, autoregressive models offer the best translation quality but not the best modeling performance. In fact, Flow-base model with a non-autoregressive decoder gives the highest held-out log-likelihood on all datasets.

Correlation between log-likelihood and BLEU across checkpoints Table 2 presents the correlation between log-likelihood and BLEU across the training checkpoints of several models. The findings are similar to Table 1: for Transformer-base, there is almost perfect correlation (0.926) across the checkpoints. For Gauss-base and Flow-base, we observe strong but not perfect correlation (0.831 and 0.678). Overall, these findings suggest that there is a high correlation between log-likelihood and BLEU when comparing models within the same family. We discuss the correlation for models trained with distillation below in §5.2.

5.2 Knowledge Distillation

In Table 2, we observe a strong negative correlation between log-likelihood and BLEU across the training checkpoints of several density estimators trained with distillation. Indeed, distillation severely hurts density estimation performance on all datasets (see Table 1). In terms of generation quality, it consistently improves non-autoregressive models, yet the amount of improvement varies across models and datasets. On WMT'14 En→De and WMT'14 De→En, distillation gives a significant 7–9 BLEU increase for diagonal Gaussian prior models, but the improvement is relatively smaller on other datasets. Flow prior models benefit less from distillation, only 3–4 BLEU scores on WMT'14 En↔De and less on other datasets. For autoregressive models, distillation results in a slight decrease in generation performance.

5.3 Iterative inference on Gaussian vs. flow prior

We analyze the effect of iterative inference on the Gaussian and the flow prior models. Table 3 shows that iterative refinement improves BLEU and ELBO for both Gaussian prior and flow prior models, but the gain is relatively smaller for the flow prior model.

Visualization of latent space In Figure 1, we visualize the latent space of the approximate prior, the prior and the delta posterior of the latent variable models using t-SNE (van der Maaten, 2014). It is clear from the figures that the delta posterior of Gauss-base has high overlap with the approximate posterior, while the overlap is relatively low for

| | | NUMBER OF REFINEMENT STEPS | | | |
		0	1	2	4
BLEU	GA-B	22.88	24.36	24.60	24.69
	FL-B	24.57	24.89	24.81	24.92
ELBO	GA-B	-1.11	-0.93	-0.90	-0.89
	FL-B	-1.22	-1.17	-1.16	-1.15

Table 3: Iterative inference with a delta posterior improves BLEU and ELBO for Gauss-base and Flow-base on IWSLT'16 De→En (without distillation).

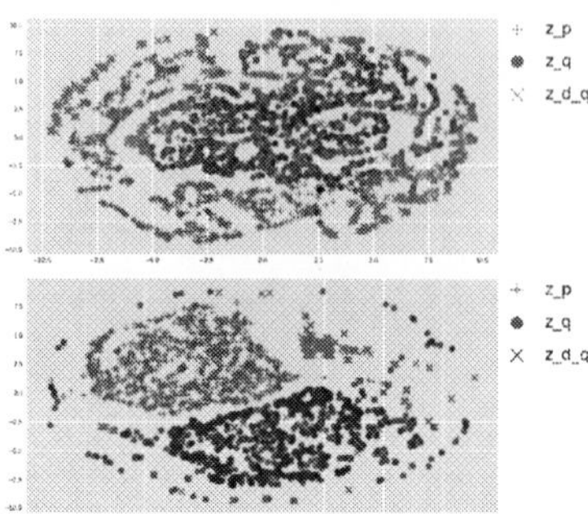

Figure 1: Visualization of the latent space with 1K samples from the prior (green plus sign), the approximate posterior (blue circle) and the delta posterior (red cross) of Gauss-base (top) and Flow-small (bottom) on a IWSLT'16 De→En test example.

Flow-small. We conjecture that while the loss surface of ELBO contains many local optima that we can reach via iterative refinement, not all of them share the support of the approximate posterior density (hence correspond to data). This is particularly pronounced for the flow prior model.

5.4 Generation speed and model size

We compare performance, generation speed and size of various models in Table 4. While autoregressive models offer the best translation quality, inference is inherently sequential and slow. Decoding from non-autoregressive latent variable models is much more efficient, and requires constant time with respect to sequence length given parallel computation. Compared to Transformer-base, Gauss-large with 1 step of iterative inference improves generation speed by 6x, at the cost of 2.6 BLEU. On WMT'14 De→En, the performance degradation is 1.9 BLEU. Flow prior models perform much worse than the Gaussian prior models despite having more parameters and slower generation speed.

$k =$	BLEU					SPEED					SIZE
	0	1	2	4	8	0	1	2	4	8	
TR-S	24.54					2.69					17M
TR-B	28.18					2.58					60M
TR-L	29.39					1.93					208M
GA-B	23.15	24.54	24.87	24.94	24.92	28.77	20.52	16.51	12.00	8.11	75M
GA-L	24.31	25.53	25.69	25.68	25.68	19.83	14.72	10.25	7.88	4.91	95M
FL-B	21.57	21.82	21.79	21.81	21.80	5.82	5.60	4.84	3.60	3.37	75M
FL-L[*]	23.72										258M

Table 4: BLEU score, generation speed and size of various models on WMT'14 En→De test set. We measure generation speed in sentence/s on a single V100 GPU with batch size 1. We perform inference of autoregressive models using beam search with width 4. For latent variable models, we train perform k steps of iterative inference (Shu et al., 2019) (where $k \in \{0, 1, 2, 4, 8\}$) and report results from models trained with distillation. (∗) results are from Ma et al. (2019).

6 Related Work

For sequence generation, the gap between log-likelihood and downstream metric has long been recognized. To address this discrepancy between density estimation and approximate inference (generation), there has largely been two lines of prior work: (1) structured perceptron training for conditional random fields (Lafferty et al., 2001; Collins, 2002; Liang et al., 2006) and (2) empirical risk minimization with approximate inference (Valtchev et al., 1997; Povey and Woodland, 2002; Och, 2003; Qiang Fu and Biing-Hwang Juang, 2007; Stoyanov et al., 2011; Hopkins and May, 2011; Shen et al., 2016). More recent work proposed to train neural sequence models directly on task-specific losses using reinforcement learning (Ranzato et al., 2016; Bahdanau et al., 2017; Jaques et al., 2017) or adversarial training (Goyal et al., 2016).

Despite such a plethora of work in bridging the gap between log-likelihood and the downstream task, the exact correlation between the two has not been established well. Our work investigates the correlation for neural sequence models (autoregressive models and latent variable models) in machine translation. Among autoregressive models for open-domain dialogue, a concurrent work (Adiwardana et al., 2020) found a strong correlation between perplexity and a human evaluation metric that awards sensibleness and specificity. This work confirms a part of our finding that log-likelihood is highly correlated with the downstream metric when we consider models within the same family.

Our work is inspired by recent work on latent variable models for non-autoregressive neural machine translation (Gu et al., 2018; Lee et al., 2018; Kaiser et al., 2018). Specifically, we compare continuous latent variable models with a diagonal Gaussian prior (Shu et al., 2019) and a normalizing flow prior (Ma et al., 2019). We find that while having an expressive prior is beneficial for density estimation, a simple prior delivers better generation quality while being smaller and faster.

7 Conclusion

In this work, we investigate the correlation between log-likelihood and the downstream evaluation metric for machine translation. We train several autoregressive models and latent variable models on five language pairs from three machine translation datasets (WMT'14 En↔De, WMT'16 En↔Ro and IWSLT'16 De→En), and find that the correlation between log-likelihood and BLEU changes drastically depending on the range of model families being compared: Among the models within the same family, log-likelihood is highly correlated with BLEU. Between models of different families, however, we observe no correlation: the flow prior model gives higher held-out log-likelihood but similar or worse BLEU score than the Gaussian prior model. Furthermore, autoregressive models give the highest BLEU scores overall but the latent variable model with a flow prior gives the highest test log-likelihoods on all datasets.

In the future, we will investigate the factors behind this discrepancy. One possibility is the inherent difficulty of inference for latent variable models, which might be resolved by designing better inference algorithms. We will also explore if the discrepancy is mainly caused by the difference in the decoding distribution (autoregressive vs. factorized) or the training objective (maximum likelihood vs. ELBO).

Acknowledgements

We thank our colleagues at the Google Translate and Brain teams, particularly Durk Kingma, Yu Zhang, Yuan Cao and Julia Kreutzer for their feedback on the draft. JL thanks Chunting Zhou, Manoj Kumar and William Chan for helpful discussions.

KC is supported by Samsung Advanced Institute of Technology (Next Generation Deep Learning: from pattern recognition to AI), Samsung Research (Improving Deep Learning using Latent Structure) and NSF Award 1922658 NRT-HDR: FUTURE Foundations, Translation, and Responsibility for Data Science. KC thanks CIFAR, eBay, Naver and NVIDIA for their support.

References

Daniel Adiwardana, Minh-Thang Luong, David R. So, Jamie Hall, Noah Fiedel, Romal Thoppilan, Zi Yang, Apoorv Kulshreshtha, Gaurav Nemade, Yifeng Lu, and Quoc V. Le. 2020. Towards a human-like open-domain chatbot. *arXiv preprint arxiv:2001.09977*.

Dzmitry Bahdanau, Philemon Brakel, Kelvin Xu, Anirudh Goyal, Ryan Lowe, Joelle Pineau, Aaron C. Courville, and Yoshua Bengio. 2017. An actor-critic algorithm for sequence prediction. In *5th International Conference on Learning Representations, ICLR*.

Dzmitry Bahdanau, Kyunghyun Cho, and Yoshua Bengio. 2015. Neural machine translation by jointly learning to align and translate. In *3rd International Conference on Learning Representations, ICLR*.

Satanjeev Banerjee and Alon Lavie. 2005. Meteor: An automatic metric for mt evaluation with improved correlation with human judgments.

Matthias Bauer and Andriy Mnih. 2019. Resampled priors for variational autoencoders. In *The 22nd International Conference on Artificial Intelligence and Statistics, AISTATS*, pages 66–75.

Samuel R. Bowman, Luke Vilnis, Oriol Vinyals, Andrew M. Dai, Rafal Józefowicz, and Samy Bengio. 2016. Generating sentences from a continuous space. In *Proceedings of the 20th SIGNLL Conference on Computational Natural Language Learning, CoNLL*, pages 10–21.

Junyoung Chung, Çaglar Gülçehre, KyungHyun Cho, and Yoshua Bengio. 2014. Empirical evaluation of gated recurrent neural networks on sequence modeling. *arXiv preprint arxiv:1412.3555*.

Michael Collins. 2002. Discriminative training methods for hidden Markov models: Theory and experiments with perceptron algorithms. In *Proceedings of the 2002 Conference on Empirical Methods in Natural Language Processing (EMNLP 2002)*, pages 1–8. Association for Computational Linguistics.

Laurent Dinh, Jascha Sohl-Dickstein, and Samy Bengio. 2017. Density estimation using real NVP. In *International Conference on Learning Representations*.

Jeffrey L. Elman. 1990. Finding structure in time. *Cognitive Science*, 14(2):179–211.

Jonas Gehring, Michael Auli, David Grangier, Denis Yarats, and Yann N. Dauphin. 2017. Convolutional sequence to sequence learning. In *Proceedings of the 34th International Conference on Machine Learning, ICML*, pages 1243–1252.

Anirudh Goyal, Alex Lamb, Ying Zhang, Saizheng Zhang, Aaron C. Courville, and Yoshua Bengio. 2016. Professor forcing: A new algorithm for training recurrent networks. In *Advances in Neural Information Processing Systems 29: Annual Conference on Neural Information Processing Systems*, pages 4601–4609.

Jiatao Gu, James Bradbury, Caiming Xiong, Victor O. K. Li, and Richard Socher. 2018. Non-autoregressive neural machine translation. In *6th International Conference on Learning Representations, ICLR*.

Irina Higgins, Loïc Matthey, Arka Pal, Christopher Burgess, Xavier Glorot, Matthew Botvinick, Shakir Mohamed, and Alexander Lerchner. 2017. beta-vae: Learning basic visual concepts with a constrained variational framework. In *5th International Conference on Learning Representations, ICLR*.

Sepp Hochreiter and Jürgen Schmidhuber. 1997. Long short-term memory. *Neural Computation*, 9(8):1735–1780.

Matthew D Hoffman and Matthew J Johnson. 2016. Elbo surgery: yet another way to carve up the variational evidence lower bound. *Workshop in Advances in Approximate Bayesian Inference, Neurips*.

Mark Hopkins and Jonathan May. 2011. Tuning as ranking. In *Proceedings of the 2011 Conference on Empirical Methods in Natural Language Processing*, pages 1352–1362. Association for Computational Linguistics.

Natasha Jaques, Shixiang Gu, Dzmitry Bahdanau, José Miguel Hernández-Lobato, Richard E. Turner, and Douglas Eck. 2017. Sequence tutor: Conservative fine-tuning of sequence generation models with kl-control. In *Proceedings of the 34th International Conference on Machine Learning, ICML*, pages 1645–1654.

Lukasz Kaiser, Samy Bengio, Aurko Roy, Ashish Vaswani, Niki Parmar, Jakob Uszkoreit, and Noam Shazeer. 2018. Fast decoding in sequence models using discrete latent variables. In *Proceedings of the*

35th International Conference on Machine Learning, ICML, pages 2395–2404.

Yoon Kim and Alexander M. Rush. 2016. Sequence-level knowledge distillation. In *Proceedings of the 2016 Conference on Empirical Methods in Natural Language Processing, EMNLP*, pages 1317–1327.

Diederik P. Kingma and Jimmy Ba. 2015. Adam: A method for stochastic optimization. In *3rd International Conference on Learning Representations, ICLR*.

Diederik P. Kingma and Prafulla Dhariwal. 2018. Glow: Generative flow with invertible 1x1 convolutions. In *Advances in Neural Information Processing Systems 31: Annual Conference on Neural Information Processing Systems*, pages 10236–10245.

Diederik P. Kingma and Max Welling. 2014. Auto-encoding variational bayes. In *2nd International Conference on Learning Representations, ICLR 2014, Banff, AB, Canada, April 14-16, 2014, Conference Track Proceedings*.

John D. Lafferty, Andrew McCallum, and Fernando C. N. Pereira. 2001. Conditional random fields: Probabilistic models for segmenting and labeling sequence data. In *Proceedings of the Eighteenth International Conference on Machine Learning (ICML 2001)*, pages 282–289.

Jason Lee, Elman Mansimov, and Kyunghyun Cho. 2018. Deterministic non-autoregressive neural sequence modeling by iterative refinement. In *Proceedings of the 2018 Conference on Empirical Methods in Natural Language Processing*, pages 1173–1182.

Percy Liang, Alexandre Bouchard-Côté, Dan Klein, and Ben Taskar. 2006. An end-to-end discriminative approach to machine translation. In *Proceedings of the 21st International Conference on Computational Linguistics and 44th Annual Meeting of the Association for Computational Linguistics*, pages 761–768.

Xuezhe Ma, Chunting Zhou, Xian Li, Graham Neubig, and Eduard H. Hovy. 2019. Flowseq: Non-autoregressive conditional sequence generation with generative flow. *arXiv preprint arxiv:1909.02480*.

Laurens van der Maaten. 2014. Accelerating t-sne using tree-based algorithms. *J. Mach. Learn. Res.*, 15(1):3221–3245.

Elman Mansimov, Omar Mahmood, Seokho Kang, and Kyunghyun Cho. 2019. Molecular geometry prediction using a deep generative graph neural network. *arXiv preprint arxiv:1904.00314*.

Franz Josef Och. 2003. Minimum error rate training in statistical machine translation. In *Proceedings of the 41st Annual Meeting of the Association for Computational Linguistics*, pages 160–167.

Aäron van den Oord, Sander Dieleman, Heiga Zen, Karen Simonyan, Oriol Vinyals, Alex Graves, Nal Kalchbrenner, Andrew W. Senior, and Koray Kavukcuoglu. 2016. Wavenet: A generative model for raw audio. In *The 9th ISCA Speech Synthesis Workshop*, page 125.

Aäron van den Oord, Yazhe Li, Igor Babuschkin, Karen Simonyan, Oriol Vinyals, Koray Kavukcuoglu, George van den Driessche, Edward Lockhart, Luis C. Cobo, Florian Stimberg, Norman Casagrande, Dominik Grewe, Seb Noury, Sander Dieleman, Erich Elsen, Nal Kalchbrenner, Heiga Zen, Alex Graves, Helen King, Tom Walters, Dan Belov, and Demis Hassabis. 2018. Parallel wavenet: Fast high-fidelity speech synthesis. In *Proceedings of the 35th International Conference on Machine Learning, ICML*, pages 3915–3923.

George Papamakarios, Eric T. Nalisnick, Danilo Jimenez Rezende, Shakir Mohamed, and Balaji Lakshminarayanan. 2019. Normalizing flows for probabilistic modeling and inference. *arXiv preprint arxiv:1912.02762*.

Kishore Papineni, Salim Roukos, Todd Ward, and Wei-Jing Zhu. 2002. Bleu: a method for automatic evaluation of machine translation. In *Proceedings of the 40th Annual Meeting of the Association for Computational Linguistics*, pages 311–318.

D. Povey and P. C. Woodland. 2002. Minimum phone error and i-smoothing for improved discriminative training. In *2002 IEEE International Conference on Acoustics, Speech, and Signal Processing*, volume 1, pages I–105–I–108.

Qiang Fu and Biing-Hwang Juang. 2007. Automatic speech recognition based on weighted minimum classification error (w-mce) training method. In *2007 IEEE Workshop on Automatic Speech Recognition Understanding (ASRU)*, pages 278–283.

Marc'Aurelio Ranzato, Sumit Chopra, Michael Auli, and Wojciech Zaremba. 2016. Sequence level training with recurrent neural networks. In *4th International Conference on Learning Representations, ICLR*.

Danilo Jimenez Rezende and Shakir Mohamed. 2015. Variational inference with normalizing flows. In *Proceedings of the 32nd International Conference on Machine Learning*, pages 1530–1538.

Mihaela Rosca, Balaji Lakshminarayanan, and Shakir Mohamed. 2018. Distribution matching in variational inference. *arXiv preprint arxiv:1802.06847*.

Tim Salimans and Diederik P. Kingma. 2016. Weight normalization: A simple reparameterization to accelerate training of deep neural networks. In *Advances in Neural Information Processing Systems 29*, page 901.

Mike Schuster and Kaisuke Nakajima. 2012. Japanese and korean voice search. In *2012 IEEE International Conference on Acoustics, Speech and Signal Processing, ICASSP*, pages 5149–5152.

Rico Sennrich, Barry Haddow, and Alexandra Birch. 2016. Edinburgh neural machine translation systems for WMT 16. In *Proceedings of the First Conference on Machine Translation, WMT*, pages 371–376.

Shiqi Shen, Yong Cheng, Zhongjun He, Wei He, Hua Wu, Maosong Sun, and Yang Liu. 2016. Minimum risk training for neural machine translation. In *Proceedings of the 54th Annual Meeting of the Association for Computational Linguistics (Volume 1: Long Papers)*, pages 1683–1692.

Raphael Shu, Jason Lee, Hideki Nakayama, and Kyunghyun Cho. 2019. Latent-variable non-autoregressive neural machine translation with deterministic inference using a delta posterior. *arXiv preprint arxiv:1908.07181*.

Veselin Stoyanov, Alexander Ropson, and Jason Eisner. 2011. Empirical risk minimization of graphical model parameters given approximate inference, decoding, and model structure. In *Proceedings of the Fourteenth International Conference on Artificial Intelligence and Statistics, AISTATS*, pages 725–733.

Ilya Sutskever, Oriol Vinyals, and Quoc V. Le. 2014. Sequence to sequence learning with neural networks. In *Advances in Neural Information Processing Systems 27: Annual Conference on Neural Information Processing Systems*, pages 3104–3112.

E. G. Tabak and Cristina V. Turner. 2013. A family of nonparametric density estimation algorithms. *Communications on Pure and Applied Mathematics*, 66(2):145–164.

Jakub M. Tomczak and Max Welling. 2018. VAE with a vampprior. In *International Conference on Artificial Intelligence and Statistics, AISTATS*, pages 1214–1223.

V. Valtchev, J. J. Odell, P. C. Woodland, and S. J. Young. 1997. Mmie training of large vocabulary recognition systems. *Speech Commun.*, 22(4):303–314.

Ashish Vaswani, Noam Shazeer, Niki Parmar, Jakob Uszkoreit, Llion Jones, Aidan N. Gomez, Lukasz Kaiser, and Illia Polosukhin. 2017. Attention is all you need. In *Advances in Neural Information Processing Systems 30: Annual Conference on Neural Information Processing Systems*, pages 5998–6008.

Oriol Vinyals and Quoc V. Le. 2015. A neural conversational model. *arXiv preprint arxiv:1506.05869*.

Oriol Vinyals, Alexander Toshev, Samy Bengio, and Dumitru Erhan. 2015. Show and tell: A neural image caption generator. In *IEEE Conference on Computer Vision and Pattern Recognition, CVPR*, pages 3156–3164.

Martin J. Wainwright and Michael I. Jordan. 2008. Graphical models, exponential families, and variational inference. *Foundations and Trends in Machine Learning*, 1(1-2):1–305.

Chunting Zhou, Graham Neubig, and Jiatao Gu. 2019. Understanding knowledge distillation in non-autoregressive machine translation. *arXiv preprint arxiv:1911.02727*.

Log-Linear Reformulation of the Noisy Channel Model for Document-Level Neural Machine Translation

Sébastien Jean
New York University
`sj2233@nyu.edu`

Kyunghyun Cho
New York University
`kyunghyun.cho@nyu.edu`

Abstract

We seek to maximally use various data sources, such as parallel and monolingual data, to build an effective and efficient document-level translation system. In particular, we start by considering a noisy channel approach (Yu et al., 2020) that combines a target-to-source translation model and a language model. By applying Bayes' rule strategically, we reformulate this approach as a log-linear combination of translation, sentence-level and document-level language model probabilities. In addition to using static coefficients for each term, this formulation alternatively allows for the learning of dynamic per-token weights to more finely control the impact of the language models. Using both static or dynamic coefficients leads to improvements over a context-agnostic baseline and a context-aware concatenation model.

1 Introduction

Neural machine translation (NMT) (Sutskever et al., 2014; Bahdanau et al., 2015) has been reported to reach near human-level performance on sentence-by-sentence translation (Läubli et al., 2018). Going beyond sentence-level, document-level NMT aims to translate sentences by taking into account neighboring source or target sentences in order to produce a more cohesive output (Jean et al., 2017; Wang et al., 2017; Maruf et al., 2019). These approaches often train new models from scratch using parallel data.

In this paper, in a similar spirit to Voita et al. (2019a); Yu et al. (2020), we seek a document-level approach that maximally uses various available corpora, such as parallel and monolingual data, leveraging models trained at the sentence and document levels, while also striving for computational efficiency. We start from the noisy channel model (Yu et al., 2020) which combines a target-to-source

translation model and a document-level language model. By applying Bayes' rule, we reformulate this approach into a log-linear model. It consists of a translation model, as well as sentence and document-level language models. This reformulation admits an auto-regressive expression of token-by-token target document probabilities, facilitating the use of existing inference algorithms such as beam search. In this log-linear model, there are coefficients modulating the impact of the language models. We first consider static coefficients and, for more fine-grained control, we train a *merging module* that dynamically adjusts the LM weights.

With either static or dynamic coefficients, we observe improvements over a context-agnostic baseline, as well as a context-aware concatenation model (Tiedemann and Scherrer, 2017). Similarly to the noisy channel model, our approach reuses off-the-shelf models and benefits from future translation or language modelling improvements.

2 Log-linear reformulation of the noisy channel model

Given the availability of various heterogeneous data sources that could be used for document-level translation, we seek a strategy to maximally use them. These sources include parallel data, at either the sentence or document level, as well as more broadly available monolingual data.

As the starting point, we consider the noisy channel approach proposed by Yu et al. (2020). Given a source document $(X^{(1)}, \ldots, X^{(N)})$ and its translation $(Y^{(1)}, \ldots, Y^{(N)})$, they assume a generation process where target sentences are produced from left to right, and where each source sentence is translated only from the corresponding target sentence. Under these assumptions, the probability of a source-target document pair is given by

95

Proceedings of 4th Workshop on Structured Prediction for NLP, pages 95–101
November 20, 2020. ©2020 Association for Computational Linguistics

$$P(X^{(1)},\ldots,X^{(N)},Y^{(1)},\ldots,Y^{(N)})$$
$$= \prod_{n=1}^{N} P(X^{(n)}|Y^{(n)})P(Y^{(n)}|Y^{(<n)})$$

As such, the conditional probability of the target document given the source is expressed by

$$P(Y^{(1)},\ldots,Y^{(N)}|X^{(1)},\ldots,X^{(N)})$$
$$\propto \prod_{n=1}^{N} P(X^{(n)}|Y^{(n)})P(Y^{(n)}|Y^{(<n)})$$
$$= \prod_{n=1}^{N} \underbrace{P(Y^{(n)}|X^{(n)})\frac{P(Y^{(n)}|Y^{(<n)})}{P(Y^{(n)})}}_{\propto P(Y^{(n)}|X^{(n)},Y^{(<n)})}.$$

We therefore generate context-aware translations by combining a translation model (TM) $P(Y^{(n)}|X^{(n)})$ with both sentence-level $P(Y^{(n)})$ and document-level $P(Y^{(n)}|Y^{(<n)})$ language models (LM). To calibrate the generation process, we introduce coefficients $\alpha \in \mathbb{R}$ and $\beta \in \mathbb{R}$ to control the contribution of each language model, which are tuned on a validation set:

$$\log P(Y^{(n)}|X^{(n)},Y^{(<n)}) \qquad (1)$$
$$= \sum_{i=1}^{L_n} \left[\log P(y_i^{(n)}|y_{<i}^{(n)},X^{(n)}) \right.$$
$$+ \alpha \log P(y_i^{(n)}|y_{<i}^{(n)},Y^{(<n)})$$
$$\left. - \beta \log P(y_i^{(n)}|y_{<i}^{(n)}) + C_i^{(n)} \right],$$

where $C_i^{(n)}$ is a normalization constant and L_n is the target sentence length.

Similarly to the noisy channel approach (Yu et al., 2020), we use off-the-shelf translation and language models. As such, future improvements to either translation or language modelling can easily be leveraged. Our reformulation however admits a more efficient search procedure, unlike that by Yu et al. (2020).

2.1 Model parameterization

The translation model is implemented as any auto-regressive neural translation model. We use the Transformer encoder-decoder architecture (Vaswani et al., 2017). Given a source sentence

$x_1,\ldots,x_L$, each token and its position are projected into a continuous embedding $s_{0,1},\ldots,s_{0,L}$. These representations are passed through a sequence of M encoder layers that each comprise self-attention and feed-forward modules, resulting in the final representations $s_{M,1},\ldots,s_{M,L}$. The decoder updates target embeddings through similar layers, which additionally attend to the encoder output, to obtain final hidden states $t_{M,1},\ldots,t_{M,L}$. Token probabilities may be obtained by projecting these representations and applying softmax normalization.

Language models are implemented as Transformer decoders without cross-attention. We use a single language model trained on sequences of consecutive sentences to obtain both sentence-level and document-level probabilities.

3 Dynamic merging

As extra-sentential information is not uniformly useful for translation, we propose dynamic coefficients for the different models by generalizing Eq. 1:

$$\mathcal{L} = -\sum_{n=1}^{N}\sum_{i=1}^{L_n} \left[\log P(y_i^{(n)}|y_{<i}^{(n)},X^{(n)}) \right.$$
$$+ \alpha_i^{(n)} \log P(y_i^{(n)}|y_{<i}^{(n)},Y^{(<n)}) \qquad (2)$$
$$\left. - \beta_i^{(n)} \log P(y_i^{(n)}|y_{<i}^{(n)}) + C_i^{(n)} \right].$$

With the translation and language models kept fixed, the coefficients $\alpha_i^{(n)}$ and $\beta_i^{(n)}$ are computed by an auxiliary neural network which uses $Y^{(<n)}$, $Y^{(n)}$ and $X^{(n)}$. We call this network a *merging module* and implement it as a feed-forward network on top of the translation and language models.

3.1 Dynamic coefficient computation

For every token, the corresponding last hidden states of the translation model, sentence-level LM and document-level LM are concatenated. Each non-final layer ($k = 1,\ldots,K-1$) is a feed-forward block

$$h_k = \mathrm{LN}(h_{k-1}+\mathrm{drop}(W_{k,2}(\mathrm{ReLU}(W_{k,1}h_{k-1})))),$$

where LN and drop respectively denote layer normalization and dropout (Ba et al., 2016; Srivastava et al., 2014). The final layer is similar, but there is no residual connection (and no dropout) as the final linear transformation projects the result to 2 dimensions, so that $(\alpha, \beta) = W_{K,2}(\text{ReLU}(W_{K,1}h_{K-1}))$.

4 Experiments

4.1 Settings

Data We run experiments on English-Russian data from OpenSubtitles (Lison et al., 2018), which was used in many recent studies on document-level translation (Voita et al., 2019b,a; Mansimov et al., 2020; Jean et al., 2019). Language models are trained on approximately 30M sequences of 4 consecutive sentences (Voita et al., 2019a).The parallel data was originally preprocessed by Voita et al. (2019b), yielding 6M examples. For 1.5M of these data points, the 3 preceding source and target sentences are provided. We use this subset to train the *merging module* that predicts the per-token coefficients for each model. We uniformly set the number of contextual sentences between 1 and 3 to match the test condition.

We apply byte-pair encoding (BPE) (Sennrich et al., 2016), with a total of 32k merge operations, separately on each language pair, as Russian and English use different sets of alphabets.

Models Translation models are standard Transformers in their base configuration (Vaswani et al., 2017). The language model is implemented as a Transformer decoder of the same size, except for a smaller feed-forward dimension $d_{ff} = 1024$. The *merging module* has 2 layers, with $d_{ff} = 1536$.

Learning The translation and language models, as well as the *merging module*, are trained with label smoothing set to 10%. The TM is trained with 20% dropout, while it is set to 10% for the LMs and *merging module*.

Evaluation Translation quality is evaluated with tokenized BLEU on lowercased data, using beam search with its width set to 5. We average 5 checkpoints for the translation models. Sentences are generated from left to right, and the beam is reset for every sentence.

4.2 Results

With our approach, using static coefficients, we reach a BLEU score of 34.31, which is a modest gain of 0.21 BLEU over the baseline and 0.8 over a model trained on concatenated sentences (Table 1). By optimizing dynamic coefficients, we reach a similar score of 34.22.

	BLEU
Baseline	34.10
Concat	33.51
Static coeffs.	34.31
Dynamic coeffs.	34.22
CADec	33.86
DocRepair	**34.60**

Table 1: Test set BLEU scores (beam width 5, all 4 sentences concatenated). CADec and DocRepair results from (Voita et al., 2019a).

β \\ α	0	0.2	0.4	0.6
0	31.5	31.0	29.3	26.9
0.2	30.7	**31.7**	31.2	29.5
0.4	23.3	30.1	31.6	31.1
0.6	14.3	21.9	26.9	30.8

Table 2: Greedy validation BLEU (last sentence only) for different static values of α and β. Both LMs are critical to the approach.

DocRepair (Voita et al., 2019a), a two-pass method that post-edits the output of a baseline system, obtains a slightly higher BLEU score of 34.60. Both approaches could be combined by instead post-editing the output of our models, which we leave for future investigation.

BLEU-NLL correlation We observe limited correlation between BLEU and reference NLL (Och, 2003; Lee et al., 2020). On the validation set, the per-token baseline loss (with label smoothing) is 13.09. Using static coefficients, it actually increases to 13.23, while it decreases to 12.86 with dynamic coefficients.

Contribution of each language model (static) Table 2 presents the BLEU scores on the validation set using greedy validation for different static values of α and β. Only using the document-level LM ($\alpha > 0, \beta = 0$) leads to worse performance than the baseline. It is critical to counter-balance the document-level LM with the sentence-level LM.

Dynamic coefficients The dynamic coefficients α and β predicted by the *merging module* are highly correlated (Figure 1 (left)). As a conjecture, this high correlation may be explained by the use of the same language model to obtain both sentence and document-level scores.

Figure 1 (right) shows the average value of the

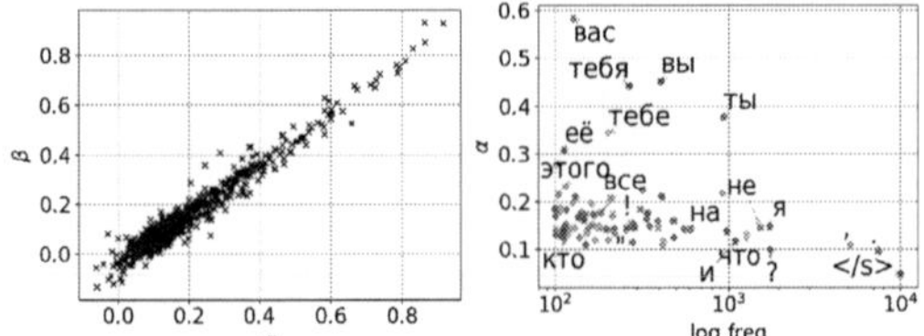

Figure 1: Scatter plot of α and β for tokens appearing at least 100 times over the validation set (left). Average dynamic coefficient α for frequent words over the validation set (right).

	D	LC	I	VP
LM difference	95.5	91.7	71.8	85.6
Baseline	50.0	45.9	53.4	26.6
Concat	84.9	47.7	84.2	78.6
Static	66.6	65.5	56.6	40.2
Dynamic	74.2	51.1	57.8	56.8
CADec	81.6	58.1	72.2	**80.0**
DocRepair	**91.8**	**80.6**	**86.4**	75.2

Table 3: Deixis (D), lexical cohesion (LC), inflection ellipsis (I) and VP ellipsis (VP) accuracy (%). Best scores from translation models only are highlighted.

dynamic coefficient α for frequent words within the validation reference set. In particular, Ты and Вы, which are translations of *you* that depend on plurality and formality, are assigned high weights.

Challenge sets While static and dynamic coefficients lead to similar BLEU, using dynamic coefficients often results in better performance on multiple-choice scoring-based challenge sets targeting specific translation phenomena (Table 3) (Voita et al., 2019b).[1] We conjecture this likely happens because dynamic coefficients can more narrowly focus on particular subsets of target sentences that benefit from document-level context.

5 Related work

Document-level NMT Neural machine translation may be extended to include extra-sentential information in many ways, as surveyed by Maruf et al. (2019). The model architecture may be modified, for example by encoding previous source sentences or generated translations and attending to them (Jean et al., 2017; Wang et al., 2017; Voita et al., 2018; Zhang et al., 2018; Miculicich et al., 2018; Maruf and Haffari, 2018; Tu

---

[1]Using the difference of language models scores gives higher accuracy, but they cannot be used in isolation to generate relevant translations.

et al., 2018). Otherwise, by simply concatenating multiple sentences together as input, existing model architectures may be used without additional changes (Tiedemann and Scherrer, 2017; Junczys-Dowmunt, 2019).

Voita et al. (2019b) and Voita et al. (2019a) propose refining the output of a context-agnostic baseline, using a new model trained from either document-level parallel data or from round-trip translated monolingual data. The noisy channel approach similarly uses large-scale monolingual data (Yu et al., 2020) to refine translations, while using arbitrary, and potentially pre-trained, translation or language models, as discussed in Sec. 2.

Our approach shares many similarities with the above, but admits a more straightforward generation process. If desired, we could still rerank the beam search output with a channel model, which might improve general translation quality for reasons not necessarily related to context.

Language modelling Language model probabilities have been used to rerank NMT hypotheses (see, e.g., Stahlberg et al., 2019). Additionally, direct integration of a language model into a translation model, using various fusion techniques, improves generation quality and admits the use of single-pass search algorithms (Gulcehre et al., 2015). To promote diversity in dialogue systems, model scores may be adjusted by negatively weighing a language model (Li et al., 2015).

6 Conclusion

In this paper, we set to use heterogeneous data sources in an effective and efficient manner for document-level NMT. We reformulated the noisy channel approach (Yu et al., 2020) and end up with a left-to-right log-linear model combining a baseline machine translation model with sentence-level and document-level language models.

To modulate the impact of the language models, we dynamically adapt their coefficients at each time step with a *merging module* taking into account the translation and language models. We observe improvements over a context-agnostic baseline and using dynamic coefficients helps capture document-level linguistic phenomena better.

Future directions include combining our approach with MT models trained on back-translated documents, exploring its applicability to other modalities such as vision and speech, and considering deeper fusion of the models.

Acknowledgements

This work was supported by Samsung Advanced Institute of Technology (Next Generation Deep Learning: from pattern recognition to AI), Samsung Research (Improving Deep Learning using Latent Structure) and NSF Award 1922658 NRT-HDR: FUTURE Foundations, Translation, and Responsibility for Data Science.

References

Jimmy Lei Ba, Jamie Ryan Kiros, and Geoffrey E Hinton. 2016. Layer normalization. *arXiv preprint arXiv:1607.06450*.

Dzmitry Bahdanau, Kyunghyun Cho, and Yoshua Bengio. 2015. Neural machine translation by jointly learning to align and translate. In *International Conference on Learning Representations (ICLR)*.

Caglar Gulcehre, Orhan Firat, Kelvin Xu, Kyunghyun Cho, Loic Barrault, Huei-Chi Lin, Fethi Bougares, Holger Schwenk, and Yoshua Bengio. 2015. On using monolingual corpora in neural machine translation. *arXiv preprint arXiv:1503.03535*.

Sébastien Jean, Ankur Bapna, and Orhan Firat. 2019. Fill in the blanks: Imputing missing sentences for larger-context neural machine translation. *arXiv preprint arXiv:1910.14075*.

Sebastien Jean, Stanislas Lauly, Orhan Firat, and Kyunghyun Cho. 2017. Does neural machine translation benefit from larger context? *arXiv preprint arXiv:1704.05135*.

Marcin Junczys-Dowmunt. 2019. Microsoft translator at wmt 2019: Towards large-scale document-level neural machine translation. In *Proceedings of the Fourth Conference on Machine Translation (Volume 2: Shared Task Papers, Day 1)*, pages 225–233, Florence, Italy. Association for Computational Linguistics.

Samuel Läubli, Rico Sennrich, and Martin Volk. 2018. Has machine translation achieved human parity? a case for document-level evaluation. In *Proceedings of the 2018 Conference on Empirical Methods in Natural Language Processing*, pages 4791–4796.

Jason Lee, Dustin Tran, Orhan Firat, and Kyunghyun Cho. 2020. On the discrepancy between density estimation and sequence generation. *arXiv preprint arXiv:2002.07233*.

Jiwei Li, Michel Galley, Chris Brockett, Jianfeng Gao, and Bill Dolan. 2015. A diversity-promoting objective function for neural conversation models. *arXiv preprint arXiv:1510.03055*.

Pierre Lison, Jörg Tiedemann, and Milen Kouylekov. 2018. Opensubtitles2018: Statistical rescoring of sentence alignments in large, noisy parallel corpora. In *Proceedings of the Eleventh International Conference on Language Resources and Evaluation (LREC-2018)*.

Elman Mansimov, Gábor Melis, and Lei Yu. 2020. Capturing document context inside sentence-level neural machine translation models with self-training. *arXiv preprint arXiv:2003.05259*.

Sameen Maruf and Gholamreza Haffari. 2018. Document context neural machine translation with memory networks. In *Proceedings of the 56th Annual Meeting of the Association for Computational Linguistics (Volume 1: Long Papers)*, volume 1, pages 1275–1284.

Sameen Maruf, Fahimeh Saleh, and Gholamreza Haffari. 2019. A survey on document-level machine translation: Methods and evaluation. *arXiv preprint arXiv:1912.08494*.

Lesly Miculicich, Dhananjay Ram, Nikolaos Pappas, and James Henderson. 2018. Document-level neural machine translation with hierarchical attention networks. In *Proceedings of the 2018 Conference on Empirical Methods in Natural Language Processing*, pages 2947–2954.

Franz Josef Och. 2003. Minimum error rate training in statistical machine translation. In *Proceedings of the 41st Annual Meeting on Association for Computational Linguistics-Volume 1*, pages 160–167. Association for Computational Linguistics.

Rico Sennrich, Barry Haddow, and Alexandra Birch. 2016. Neural machine translation of rare words with subword units. In *Proceedings of the 54th Annual Meeting of the Association for Computational Linguistics (Volume 1: Long Papers)*, volume 1, pages 1715–1725.

Nitish Srivastava, Geoffrey Hinton, Alex Krizhevsky, Ilya Sutskever, and Ruslan Salakhutdinov. 2014. Dropout: a simple way to prevent neural networks from overfitting. *The journal of machine learning research*, 15(1):1929–1958.

Felix Stahlberg, Danielle Saunders, Adrià de Gispert, and Bill Byrne. 2019. Cued@ wmt19: Ewc&lms. In *Proceedings of the Fourth Conference on Machine Translation (Volume 2: Shared Task Papers, Day 1)*, pages 364–373.

Ilya Sutskever, Oriol Vinyals, and Quoc V Le. 2014. Sequence to sequence learning with neural networks. *NIPS*.

Jörg Tiedemann and Yves Scherrer. 2017. Neural machine translation with extended context. In *Proceedings of the Third Workshop on Discourse in Machine Translation*, pages 82–92.

Zhaopeng Tu, Yang Liu, Shuming Shi, and Tong Zhang. 2018. Learning to remember translation history with a continuous cache. *Transactions of the Association of Computational Linguistics*, 6:407–420.

Ashish Vaswani, Noam Shazeer, Niki Parmar, Jakob Uszkoreit, Llion Jones, Aidan N Gomez, Łukasz Kaiser, and Illia Polosukhin. 2017. Attention is all you need. In *Advances in Neural Information Processing Systems*, pages 5998–6008.

Elena Voita, Rico Sennrich, and Ivan Titov. 2019a. Context-aware monolingual repair for neural machine translation. In *Proceedings of the 2019 Conference on Empirical Methods in Natural Language Processing and 9th International Joint Conference on Natural Language Processing*, Hong Kong, China. Association for Computational Linguistics.

Elena Voita, Rico Sennrich, and Ivan Titov. 2019b. When a Good Translation is Wrong in Context: Context-Aware Machine Translation Improves on Deixis, Ellipsis, and Lexical Cohesion. In *Proceedings of the 57th Annual Meeting of the Association for Computational Linguistics*, Florence, Italy. Association for Computational Linguistics.

Elena Voita, Pavel Serdyukov, Rico Sennrich, and Ivan Titov. 2018. Context-aware neural machine translation learns anaphora resolution. In *Proceedings of the 56th Annual Meeting of the Association for Computational Linguistics (Volume 1: Long Papers)*, volume 1, pages 1264–1274.

Longyue Wang, Zhaopeng Tu, Andy Way, and Qun Liu. 2017. Exploiting cross-sentence context for neural machine translation. In *Proceedings of the 2017 Conference on Empirical Methods in Natural Language Processing*, pages 2826–2831.

Lei Yu, Laurent Sartran, Wojciech Stokowiec, Wang Ling, Lingpeng Kong, Phil Blunsom, and Chris Dyer. 2020. Putting machine translation in context with the noisy channel model. *TACL*.

Jiacheng Zhang, Huanbo Luan, Maosong Sun, Feifei Zhai, Jingfang Xu, Min Zhang, and Yang Liu. 2018. Improving the transformer translation model with document-level context. In *Proceedings of the 2018 Conference on Empirical Methods in Natural Language Processing*, pages 533–542.

A Expanded derivation

The conditional probability of the target document given the source is expressed by

$$P(Y^{(1)}, ...Y^{(N)} | X^{(1)}, ..., X^{(N)}) =$$
$$\frac{\prod_{n=1}^{N} P(X^{(n)}|Y^{(n)}) P(Y^{(n)}|Y^{(<n)})}{P(X^{(1)}, ..., X^{(N)})} =$$
$$\frac{\prod_{n=1}^{N} \frac{P(Y^{(n)}|X^{(n)}) P(X^{(n)})}{P(Y^{(n)})} P(Y^{(n)}|Y^{(<n)})}{P(X^{(1)}, ..., X^{(N)})} =$$
$$C(X) \prod_{n=1}^{N} P(Y^{(n)}|X^{(n)}) \frac{P(Y^{(n)}|Y^{(<n)})}{P(Y^{(n)})},$$

where $C(X) = \frac{\prod_{n=1}^{N} P(X^{(n)})}{P(X^{(1)}, ..., X^{(N)})}$ does not affect the optimal target sentences given a source document.

B Hyper-parameters

Translation model We validate models with greedy search. We use the base transformer configuration (Vaswani et al., 2017). We use effective batches of approximately 31500 source tokens and optimize models with Adam (Kingma and Ba, 2014). We follow a learning rate schedule similar to Vaswani et al. (2017), with 16,000 warmup steps and scaled by 4. We experimented with 10% and 20% dropout, obtaining higher validation BLEU with the latter. We use pre-LN transformer layers (Xiong et al., 2020).

Language model We use a similar configuration to the translation model, except with 64,000 warmup steps and post-LN transformer layers (Xiong et al., 2020).

Static coefficients We evaluate greedy validation BLEU with a grid search over $(\alpha, \beta) \in \{0, 0.1, \ldots, 1\} \times \{0, 0.1, \ldots, 1\}$.

Dynamic coefficients We varied the number of layers between 1 and 3. We also considered adding cross-attention within the *merging module*, but we did not observe improvements in preliminary experiments.

C Label smoothing

If we train the *merging module* without label smoothing (instead of 10%), greedy validation BLEU drops by approximately 1 BLEU point. We also observe much higher variability in the coefficients, which may be caused by the unbounded optimal value of α when a target token is the most likely according to the document-level LM.

D Challenge set validation scores

	D	LC
LM difference	95.4	92.6
Baseline	50.0	46.2
Concat	86.6	47.8
Static	65.6	67.8
Dynamic	74.6	50.4

Table 1: Deixis (D) and lexical cohesion (LC) validation accuracy (%).

E Number of parameters

TM: 77,633,536 LM: 29,399,040, *Merging module*: 7,088,642

F Computing infrastructure

We train models with PyTorch 1.2.0 (Paszke et al., 2019). We use a single NVIDIA 1080 Ti or 2080 Ti, running CUDA 10.2 on CentOS Linux 7 (Core).

G Links

Data:
```
https://box.com/shared/static/
qmad0j3e6qknas9nwznyw1w0l5vgpdf4.
zip
```
multi_bleu.perl:
```
https://raw.githubusercontent.
com/moses-smt/mosesdecoder/
master/scripts/generic/
multi-bleu.perl
```

Deeply Embedded Knowledge Representation & Reasoning For Natural Language Question Answering: A Practitioner's Perspective

Arindam Mitra[1] and **Sanjay Narayana**[2] and **Chitta Baral**[2]
[1]Microsoft
[2]Arizona State University
arindam.mitra@microsoft.com, {snaray48, chitta}@asu.edu

Abstract

Successful application of Knowledge Representation and Reasoning (KR) in Natural Language Understanding (NLU) is largely limited by the availability of a robust and general purpose natural language parser. Even though several projects have been launched in the pursuit of developing a universal meaning representation language, the existence of an accurate universal parser is far from reality. This has severely limited the application of knowledge representation and reasoning (KR) in the field of NLP and also prevented a proper evaluation of KR based NLU systems.

Our goal is to build KR based systems for Natural Language Understanding without relying on a parser. Towards this we propose a method named Deeply Embedded Knowledge Representation & Reasoning (DeepEKR) where we replace the parser by a neural network, soften the symbolic representation so that a deterministic mapping exists between the parser neural network and the interpretable logical form, and finally replace the symbolic solver by an equivalent neural network, so the model can be trained end-to-end.

We evaluate our method with respect to the task of Qualitative Word Problem Solving on the two available datasets (QuaRTz and QuaRel). Our system achieves same accuracy as that of the state-of-the-art accuracy on QuaRTz, outperforms the state-of-the-art on QuaRel and severely outperforms a traditional KR based system. The results show that the bias introduced by a KR solution does not prevent it from doing a better job at the end task. Moreover, our method is interpretable due to the bias introduced by the KR approach.

1 Introduction

Developing agents that understand natural language is a long standing challenge in AI. Towards this, several question answering challenges have been proposed, namely SQuAD (Rajpurkar et al., 2016) containing reading comprehension problems, OBQA (Mihaylov et al., 2018), QASC (Khot et al., 2019) containing science questions requiring inference over multiple facts, ProPara (Mishra et al., 2018), SocialIQA (Sap et al., 2019), RecipeQA (Yagcioglu et al., 2018) requiring understanding of events and effects, QuaRTz (Tafjord et al., 2019b), QuaRel (Tafjord et al., 2019a) requiring qualitative reasoning and bAbI (Weston et al., 2015) containing a broad set of synthetic tasks.

For most of these challenges there exists a KR based methodology which typically says, if "the problem and the associated knowledge is represented as 'R', then there exists an algorithm 'A' which can compute the answer". However, almost no end-to-end system that executes such a solution exists (except for bAbI and QuaRel), as obtaining the desired representation 'R' with precision is a challenging task. For the dataset bAbI, which contains synthetically generated simple sentences, existing semantic parsers work well and thus several KR systems (Mitra and Baral, 2016; Chabierski et al., 2017; Wu et al., 2018) have been implemented for it. But for other datasets, researchers have had to build their own semantic parser when implementing a KR solution. For e.g., the work in (Tafjord et al., 2019a) has developed the QuaSP[+] translation system for QuaRel. Data collection for training a semantic parser is a costly process and often parser error becomes a bottleneck to the final system performance. Our goal is eliminate reliance on a semantic parser and to allow rapid implementation of KR based solutions so that the gap between "there is a KR solution" and "there is a system implementing a KR solution" diminishes.

Roughly speaking, our proposed approach takes a KR solution and simulates it in a Neural Network. There are three design choices that are involved in the construction of the simulator Neural Net-

Proceedings of 4th Workshop on Structured Prediction for NLP, pages 102–111
November 20, 2020. ©2020 Association for Computational Linguistics

work. The first design process aims to answer the following question: "How to encode the symbolic representation 'R' in terms of vectors so that a deterministic process can convert the vectors back to the original symbolic form?". The second design process aims to construct a neural network which is responsible for computing the desired vector encoding of 'R'. The third process, implements the reasoning algorithm 'A' in a neural network which takes as input the vector encoding of the symbolic representation 'R'. The parameters of the networks are learned jointly in an end-to-end fashion. We call this approach, Deeply Embedded Knowledge Representation & Reasoning (DeepEKR).

In this work, we describe a DeepEKR solution for the task of qualitative problem solving (Table 1). We describe a standard KR solution and then describe a way to encode it in a Neural Network. The resulting system is evaluated on the two available datasets, namely Quarel and Quartz. In our evaluation we seek the answer to the following two questions: 1) Can the DeepEKR system outperform the available KR baseline? We find the answer to be yes. 2) Can the DeepEKR system outperform the state-of-the-art? We find the answer to be yes for the QuaRel dataset, for the QuaRTz dataset the performance is same as that of the existing state-of-the-art system. The main contributions of our work is that we propose a novel method to implement a KR solution without relying on a natural language parser and provide a proof of concept towards that.

2 Qualitative Word Problem Solving

A noticeable portion of textual knowledge, particularly in science, economics, and medicine, are qualitative in nature, i.e. they describe how changing one entity (e.g., diesel car) affects another (e.g., air pollution). To help NLU systems become better at understanding such sentences, recently two datasets, Quarel and Quartz, containing Qualitative Word Problems (Table 1) have been developed. Each qualitative word problem is a multiple choice question (Table 1) and is accompanied by a sentence containing necessary qualitative knowledge, both of which are given as input. The hope is that if the system correctly answers the question, it most likely understands the accompanied knowledge.

3 A KR Solution

A KR solution typically describes a high level language where a parser translates the natural lan-

K_1	Bigger stars produce more energy, so their surfaces are hotter.
Q_1	Jan is comparing stars, specifically a small star and the larger Sun. Given the size of each, Jan can tell that the Sun puts out heat that is (A) greater (B) lesser
K_2	An object with greater mass or greater velocity has more kinetic energy.
Q_2	Milo threw both a basketball and a baseball through the air. if the basketball has more mass then the baseball, which ball has more kinetic energy (A) basketball (B) baseball
K_3	A sunscreen with a higher spf protects the skin longer.
Q_3	Billy is wearing sunscreen with a higher spf than Lucy. who will be protected from the sun for longer? (A) Lucy (B) Billy

Table 1: Examples of Qualitative word problems

guage input and a set of rules which then computes the answer given the translated input.

3.1 Representation

For Qualitative Word Problems, the input contains two parts. One is the qualitative knowledge sentence and another is the multiple choice question. The qualitative knowledge sentence can be compactly represented as a four tuple :

```
(concept 1 value,
 concept 1 description,
 concept 2 value,
 concept 2 description)
```

The "concept 1 value" and "concept 2 value" takes value from the set {"more","less"} whereas the concept descriptions are arbitrary. Each tuple basically describes whether "concept 1" and "concept 2" are proportional to each other or inversely proportional to each other. Table 2 shows the the 4-tuple representation of the knowledge sentences for the problems in Table 1.

| (more, size of star, more, production of energy) |
| (more, mass, more, kinetic energy) |
| (more, spf of sunscreen, more, skin protection) |

Table 2: Representation of the knowledge sentences as 4-tuple. We omit a predicate name (e.g., *knowledge*) for brevity.

Each qualitative fact e.g., "Billy is wearing sunscreen with a higher spf"), or a query with option (hereafter, "claim") such as "who will be protected from the sun for longer? (option) Lucy" can be compactly represented as a 3-tuple :

```
(concept value,
 concept description,
```

A 3-tuple either states or claims that some concept (e.g., " spf of sunscreen") attains certain value (e.g. "more") for some reference of frame (e.g., "Billy"). The multiple choice question in the input describes two claims (Claim A and Claim B) one for each answer option A and B and one key fact (hereafter *Fact*) to distinguish the correct claim. Each multiple choice question for the qualitative word problem thus can be represented as a collection of three 3-tuples as shown in Table 3.

Fact	(more, size, sun)
Claim A	(more, heat, sun)
Claim B	(less, heat, sun)
Fact	(more, mass, basketball)
Claim A	(more, kinetic energy, basketball)
Claim B	(more, kinetic energy, baseball)
Fact	(more, spf of sunscreen, Billy)
Claim A	(more, protection, Billy)
Claim B	(more, protection, Lucy)

Table 3: Representation of multiple choice questions

Each qualitative word problem of interest thus can be represented by $4 + 3 \times 3 = 13$ terms. Out of these, the two terms, *Claim A concept description* and *Claim B concept description* always have the same value in the Quarel and Quartz dataset (See Table 3). Thus there are 12 unique terms. We will refer to this set as T. Among these 12 terms, there exist five special terms, namely {*concept 1 value, concept 2 value, Fact Concept Value, Claim A Concept Value, Claim B Concept Value*} which takes values from the set {"more","less"}. We will refer to this set containing these five special terms as sT.

3.2 Reasoning

The reasoning algorithm is quite straightforward for the qualitative word problems if the input is presented in the desired symbolic representation. To identify the correct answer choice, one can compute and utilize five indicator variables (propositions) as described below.

Let $I_{Rel|K}$ denote an indicator variable which when *true* denotes that according to the knowledge K, the qualitative concepts (e.g., "size of star" and "production of energy") in the word problem P is **proportional** to each other and if *false* then **inversely proportional**. For each answer choice X (where $X \in A, B$), let $I^{X}_{Rel|F}$ be another indicator variable which denotes if the concept in claim X is proportionally related to the concept in the given Fact or inversely related. Similarly, for each answer choice X (where $X \in A, B$) let $I^{X}_{Reference|F}$ denote if the frame of reference in the claim X, e.g., "Billy", (Hereafter, *Claim X Ref*) matches with the frame of reference in the given fact (Hereafter, *Fact Ref*) or not. Each of these indicator variables are computed as follows:

$I_{Rel	K}$	*Concept 1 Value = Concept 2 Value*
$I^{X}_{Rel	F}$	*Claim X Concept Value = Fact Concept Value*
$I^{X}_{Reference	F}$	*Claim X Ref = Fact Ref*

Table 4: Definition of Indicator variables

The decision function for an answer choice X, $answer(X)$ can then be defined as follows:

$I_{Rel|K}$	$I^{X}_{Rel|F}$	$I^{X}_{Reference|F}$	Correct Answer?
F	F	F	F
F	F	T	T
F	T	F	T
F	T	T	F
T	F	F	T
T	F	T	F
T	T	F	F
T	T	T	T

Table 5: Decision function: If answer choice X is the correct answer

For the example 3 in Table 1, $I_{Rel|K}$ is *true*, $I^{A}_{Rel|F}$ is *true*, $I^{B}_{Rel|F}$ is *true*, $I^{A}_{Reference|F}$ is *true*, $I^{B}_{Reference|F}$ is *false*, thus according to Table 5, $answer(A)$ is *true* but $answer(B)$ is *false*.

4 Encoding the Symbolic Representation with Vectors

In this section we describe, how we encode the symbolic representation in terms of vectors. We model each term t whether it is a concept description (e.g., "spf of sunscreen") , a concept value (e.g., "more") or a frame of reference (e.g., "Billy") in terms of two vectors, namely the term surface vector, a^t and the term content vector, v^t. The term surface vector, a^t captures the attention over the natural language input and surrogates for the symbolic description (in our case, phrases like "spf of sunscreen"). The term content vector v^t surrogates for its meaning. For the terms in sT, such as *Concept 1 value*, which take values from a close set, the dimension of the term content vector v^t is equal to the size of that close set, essentially describing a distribution over the members of the set.

In the symbolic form, each qualitative word problem is represented in terms of 12 terms. In its vector form, each problem is thus represented as 12 pair of vectors. Let m be the length of the input sequence tokens (words or sub-words) containing both the knowledge sentence and the multiple choice question (See Figure 1). Each term surface vectors a^t is then a member of the set $[0, 1]^n$ (Figure 1). Ideally, we want a^t to be $\in \{0, 1\}^n$, however we don't put such an hard constraint to keep the algorithm differentiable and expect that the learned model will exhibit such behavior.

4.1 Encoding Symbolic Reasoning over Vector Space

The decision function for the symbolic representation works with five boolean indicator variables. To work in the continuous space we relax the boolean indicator variables to take any real value in the range of $[-\infty, 0) \cup (0, +\infty]$. If the value of an indicator variable is less than 0, we assume it is *false* and otherwise it is assumed to be *true*. We first obtain a compact formula for the decision function described by the truth table in Table 5. Even though any truth table can be implemented by layers of *and, or* and *not* gates with neural networks, we try to minimize number of such gates to simplify the model. For the truth table in Table 5, the entire truth table can be modelled with two 2-input XNOR gates as follows: $ans(X) = ((I^X_{Rel|F} \; XNOR \; I^X_{Rel|F}) \; XNOR \; I^X_{Reference|F})$. Recall that, a 2-input XNOR gate denotes equivalence and has the following truth table:

A	B	A XNOR B
F	F	T
F	T	F
T	F	F
T	T	T

Table 6: Truth table of a 2-input XNOR gate

With our choice of all negative vales as *false* and all positive values as *true*, we use simple multiplication to model the XNOR gate, thus the decision function $ans(X)$, which denotes if X is the correct answer, takes the following simplified form in the continuous space:

$$anser(X) = I^X_{Rel|F} \times I^X_{Rel|F} \times I^X_{Reference|F}$$

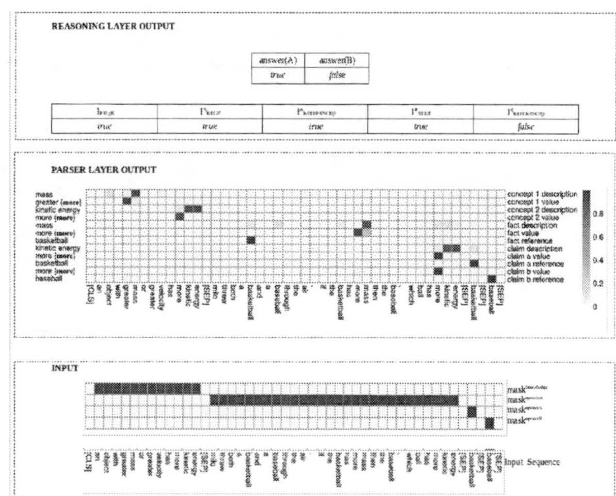

Figure 1: Figure shows a sample input to our model and the predicted output of the parser layer and the reasoning layer. The input masks and the surface term vectors a^t are shown with a heat map over the input sequence. For each of the surface term a^t we also show on the left, the tokens with a weight of more than 0.8. For the five terms in sT we show the value v^t within $\{\}$ which is "more" for all the five terms for this example.

5 Model

In this section we provide the complete detail about how the term vectors, the indicator variables and the correct answer choice is calculated using the tokenized input containing the qualitative knowledge and the multiple choice question.

Model Input The knowledge sentence (k) and the multiple choice question (*question (A) optionA (B) optionB*) are concatenated together as a single sequence "[CLS] k [SEP] *question (A) optionA (B) optionB [SEP]*" and is passed to the Model (Figure 1). Let the length of the input sequence be m. The model then additionally takes as input, four binary masks $\in \{0, 1\}^m$, namely $mask_{knowledge}$, $mask_{question}$, $mask_{optionA}$ and $mask_{optionB}$, respectively describing which part of the input belongs to knowledge, question, option A and option B. See Figure 1 for example.

Layer 1: Parser Layer The goal of the parser layer is to recognize 12 important term vector pairs from the input sequence $w_1, ..., w_m$. Towards that, the parser layer first obtains contextual embeddings for each of the token w_i using BERT. Let $e_i \in R^d$ be the embedding for w_i. Those vectors are calculated as follows:

$$e_1, ..., e_m = BERT(w_1, ..., w_m)$$

105

Let E denote a two dimensional embedding matrix $\in R^{d \times m}$ whose i-th column is e_i.

Using the embeddings in E and the binary masks provided in the input, first the term surface vector $a^t \in [0, 1]^m$ are computed for each of the 12 terms in T. Let $f^t(e) : R^d \to R$ be a linear function of the form $W^t e + b^t$. The j-th component of a vector a^t, i.e., $a^t[j]$ is computed as follows:

$$a^t[j] = \frac{exp(f^t(e_j))}{1 + exp(f^t(e_j))} \times mask^t[j]$$

t	$mask^t$
concept 1 value, concept 1 description, concept 2 value, concept 2 description	$mask_{knowledge}$
Fact description, Claim description, Fact Frame of Reference	$mask_{question}$
Claim A value, Claim A Frame of Reference	$mask_{question}$ + $mask_{optionA}$
Claim B value, Claim B Frame of Reference	$mask_{question}$ + $mask_{optionB}$

Table 7: Describes the value of $mask^t$ for each of the 12 terms.

Table 7 provides the value of $mask^t$ for each of the 12 terms. The $mask^t$ restricts the part of the input sequence that can contain the surface form for the associated term. Since the surface form of each of *Concept 1 value, Concept 1 description, Concept 2 value, Concept 2 description*, should contain tokens from *knowledge sentence* part of the input sequence, $mask^t$ for these four terms are set to be the $mask_{knowledge}$. Other values of $mask^t$ are set accordingly.

The term content (v^t) vector for each of the 7 terms in $T \setminus sT$ which do not take values from the closed set {*more, less*} is computed as follows:

$$v^t = \sum_{j=0}^{m} e_j \times a^t[j]$$

For the remaining 5 terms in sT, we employ a linear function $f^{value} : R^d \to R$ to obtain the mapping to the closed set {*more, less*}. The term content vector, v^t for each of these 5 terms are defined as follows:

$$v^t = f^{value}(\sum_{j=0}^{m} e_j \times a^t[j])$$

If the value of v^t for these 5 terms are less than 0, we assume that it is aligned towards the value *less*, otherwise it is aligned towards the value *more*.

Layer 2: Reasoning Layer The reasoning layer takes the output from the parser layer and outputs 0 if the correct answer choice is A otherwise it outputs 1. To compute the correct answer, it first obtains the values of the five indicator variables. It computes the value of $I_{Rel|K}, I^A_{Rel|F}, I^B_{Rel|F}$ as follows:

$$I_{Rel|K} = v^{concept\ 1\ value} * v^{concept\ 2\ value}$$

$$I^A_{Rel|F} = v^{fact\ concept\ value} * v^{claim\ a\ concept\ value}$$

$$I^B_{Rel|F} = v^{fact\ concept\ value} * v^{claim\ b\ concept\ value}$$

Recall that each of $I_{Rel|K}, I^A_{Rel|F}, I^B_{Rel|F}$ denotes if a pair of qualitative values are same or not (see Table 4 for definition). With our interpretation of negative meaning *false* and positive denoting *true*, multiplication operator is employed to detect equality.

The value of $I^A_{Reference|F}$ is always set to 1 as we assume the terms in the fact tuple should be translated with respect to the frame of reference in claim A to have an unique translation. Then the value of $I^B_{Reference|F}$ is *true* if the frame of reference in claim A matches the frame of reference in claim B and *false* otherwise. We compute the value of $I^B_{Reference|F}$ as follows:

$$1 - sum_{j=0}^{m} |a^{claim-a-ref}[j] - a^{claim-b-ref}[j]|$$

Note that we use term surface vector to detect equality. If the two terms (roughly) attends to same positions which should be the case when claim a frame of reference and claim b frame of reference are same (see examples in Table 1 for clarity), the value of $I^B_{Reference|F}$ is positive and thus interpreted as *true*. When the two surface term vectors are disjoint, the value of $I^B_{Reference|F}$ is -1 as $sum_{j=0}^{m} a^{claim-a-ref}[j] = sum_{j=0}^{m} a^{claim-b-ref}[j] = 1$. and is interpreted as *false*.

The score for option A and B is computed as follows,

$$answer(A) = I^X_{Rel|F} \times I^A_{Rel|F} \times I^A_{Reference|F}$$

$$answer(B) = I^X_{Rel|F} \times I^B_{Rel|F} \times I^B_{Reference|F}$$

The answer is 0 if $answer(A) > answer(B)$ other the answer is 1. See Figure 1 for the trace of the reasoning process for the problem 2 in Table 1.

6 Training

Both the Quartz and Quarel dataset provide the correct answer choice for each qualitative word problem. The Quartz dataset additionally provides the concept description (i.e. a^t) and concept value (v^t) annotation for the five terms in sT which we use as additional supervision. This additional information is not supplied for all the word problems in the training dataset. 2280 number of problems out of 2696 problems in the training dataset contain this annotation. The Quarel dataset provides annotation for the concept value for the terms in sT.

In this section we describe our loss function which uses these supervisions and some additional constraints. The loss functions takes as input the following information:

1. $y \in R^2$ contains the confidence score for answer choice A and answer choice B, i.e., $\hat{y} = [answer(A), answer(B)]$.

2. $c \in \{0, 1\}$ which denotes the correct answer.

3. $\hat{v}^t \in \{-1, 1\}$ for the the qualitative values.

4. $\gamma^t \in \{0, 1\}$ which denotes whether the loss function should use the annotation $\hat{v}^t$. This helps to deal with the missing annotation scenario and also in performing some ablation studies.

5. $\hat{a}^t \in \{0, 1\}^m$ for the target value of a^t.

6. $\lambda^t \in \{0, 1\}$ which denotes whether the loss function should use the annotation $\hat{a}^t$.

The loss value L is then computed as follows:

$$
\begin{aligned}
L = {} & loss^{answer}(y, c) \\
& + \sum_{t \in Cl} \gamma^t * loss^{content}(v^t, \hat{v}^t) \\
& + \sum_{t \in Cl} \lambda^t * loss^{surface}(a^t, \hat{a}^t) \\
& + loss^{constraint^1} \\
& + loss^{constraint^2}
\end{aligned} \tag{1}
$$

We use the standard cross entropy function as $loss^{answer}(y, c)$, L1 loss for $loss^{content}$ i.e., $loss^{content}(v^t, \hat{v}^t) = |v^t - \hat{v}^t|$ and binary cross entropy loss function for $loss^{surface}(a^t, \hat{a}^t)$.

The $loss^{constraint^1}$ tells the model that the $a^{concept\ 1\ value}$ and $a^{concept\ 2\ value}$ should be disjoint and similarly $a^{concept\ 1\ description}$ and $a^{concept\ 2\ description}$ should be disjoint. This is computed as follows:

$$
\begin{aligned}
loss^{constraint^1} = {} & \\
mean(a^{concept\ 1\ value} & \circ a^{concept\ 2\ value}) + \\
mean(a^{concept\ 1\ description} & \circ a^{concept\ 2\ description})
\end{aligned}
$$

Here, $\circ$ denotes element-wise multiplication, $mean(x) : R^m \to R$ computes the average of all the elements of the input vector x.

Recall that the two options in the multiple choice question either contain two different concept values or two different frame of references. Using this information we add constraints over the term surface vector $a^{claim\ a\ ref}$ and $a^{claim\ b\ ref}$. Let, β if 1 denote that the option choices contain two different frame of reference and 0 otherwise. Note that β can be computed by using the masks $\hat{a}^t$. The $loss^{constraint^2}$ is then computed as follows:

$$
\begin{aligned}
loss^{constraint^2} = {} & \\
\beta * subset(a^{claim\ a\ ref}, & mask_{optionA}) + \\
\beta * subset(a^{claim\ b\ ref}, & mask_{optionB}) + \\
(1 - \beta) * subset(a^{claim\ a\ ref}, & mask_{question}) + \\
(1 - \beta) * *subset(a^{claim\ b\ ref}, & mask_{question}) + \\
(1 - \beta) * mean(|a^{claim\ a\ ref} & - a^{claim\ b\ ref}|)
\end{aligned}
$$

The $subset(a, b)$ function returns 0 if the surface vector a is "subset" of the binary mask b and a positive value otherwise and is defined as follows:

$$
subset(a, b) = sum((1 - b) \circ a)
$$

Here, $sum(x) : R^m \to R$ computes the sum of all the elements of the input vector x.

7 Related Work

Our work is related to all the works in Neuro-Symbolic reasoning (Serafini and Garcez, 2016; Cohen et al., 2020; Rocktäschel and Riedel, 2017; Kazemi and Poole, 2018; Aspis et al., 2018; Ebrahimi et al., 2018; Evans and Grefenstette, 2018) that aims at implementing a symbolic theorem prover with Neural Networks. These works provides proof that more complicated symbolic reasoning algorithms than the one used in this work, can be implemented using neural nets. However the algorithms proposed in these work operates over symbolic input, which again calls for a parser. On the other hand several neural systems have been developed for constituency parsing (Stern et al., 2017; Shen et al., 2018), dependency parsing (Chen and Manning, 2014; Dyer et al., 2015), Semantic Role

Constraints	Test Acc %	Concept 1 Value	Concept 2 Value	Fact Concept Value	Claim A Value	Claim B Value
$loss^{answer}$	50	80	82	50	37	60
$loss^{answer}, loss^{constraint^2}$	50	78	82	49	37	60
$loss^{answer}, loss^{constraint^1}$	50	19	18	50	62	39
$loss^{answer}, loss^{surface}$	74.1	16	17	50	50	50
$loss^{answer}, loss^{constraint^1}, loss^{constraint^2}$	50	80	82	50	62	39
$loss^{answer}, loss^{constraint^1}, loss^{constraint^2}, loss^{content}$	50	80	88	50	62	39
$loss^{answer}, loss^{constraint^1}, loss^{constraint^2}, loss^{content}, loss^{surface}$	**79.84**	89	92	80	94	95
$loss^{answer}, loss^{surface}, loss^{content}$	78.18	91	88	78	91	94

Table 8: Ablation Analysis of different supervisions

Labelling (He et al., 2018), parsing to the language of Abstract Meaning Representation (Konstas et al., 2017) or task specific semantic parsing(Dong and Lapata, 2018; Krishnamurthy et al., 2017). These works also provide useful knowledge while constructing a DeepEKR solution.

In this work, the input problem is translated to a set of fixed number of terms. However, depending on the end application the representation format could be a graph, stack, table. Thus the work in Graph Neural Networks (Scarselli et al., 2008; Lamb et al., 2020), which operates over graphs or the Neural State Machine (Hudson and Manning, 2019) that operates over automata is also related to our work.

In this work we have proposed to replace the symbolic representation by vectors so that dependency over an accurate parser can be avoided. With a similar goal, the work in (Mitra et al., 2019b) proposes to use textual entailment to replace the parser. The central idea behind the proposal is, if the input is supposed to be translated to a predicate e.g., *claimA("protection", "more", "Billy")*, instead of asking the parser to translate it to the symbolic form, generate a textual description for the predicate e.g., "protection is more for Billy" and use a textual entailment system to check if the input string entails it. A drawback of this approach is that generation of the textual description of a symbolic term currently requires handwritten templates. A system, namely **gvQPS** (Mitra et al., 2019a) following this approach has been built for the QuaRel dataset.

Our work is directly related to the QUASP$^+$ system (Tafjord et al., 2019a) for QuaRel that trains a parser to obtain a symbolic representation of a qualitative word problem and uses a symbolic reasoner implemented in Prolog to obtain the answer. Our work is also related to the BERT (Devlin et al., 2018) based multiple choice question solver that takes as input "[CLS] knowledge [SEP] question [SEP] option X [SEP]" and computes the score for option X.

8 Experiments

We evaluate our system on the QuaRTz and QuaRel dataset. The QuaRTz dataset contains a total of 3864 problems. The train, dev and test split respectively contain 2696, 384 and 784 problems. The QuaRel dataset contains a total of 2771 problems. The train, dev and test split respectively contain 1941, 278 and 552 problems. We have used the *bert-large-uncased-whole-word-masking* model in our experimentation.

Performance on QuaRTz Table 9 compares the accuracy of our system (DeepEKR) with the two reported solvers, namely BERT (standard BERT multiple choice question solver trained on the QuaRTz dataset) and BERT-PFT-Race (BERT multiple choice question solver trained on the Race dataset (Lai et al., 2017) and then on the QuaRTz dataset) . Our system achieves same accuracy to that of the BERT-PFT-Race model. However, DeepEKR provides better interpretability.

Models ↓	Test Acc.
BERT	67.7
BERT-PFT-Race	79.8
DeepEKR	79.8

Table 9: Performance of various models on QuaRTz

Ablation Analysis on Supervision The loss function takes five different supervisions as described in equation 1. Table 8 displays the effect of different combination of supervisions on the question-answering accuracy on the test set and the accuracy of $v^t \in \{$"less","more"$\}$ for the $t \in sT$. We observe that a combination of all constraints results in the best test accuracy. However, $loss^{surface}$ i.e. the supervision for term surface vector is the most significant one, as without this supervision accuracy remains stuck at 50%. Due to this, while training on QuaRel, we either pre-train the model on QuaRTz or expand the QuaRel training data with QuaRTz training data.

Performance on QuaRel Table 10 compares the accuracy of our system on the QuaRel dataset. DeepEKR model first trained on QuaRTz and then later fine-tuned on QuaRel achieves the state-of-the-art-accuracy.

Models ↓	Test Acc.
BERT	53
BERT-PFT-Race	79.89
BERT-PFT-QuaRTz	53
BERT-PFT-Race and PFT-QuarTz	77
QuaSP+	68.7
gvQPS	76.63
DeepEKR PFT on QuaRTz	**81.15**
DeepEKR augmented with QuaRTz training data	78.98

Table 10: Performance of various models on Quarel

8.1 Error Analysis

We carefully examine all the 87 examples in the dev set of the QuaRTz dataset where the system picks the incorrect answer. We break down the errors in 5 categories.

Incorrect Value Prediction The majority of the errors (41) fall in this category where a^t is correctly computed for the terms t in sT but one of $I_{Rel|K}$ or $I^X_{Rel|F}$ is wrong. Table 11 displays an example with this error. Here, the two concepts being compared are *energy of vibrations* and *proximity of particles*. Our system incorrectly classifies $v^{fact\ concept\ value}$ ("further") as "more" even though the associated concept is *proximity of particles* resulting in an error in the computation. This happens as "farther" often correlates with "more" in the dataset. We believe adding more examples to teach the model that $v^{fact\ concept\ value}$ sometimes depends on concept description is necessary to deal with this issue.

K	When particles of matter are closer together, they can more quickly pass the energy of vibrations to nearby particles.
Q	If jim moves some particles of matter **farther** apart, what will happen to the rate at which they can pass vibrations on to nearby particles? (A) decrease (B) increase

Table 11: An Example of Incorrect Value Prediction

Attention over Incorrect Tokens For 28 problems, the incorrect token gets a high attention score i.e. a^t is wrong, leading to incorrect v^t and ultimately in an incorrect prediction. This occurs for the example in Table 12, where $a^{fact\ concept\ value}$ points to the token "increases" but does not contain "removing" which results in incorrect v^t.

K	When particles of matter are closer together, they can more quickly pass the energy of vibrations to nearby particles.
Q	If mona is removing helium from a balloon and she **increases** the amount she is **removing**, what happens to the amount of energy the helium particles can pass amongst each other? (A) decrease (B) increase

Table 12: An example of Attention over Incorrect Tokens.

Others For the reaming 18 problems, 9 requires numerical reasoning (number comparisons), 4 requires commonsense knowledge such as "K=Objects that are closer together have a stronger force of gravity. Q = Which planet has the most gravity exerted on it from the sun?(A) Mercury (B) Mars". For 5 problems the gold answer provided is actually wrong and the model actually predicted the correct answer.

9 Conclusion

Knowledge Representation and Reasoning (KR) based solutions are interesting for Natural Language Understanding as they are interpretable and can work with declarative knowledge. However, systems that implement KR solution with traditional parser and symbolic solvers normally fall short on performance when compared to neural systems. These observations and issues related to parser and symbolic reasoning have resulted in less interest towards KR solutions. However, we show that we can take a KR solution and implement in a way that is competitive with neural systems and is also explainable. For the qualitative word problems, the reasoning is fairly simple. Our future work includes applying this method to other areas requiring more complex reasoning.

References

Yaniv Aspis, Krysia Broda, and Alessandra Russo. 2018. Tensor-based abduction in horn propositional programs. CEUR Workshop Proceedings.

Piotr Chabierski, Alessandra Russo, and Mark Law. 2017. Logic-based approach to machine comprehension of text.

Danqi Chen and Christopher D Manning. 2014. A fast and accurate dependency parser using neural networks. In *Proceedings of the 2014 conference on empirical methods in natural language processing (EMNLP)*, pages 740–750.

William Cohen, Fan Yang, and Kathryn Rivard Mazaitis. 2020. Tensorlog: A probabilistic database implemented using deep-learning infrastructure. *Journal of Artificial Intelligence Research*, 67:285–325.

Jacob Devlin, Ming-Wei Chang, Kenton Lee, and Kristina Toutanova. 2018. Bert: Pre-training of deep bidirectional transformers for language understanding. *arXiv preprint arXiv:1810.04805*.

Li Dong and Mirella Lapata. 2018. Coarse-to-fine decoding for neural semantic parsing. *arXiv preprint arXiv:1805.04793*.

Chris Dyer, Miguel Ballesteros, Wang Ling, Austin Matthews, and Noah A Smith. 2015. Transition-based dependency parsing with stack long short-term memory. *arXiv preprint arXiv:1505.08075*.

Monireh Ebrahimi, Md Kamruzzaman Sarker, Federico Bianchi, Ning Xie, Derek Doran, and Pascal Hitzler. 2018. Reasoning over rdf knowledge bases using deep learning. *arXiv preprint arXiv:1811.04132*.

Richard Evans and Edward Grefenstette. 2018. Learning explanatory rules from noisy data. *Journal of Artificial Intelligence Research*, 61:1–64.

Luheng He, Kenton Lee, Omer Levy, and Luke Zettlemoyer. 2018. Jointly predicting predicates and arguments in neural semantic role labeling. *arXiv preprint arXiv:1805.04787*.

Drew Hudson and Christopher D Manning. 2019. Learning by abstraction: The neural state machine. In *Advances in Neural Information Processing Systems*, pages 5901–5914.

Seyed Mehran Kazemi and David Poole. 2018. Relnn: A deep neural model for relational learning. In *Thirty-Second AAAI Conference on Artificial Intelligence*.

Tushar Khot, Peter Clark, Michal Guerquin, Peter Jansen, and Ashish Sabharwal. 2019. Qasc: A dataset for question answering via sentence composition. *arXiv preprint arXiv:1910.11473*.

Ioannis Konstas, Srinivasan Iyer, Mark Yatskar, Yejin Choi, and Luke Zettlemoyer. 2017. Neural amr: Sequence-to-sequence models for parsing and generation. *arXiv preprint arXiv:1704.08381*.

Jayant Krishnamurthy, Pradeep Dasigi, and Matt Gardner. 2017. Neural semantic parsing with type constraints for semi-structured tables. In *Proceedings of the 2017 Conference on Empirical Methods in Natural Language Processing*, pages 1516–1526.

Guokun Lai, Qizhe Xie, Hanxiao Liu, Yiming Yang, and Eduard Hovy. 2017. Race: Large-scale reading comprehension dataset from examinations. *arXiv preprint arXiv:1704.04683*.

Luis Lamb, Artur Garcez, Marco Gori, Marcelo Prates, Pedro Avelar, and Moshe Vardi. 2020. Graph neural networks meet neural-symbolic computing: A survey and perspective. *arXiv preprint arXiv:2003.00330*.

Todor Mihaylov, Peter Clark, Tushar Khot, and Ashish Sabharwal. 2018. Can a suit of armor conduct electricity? a new dataset for open book question answering. *arXiv preprint arXiv:1809.02789*.

Bhavana Dalvi Mishra, Lifu Huang, Niket Tandon, Wen-tau Yih, and Peter Clark. 2018. Tracking state changes in procedural text: a challenge dataset and models for process paragraph comprehension. *arXiv preprint arXiv:1805.06975*.

Arindam Mitra and Chitta Baral. 2016. Addressing a question answering challenge by combining statistical methods with inductive rule learning and reasoning. In *Thirtieth AAAI Conference on Artificial Intelligence*.

Arindam Mitra, Chitta Baral, Aurgho Bhattacharjee, and Ishan Shrivastava. 2019a. A generate-validate approach to answering questions about qualitative relationships. *arXiv preprint arXiv:1908.03645*.

Arindam Mitra, Peter Clark, Oyvind Tafjord, and Chitta Baral. 2019b. Declarative question answering over knowledge bases containing natural language text with answer set programming. In *Proceedings of the AAAI Conference on Artificial Intelligence*, volume 33, pages 3003–3010.

Pranav Rajpurkar, Jian Zhang, Konstantin Lopyrev, and Percy Liang. 2016. Squad: 100,000+ questions for machine comprehension of text. *arXiv preprint arXiv:1606.05250*.

Tim Rocktäschel and Sebastian Riedel. 2017. End-to-end differentiable proving. In *Advances in Neural Information Processing Systems*, pages 3788–3800.

Maarten Sap, Hannah Rashkin, Derek Chen, Ronan Le Bras, and Yejin Choi. 2019. Social iqa: Commonsense reasoning about social interactions. In *EMNLP 2019*.

Franco Scarselli, Marco Gori, Ah Chung Tsoi, Markus Hagenbuchner, and Gabriele Monfardini. 2008. The graph neural network model. *IEEE Transactions on Neural Networks*, 20(1):61–80.

Luciano Serafini and Artur S d'Avila Garcez. 2016. Learning and reasoning with logic tensor networks. In *Conference of the Italian Association for Artificial Intelligence*, pages 334–348. Springer.

Yikang Shen, Zhouhan Lin, Athul Paul Jacob, Alessandro Sordoni, Aaron Courville, and Yoshua Bengio. 2018. Straight to the tree: Constituency parsing with neural syntactic distance. *arXiv preprint arXiv:1806.04168*.

Mitchell Stern, Jacob Andreas, and Dan Klein. 2017. A minimal span-based neural constituency parser. *arXiv preprint arXiv:1705.03919*.

Oyvind Tafjord, Peter Clark, Matt Gardner, Wen-tau Yih, and Ashish Sabharwal. 2019a. Quarel: A dataset and models for answering questions about qualitative relationships. In *Proceedings of the AAAI Conference on Artificial Intelligence*, volume 33, pages 7063–7071.

Oyvind Tafjord, Matt Gardner, Kevin Lin, and Peter Clark. 2019b. Quartz: An open-domain dataset of qualitative relationship questions. *ArXiv*, abs/1909.03553.

Jason Weston, Antoine Bordes, Sumit Chopra, Alexander M Rush, Bart van Merriënboer, Armand Joulin, and Tomas Mikolov. 2015. Towards ai-complete question answering: A set of prerequisite toy tasks. *arXiv preprint arXiv:1502.05698*.

Benjamin Wu, Alessandra Russo, Mark Law, and Katsumi Inoue. 2018. Learning commonsense knowledge through interactive dialogue. In *Technical Communications of the 34th International Conference on Logic Programming (ICLP 2018)*. Schloss Dagstuhl-Leibniz-Zentrum fuer Informatik.

Semih Yagcioglu, Aykut Erdem, Erkut Erdem, and Nazli Ikizler-Cinbis. 2018. Recipeqa: A challenge dataset for multimodal comprehension of cooking recipes. *arXiv preprint arXiv:1809.00812*.